WEST DERBY, OLD SWAN
AND
WAVERTREE

BY
JAMES HOULT

The City of Liverpool

First published 1913

This edition specially produced by
Liverpool Libraries & Information Services
William Brown Street, Liverpool L3 8EW
2005

ISBN 0 902990 27 6

Printed in Great Britain by
The Cromwell Press Ltd., Trowbridge, Wilts

FOREWORD

I am pleased that Liverpool Libraries and Information Services has reproduced this book, which is the fifth in a series of reprints leading up to the 800th anniversary of Liverpool in 2007.

The book was first published in 1913. The author, James Hoult, F.R. Hist.S., F.S.A. (Scot.), F.R.S.A. (Ireland), lived from 1864 to 1943. He was the son of James Hoult, provision dealer of Prescot Road, Old Swan, and the grandson of James Hoult, proprietor of the Old Swan Inn and Posting House. He succeeded his father in the provision business with extensive premises at the corner of Prescot Road and St. Oswald Street, a local landmark popularly known as Hoult's Corner. The Liverpool Street Directory of 1912 describes the business as provision dealers, bakers and flour dealers, ironmongers and butchers. In the late 1930s the premises were rebuilt as Corporation flats, St Oswald's Gardens, which have in turn been rebuilt as a Tesco supermarket.

Outside of his business, Hoult's main interests were antiquarian and he possessed an unrivalled knowledge of Old Swan and its neighbourhood. He contributed many articles and letters to the local press and frequently lectured on local history. He also gave some broadcast talks for the BBC. His other books included *West Derby and Old Swan: historical and topographical* first published without illustrations in 1911; *West Derby Hundred: early highways and byways*, 1923; *Lancashire* local history: *The Vill, Manor and Township of Knowsley*, 1930; and *A Short Story of Stoneycroft*, 1939.

Hoult was a member of the Historic Society of Lancashire and Cheshire from 1911 to 1919 and 1924 to 1929. His papers which appeared in the *Transactions* of the Society were "Old Swan Charity School" (1912, Volume 64); "Travelling post" (1920, Volume 72); "Prescot watchmaking in the 18th century" (1925, Volume 77); and "Prescot in Tudor times" (1927, Volume 79).

As well as having copies of his books and articles, Liverpool Record Office has a scrapbook of the Hoult family which includes newspaper cuttings, copies of letters and articles in the press, certificates, notices of lectures, and a small number of photographs (reference Hq920 HOU).

Hoult was also a prominent Wesleyan lay preacher. He was closely associated with St. Paul's Wesleyan Church at Stoneycroft. A Liberal in politics, he was at one time chairman of the Old Swan Liberal Association and had unsuccessfully contested the division as a municipal candidate in 1905.

The author himself appears in the photograph of Cronton Stocks at the end of the book (after page 154). He is pictured, seated, on the right of the photograph.

Illustrations have been added to the original edition from the extensive collections of Liverpool Record Office. An index which was compiled by Liverpool

Libraries some years ago has been edited and re-typed by Gina Kehoe.

I would like to thank David Stoker, Paul Webster, Kay Parrott, Gina Kehoe and all of the staff of Liverpool Record Office for seeing this reprint through.

I hope that you will enjoy this book and find the information useful.

Councillor Warren Bradley
Executive Member – Leisure

September 2005

ILLUSTRATIONS ADDED TO THE 2005 EDITION

Jacket: West Derby village from Mill Lane looking north-west, 1883.
Watercolour by H. Magenis.
Binns Collection C122.

Between pages 90 and 91

1. Prescot Road, south side, at the corner of St. Oswald Street, showing Hoult's corner, 1938.
Photograph by W.H. Tomkinson of watercolour by John Pride belonging to James Hoult.(Library copy of watercolour destroyed by enemy action May 1941.)
Pride Collection 75b.

2. West Derby village, 1858.
Watercolour by W. Herdman.
Herdman Collection 181.

3. East Prescot Road, numbers 204-270, 1950.
Two watercolours by A. P. Tankard.
Binns Collection C249.

4. St. Oswald Street, Old Swan, 1938.
Watercolour by John Pride.
Pride Collection 72.

5. Prescot Road, south side, showing old property between Thomas Lane and Pilch Lane opposite Eaton Road, 1911.
Watercolour by F. Beattie.
Beattie Collection 34.

6. Swan Row, south side of Prescot Road, Old Swan, 1911.
Watercolour by F. Beattie.
Beattie Collection 294.

7. Black Horse Lane, looking south, with Highfield Lodges, Prescot Road, in the distance, 1912.
Watercolour by F. Beattie.
Beattie Collection C32.

8. View from New Hall Lane, Clubmoor, at its junction with Back Lane, looking south-west and showing West Derby Parish Church in the distance, 1909.
Watercolour by F. Beattie.
Beattie Collection 322.

9. Wavertree Green, 1910.
Watercolour by F. Beattie.
Beattie Collection 47.

10. Wavertree Mill, 1884.
Watercolour by H. Magenis.
Herdman Collection 1015.

WEST DERBY, OLD SWAN

AND

WAVERTREE

HISTORICAL AND TOPOGRAPHICAL.

BY

JAMES HOULT.

ILLUSTRATED,

LIVERPOOL:
C. TINLING & CO., LTD., PRINTERS, 53, VICTORIA STREET.

1913

PREFACE.

The majority of the enclosed notes on Local History and Topography had been originally written for the columns of a local newspaper. The idea of collecting these items came from friendly critics, who frequently added fresh antiquarian lore which the writer has incorporated into his articles.

The Local Historian has his place in the literature of his country. He records things as they were in his own locality. It is desirable that there should be milestones upon the road of progress, so that in days of material and intellectual advancement, it should be possible to look back and see on what lines this development has travelled. It is well for us sometimes to review the processes of evolution which have led up to the civilisation of 1913. But this, think of it how you will, is only one of the charms of history. Two thousand years ago and more, one before whom, according to Macaulay, all other historians pale their ineffectual fires, Thucydides, the Athenian, gave tersely the greatest of claims that history has on mankind. By learning the truth about the past, he wrote, one may judge what is likely to happen in the future. Human nature changes slowly as the face of a mountain. Given the same causes, the same events will follow. In these days of the multiplication of newspapers we are apt to treat every event as if its like had never happened in the world before. Every little war is the greatest that ever was waged. Every division in Parliament is a crisis for the Constitution. Now, of course, there are some things new under the sun, but not so very many; and, of course, there are times of crises in history, but not so very often. The man who knows the story of the events of the past is far better able to see things as they are, in their true size, in their true relation, than he whose history is doled out in the daily newspaper.

The writer has been indebted to Mr. R. D. Radcliffe, M.A., F.S.A., a gentleman whom it would be difficult to equal as an antiquary; to his grandmother, a bright and very intelligent old lady who could provide a large amount of local lore from the family connections with the Pack Horse business, the toll bars, the early 'buses, West Derby Chapel, Old Swan Charity School, etc.; to Mr. George Watson, fifty years of Cunningham's Nursery, and to a number of old folk, many of whom are now dead.   J. H.

12, Brookland Road,
  Old Swan.

CONTENTS.

WEST DERBY.
PAGE

Manor of West Derby	1
West Derby Hundred	3
Local Recreations	4
Blundell Family	5
Parish Constable, West Derby	6
Country Lanes	7
West Derby Parsonage	8
West Derby Stocks	8
,, ,, Castle	9
Fir Grove	10
Bellfield	13
The Old Hall	14
Vanishing Footpaths	16
Deysbrook	16
Moss House	17
The Yew Tree	18
West Derby Wakes	18

WALTON.

In 14th Century	20
School	23
Church	24
Hall	26
Churchyard	27

OLD SWAN.

Pioneers	28
Oak Hill House	29
Highfield	30
Early Postal Arrangements	34
Methodism	35
May Place	39
Lesson from Charity School	40
Glass Making	43
Swan Hill Farm	44
Baptist Chapel	44
The Name, Old Swan	45
Cock Pit	46
Bridewell	46
Story of an Old Swan Constable	47
Rock House, Old Swan	48
First Omnibus	48
Old Swan Water Tower	49
An Old Swan Sunday School	49
St. Oswald's Church	50

WAVERTREE.

Antiquity of	51
Hall	53
Means of Communication	53
Constable's Duties	54

WAVERTREE —*continued.*   PAGE

Rural 55
Chapel 56
Local Administration 58
Poor Relief 59
Notable Townsmen 60
Constables 63
Lock-up 64
A Free Quarry 65
Town's Well 66
Old Roads 67
Select Vestry 68
Augustine Birrell's Birthplace 69
George Brown and Bluecoat School 70
Village Greens 71

BROAD GREEN.

Score Lane 72
Early Pigs from China 73
Ash House and Dr. Christy 74
Staplands 75
Thingwall Hall 75
Thingwall 77
Early Railway Memories 79
A Forgotten Station 80
A Famous Nursery 81
The First Irish Yew 82
Broad Green Hall and Dr. Brandreth 83

KNOTTY ASH.

Dovecot 85
Finch House 90
Corporal Shaw 90
Monument at Springfield 91
Church Bell 91
Memories of Ashfield 92

S.W. LANCASHIRE.

Edge Lane Hall 93
Gill Moss 96
King John and S.W. Lancashire 98
Early English Houses 101
Local Families 102
Inland Traffic 103
Early Pack Tracks 105
A Liverpool Turnpike 106
Liverpool, near Prescot 111
Prescot Road 100 years ago 111
Croxteth and Sefton 113
Derby and Molyneux 114
John Wesley and Prescot 115
America and S.W. Lancashire 116
Famous Local Wells 119
S.W. Lancashire and the Wars with Scotland 121

MISCELLANEOUS. PAGE.

At a Pack Horse Bridge 123
Alderman Snape's Staff 123
A 1778 Ballad 124
Byrom Hall 125
Maghull Font 126
St. Anne's Church 126
Kirkby and St. Chad 128
Friar's Croft 129
Childwall 129
Relics of the Past 132
Fonts in Nonconformist Chapels 133
Early Nonconformity 134
1662 in S.W. Lancashire 135
The Church in 1662 137
Early Dissent 138
Early Nonconformist Meeting Houses 139
Hill Cliff 139
Most Ancient Chapel in Lancashire 140
Communion Rails 141
Millbrook 141
Lime Street Chapel 143
Mediæval Fonts 144
Stone Crosses 147

APPENDIX.

Ancient Chapel of West Derby 151
Miller's House, West Derby 152
Fairfield Hall 152
King's Mill, Wavertree 153

ILLUSTRATIONS.

Manor Court House, West Derby.

West Derby Stocks, before removal from garden.

West Derby Parsonage.

Plan of West Derby in 1768.

Fir Grove.

Bellefield, West Derby.

Sandfield.

Deysbrook, West Derby.

The Yew Tree, West Derby.

Moss House, West Derby.

Walton Old Grammar School.

A 14th Century Document relating to Walton and Liverpool.

Old Walton Church, now demolished.

Scandinavian Font, Walton.

Walton Hall, now demolished.

Oak Hill, Old Swan, now demolished.

Wesley Chapel, Old Swan, now Catholic Club.

Highfield, Old Swan.

Old Swan Charity School.

Old Swan Bill-head in 1842.

Bridewell, Old Swan, now demolished.

Historic Blacksmith's Shop, Old Swan.

A Lawrence and Catherine Davies Jug.

Pre-historic Urn, Wavertree.

Urns, Scraper, and Arrow Head from Wavertree.

Urn found at Wavertree.

Gates of Wavertree Hall.

Wavertree Lock-up, 1840.

Wavertree Church.

Sandown Hall, Wavertree.

Entrance to Thingwall.

First Rocket Inn, Broad Green

House in Oak Vale Nursery.

Dove-cote, now demolished.

The First Irish Yew.

Edge Lane Hall, demolished 1913.

Prescot Market Place in 1750.

Ancient Knowsley.

Monk's Well, Wavertree.

Speke Hall.

St. Anne's Church, Stanley, now demolished.

A Childwall Tithe Barn.

Childwall Abbey Inn.

Childwall Almshouses and Columbarium.

Childwall Hall.

Childwall Church and Hearse House.

Leper's Squint, Childwall Church.

Base of Cross, Childwall.

Scandinavian Font, Kirkby Church.

Cross at Rainhill.

Cronton Cross.

Cronton Stocks.

Old West Derby Chapel, now demolished.

Fairfield Hall, demolished 1913.

Boltons, West Derby.

Boltons, West Derby, the Miller's House.

King's Mill, Wavertree.

West Derby, Old Swan, and Wavertree.

Historical and Topographical.

WEST DERBY.

MANOR OF WEST DERBY.

The Manor of West Derby in Domesday Book is ranked as first, and most important, in the list of manors lying between the Mersey and the Ribble. It was a Royal manor, and belonged to the last King of the old English stock, the saintly Edward the Confessor. It is impossible to assert that King Edward was ever in West Derby, but it is extremely probable, for its Royal manor, where farmed, had special privileges. There was a game preserve, a forest and a wood, the latter measuring two leagues long by one league broad. There was also a hawks' aery. The lesser theyns in the manor held land, partly by service, and among other duties they had to look after the King's fisheries— i.e., to make weirs and eel traps; to make enclosures in the wood and deer Heys—places where the deer might be aimed at and taken with little difficulty. They had to work upon the King's house and what appertained thereto, and they were also compelled to send mowers one day in August to cut the King's corn. A significant fact is that one of King Edward's favourite priests, Ernuin, had land in West Derby. The Confessor also had manors at Warrington, Blackburn, and Preston, and it is almost inconceivable that he should not visit them. The manor of Childwall was held by two radmanii, literally riders. These men were more free than the theyns of West Derby, for they only did one day's service at the Royal farm in the year; but they were to be at call to ride with the King as escort when travelling from manor to manor. The order of radmanii was instituted by King Edgar, he who brought England into political unity, and who on one occasion was rowed in his state barge on the Dee by eight vassal kings.

The court-house at West Derby is to be seen to-day, facing the tram terminus. It is near to the stocks, which at one time were affixed to it. It, however, has never been used either as a police court or as a county court, although in its interior it closely resembles both. It has been, since it was built, shortly before the Restoration, a manor court-house, and its judge has been the lord of the manor or his steward.   After the Conquest the Manor of West Derby changed hands pretty often, its early holders, in turn, being rebellious. However, when Bolingbroke became King it reverted to the Crown, with which it remained until Charles I. sold it to Charles Ditchfield and other citizens of London, who sold it again to James, seventh Lord Derby. The court-house was probably built to enable the large and important business of the copy holders under the manor to be transacted with every appearance of legality.   The only evidence which the owner of an estate (copyhold) has of his right thereto is the copy of an entry in the court rolls of the manor, which the lord is bound to allow the tenant to inspect and take copies of; hence the term copyhold.   But although the estate is said to be held at the will of the lord of the manor, this is only so in theory; practically the copyholder's estate to-day is as fixed and secure as that of any other holder of land.   There was a time, however, when the lord of the manor could insist upon his copyholders or tenants swearing fealty to him, cutting his grass and corn, grinding corn at his mill, etc.   In course of time all forms of service became altered to payments of money in lieu thereof.   The story of how the Manor of West Derby came into the hands of Lord Salisbury, the present owner, is worth repeating. Henrietta Countess of Ashburnham, the only surviving daughter of William, the ninth Lord Derby, sold it to a Prescot attorney, a Mr. Isaac Green.   Mr. Isaac Green was a marvellous man, of the stuff that millionaires are made of. He was born in Liverpool in 1678, being christened at St. Nicholas's Church.   At the age of fifty he had acquired many of the manors of the West Derby Hundred.   It is recorded of him " that in cases of surrender at times of death or sale," which was the legal process, that he used to put a deputy into the seat of the judge and acted himself as lawyer —i.e., on behalf of his own manorial privileges.   By various means he became very wealthy, and owned, when he died in 1749, the following manors—Childwall, Everton, Hale, Speke, Much Woolton, Little Woolton and West Derby. He boasted that if he could but live long enough he would get all the manor lands of South Lancashire.   Mr. Isaac Green had no sons to succeed him, and his daughter Mary, heiress of the Manor of West Derby, etc., married Bamber Gascoyne, M.P. for Truro.   They had two sons, and the eldest, " Bamber," was M.P. for Liverpool from 1780 to

1796, and built Childwall Hall. He had one daughter, Frances Mary, and again an heiress brought the manors, etc., to her husband, who was the second Marquis of Salisbury, the grandfather of the present owner. The court-house is now used but once a year, and on that occasion all copyholders are summoned to attend their lord's court, but they do not go. General Isaac Gascoyne, who succeeded his brother as M.P. for Liverpool, married Miss Mary Williamson, of Roby Hall (now Bowring Park), and in his day, as a leader of the Tories, moved the rejection of the great Reform Bill.

WEST DERBY HUNDRED.

The Wapentake Court of the Hundred of West Derby existed before County Courts, Courts of Passage, etc., came into existence. The head official, or " sergeant," in his day was the most important man of the large district called the hundred. The court is practically defunct, but the title of " Sergeant of the Wapentake " is still recognised, its present holder being King George V., who received the sergeantry as part of the titles and emoluments of the Duchy of Lancaster. The division of the country into hundreds took place in Saxon days, and is generally credited to Alfred the Great. It was an attempt to bring the whole country under military rule, each " hundred " being responsible for one hundred fighting men. The Wapentake Court was of Danish origin, and it was an ingenious attempt to use the organisation which they found in existence for an improved system of administration of the law; it dealt with matters of dispute between man and man, collection of debts, etc. The court was held for centuries; the sergeant was usually the steward of the hundred, holding both military and judicial powers. There is a document in existence in which King John, in 1199, confirmed the grant of these offices (originally made by William, Count of Boulogne) to Henry de Walton, besides grants of lands in Walton and Newsham made by the King. This Henry de Walton was entitled to a profit, called " foldage," from cattle impounded in execution at the rate of a halfpenny per night in winter, and a farthing per night in summer, as well as certain court fees. When King John granted his famous charter of incorporation to Liverpool, he ordered that the Wapentake Court should be held in future in Liverpool instead of West Derby, where it had been held formerly. The word " Wapentake " in plain English means

" weapon-touch," from the custom that when the lord or
sergeant held his court he stuck his spear into the ground,
and all the assembled liege men, by touching the spear with
their weapons, acknowledged their fealty.

Sir T. Smith says that musters were made of the armour
and weapons of the inhabitants of every Wapentake, and
from those that could not find sufficient pledges for their
good conduct, their weapons were taken away from them
and given to others.

LOCAL RECREATIONS AND PASE EGGING.

A study of the recreations and sports of our ancestors
here in S.W. Lancashire, compels one to think that there was
a good deal of pleasure in the life which they lived. Strange
it is but true, that they had more holidays than even we
moderns.

The year started with first footings and general merriment. In February there was Candlemas Day, and the
customs associated with St. Valentine were observed. A
little later in the spring came the fine custom remembered
in Mothering Sunday, Palm Sunday, Easter with its joy, its
buns, eggs and pase eggers. Then May with its Maypole
festivities. Ascension Day was a holiday, as also was Oak
Apple Day. Whitsuntide and June were the great times for
marriages. St. Swithin was remembered in July, then, a
little later, would be the Harvest Home, with its feasting
and dancing. The wakes were usually held in August or
September. In the autumn Hunting and out-door sports
were general, then, as the days grew short and dreary, there
was Gunpowder Plot to be remembered. Martinmas reminded each generation of a saint who had been extra good to
the poor, then, the grand climax of the year, Christmas, its
Yule Log, the family gathering, the present giving, feasting,
waits, etc., and to close all the bells of the Parish Churches
rang the old year out.

An Easter custom which was observed up to about forty
years ago in West Derby, Wavertree, and perhaps other
places near to, was Pase-Egging. It had degenerated into
a play performed by bands of boys dressed up with coloured
ribbons, with tinsel and paper caps, and armed with wooden
or tin swords. A hundred years ago strong young men,
similar to the ones who dance the Morris Dance at Knuts-
ford, travelled through the villages performing on the green,
and in front of the larger houses. They were well dressed
in coloured suits, sometimes wearing satin. The Dramatis

Personae were a Black Morocco King, a Noble Turk, the bold slasher, St. George, the Doctor and Beelzebub. St. George was the hero, and between items of dialogue, he fights first the bold slasher, who was killed; afterwards he encounters the Black Morocco King and wounds him. He then has a desperate struggle with the Noble Turk and brings him down wounded. Satan does not appear to be an enemy, for during the dialogue between him and St. George, there is no fighting, the two only repeatedly crossing weapons. It appeared in fact as if he were quite an acquaintance and almost a friend. He announces himself thus :—

"Here comes in old Beelzebub
And in my hand I carry a club."

Satan was not armed with swords like the fighting men, but carried a stout stick. The Doctor cures both the wounded and the dead slasher, and the play, as the stories and plays of those days usually did, finished happily, all joining in a dance.

The Pase-eggers of West Derby were esteemed to be the best in the district around Liverpool, Wavertree coming a close second.

THE BLUNDELL FAMILY.

Among local family names none is more honoured than that of Blundell. Perhaps the most distinguished was William Blundell—"the Cavalier"—born at Crosby Hall in 1620. He, at fifteen years of age, married. When King Charles was rallying his adherents William Blundell raised 100 Dragoons for the Royal cause, which he commanded. In the attack on Lancaster he was seriously wounded, having his thigh shattered with a musket ball. He was rendered a cripple, and was nicknamed by his tenants "Halt Will." William Blundell was the author of a few literary works, among them "A History of the Isle of Man," a treatise on the penal laws, and, best of all, a diary which is full of interest, as it describes in quaint language life of South-west Lancashire in the seventeenth century. Squire Blundell died in 1698, full of years and respected by all, and was buried in the Blundell Chapel, Sefton Church. Bryan Blundell was captain of a Liverpool ship. He was a man of sympathy, and became founder of the Bluecoat School, paying in 1708 for the original building himself. He says:—"I saw children begging about the streets, their parents being so poor as not to have bread for them, which gave me great concern," etc. The first building only cost £35, but it accommodated ten children. Bryan Blundell went among his friends and pursuaded a number of them to become subscribers, he himself undertaking to contribute one-tenth of his income to the charity. His business thrived, and he was able eventually to contribute £2,000. He lived to see a large building erected, and his charity became an institution of which Liverpool has been justly proud. A descendant of Bryan Blundell is the owner of Deysbrook, West Derby, now a children's hospital. Of more recent days is the name of Jonathan Blundell, "the coal king." He came of the Ince family, and built Larkhill, West Derby. The new Queen's Drive, running between Old Swan and Walton, passes it, it being on the west side. He was very wealthy, and had his town house. It was in Water Street and Rumford Street, his backyard opening into the latter. The building is at present used as the Cunard Offices.

WEST DERBY PARISH CONSTABLE.

Of the Parish of Walton, in the township of West Derby and stationed at Old Swan, the last of the parish constables lived in his day, prior to Sir Robert Peel's great Act for the formation of the police force. He was an important official in the little community. Chosen for his size and strength, he inspired respect from those who had reason to fear the majesty of the law. He was illiterate, could not read or write, and had very elementary ideas as to his duties. He knew, however, that thieves had to be caught, that peace had to be kept in the streets, and drunken people were best in the lock-up, which was conveniently situated in Old Swan. Strange stories are told of his doings. On one occasion some frightened women ran to tell him to come and stop a fight which was in course of progress in a field at Black Horse Lane. He hastened to the spot, and being a sportsman of the old school, thought it a pity to stop the fight, and, instead of interfering in the cause of peace, gave it out that he would lock up the defeated man and that they must fight it out. The old order changeth, giving place to new, and at last the constable had to find out that his methods would not be tolerated. He came, eventually, under the authority of up-to-date magistrates, who tried to instil into him their ideas. His dismissal was typical of the man and his times. He was fond of beer, and some of his neighbours, taking advantage of this weakness, played a practical joke upon him. Making him drunk, they persuaded

Manor Court House, West Derby (Page 1.)

West Derby Stocks, before removal from garden. (Page 8.)

West Derby Parsonage. (Page 8.)

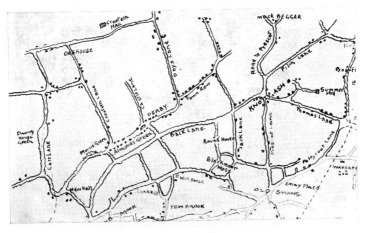

Plan of West Derby in 1768. (Page 9.)

Fir Grove. (Page 10.)

Bellefield, West Derby. (Page 13.)

Sandfield. (Page 14.)

Deysbrook, West Derby. (Page 16.)

a barber to shave one side of his face only; they then placed him in the Knotty Ash 'bus, in which was Mr. Lawrence Heyworth, J.P., of Yewtree, a Liverpool Merchant, and also a large shareholder in the Great Western Railway Company, who was in authority over the foolish constable. The drunken man immediately addressed his superior in "familiar and objectionable" terms, calling him "Old Cock," etc. After his dismissal he gave way to drink, interfered with his successor in the execution of his duty, and eventually had to be an inmate of the same lock-up in which he had incarcerated so many in the days of his authority.

COUNTRY LANES.

The passing of the country lanes of suburban Liverpool is proceeding apace, but especially is it noticeable in the eastern end of the city. Wavertree, Old Swan, and West Derby, recently villages, are now part of the town. With the village goes the lane. In Old Swan, what was originally part of Edge Lane, is now St. Oswald Street. This lane at its highest point (over 600ft. high) had a small lake or tarn. This supplied a stream of water, which ran down the lane, down Prescot Road, and into the Tue Brook at Stanley. Trees grew along the banks of the little stream. The old Manor House (which was sketched by Herdman), a few picturesque cottages, the schoolhouse, and a toll bar at the entrance to the lane, provided the life of the locality one hundred years ago. Looking from the elevated lands around towards Liverpool the view was extensive and rather pretty. The country was well wooded, and variety was supplied by two or three farms and a few gentlemen's houses or halls. There are people still living who remember seeing hares, rabbits, and pheasants in the fields which lay in the hollow between Old Swan Hill and Kensington.

Other lanes which have passed are Petticoat Lane (now Broadgreen Road) and Prescot Lane (now Prescot Road); while at the present time Derby Lane is going through the process of being made into a modern road, drive, or avenue; its hedges have been pulled up and houses and shops are being built in their place. Trees, however, are still there, but are now growing out of the pavement. There was a time when in it great trees arched overhead, when the cart track was only wide enough for one cart at a time, when there was a stretch of grass and bush at one side with the trunk of a fallen tree here and there for a seat, and when visitors drove out from Liverpool to ramble within its shades

and enjoy its rural beauties. Sailors, after the long voyages
of those days, were fond of coming to Old Swan, sometimes,
however, spending too much time at the inn. They often
had the accumulated earnings of a year's voyage and were
careless of their money. An old gentleman informed the
writer of how his mother once found a £5 note fluttering
in a blackberry bush in the lane. It had most probably been
lost by a sailor.

WEST DERBY PARSONAGE.

Early in the 18th century, certainly before 1723, the
township of West Derby built a Parsonage for the Curate
of the Chapel on a piece of waste land on the road between
the Mill and Old Swan. It was a time of religious stagna-
tion in other parts of the country, just prior to the revival
associated with the names of Wesley and Whitfield. Here,
however, the claims of the Church were recognised. In 1688
William Atherton was Curate of West Derby and Liverpool,
serving both Chapels, but in 1723 William Worthington
had sole charge, and for him the Parsonage was built. After
his day the township claimed a nominal rent of 6d. per year
from the Curate for the House and presumably the fields
at the rear, for in the Croxteth plan of 1769 the lot is marked
as glebe. For many years the garden was used by a Japhet
Roberts as a nursery garden, but now, in 1913, the whole
place is showing signs of neglect and the outhouses are
crumbling to ruin.

WEST DERBY STOCKS AND POUND.

West Derby village has still in its midst the old-time
instrument of punishment, the stocks. Our forefathers had
much sense in their treatment of offenders, for the stocks
were economy itself compared to prisons, and as a means of
correction and punishment, were most efficient. Drunken-
ness, for instance, was one of the sins of mankind which the
shame and ridicule of exposure in them made atonement
for. In 1605 an Act of Parliament was passed making the
offence of being drunk punishable by a fine of 5s. or six hours
in the stocks. The original West Derby stocks were made
of wood, but much usage and the ravages of time ultimately
necessitated new ones being provided, and about the year
1800 the iron stocks, which are to be seen to-day, were made
and fixed at the north of the old Court House. The new
stocks had a little adventure, for they were at one time
removed from their public position and placed in the back

garden of a gentleman's house in West Derby, where the writer first saw them, objects neither of use nor ornament and almost overgrown with weeds. They were, however, restored by the representatives of the possessor of them, and now stand in a small garden laid out on the site of the ancient pinfold or pound. A stone set up in front of the stocks bears the inscription :—" To commemorate the long and happy reign of Queen Victoria and the Coronation of Edward VII., this site of the ancient pound of the Dukes of Lancaster and other Lords of the Manor of West Derby was enclosed and planted and the village stocks set herein, Easter, 1904."

Stocks were anciently movable and kept in castles, they were usually by the inner gate. They were used to hold prisoners, who were brought from outside and who were detained in them until committed to the dungeon of the castle. The Pound was looked upon as a valuable piece of property. It belonged to the Dukes of Lancaster. In 1321 it brought into his coffers the sum of £9 13s. 4d., which represents a much larger sum than its present value. Cattle, etc., impounded were charged for at the rate of ½d. per night in winter and ¼d. per night in summer.

WEST DERBY CASTLE.

From the tower of West Derby Parish Church the field known as Castle Field can be distinctly seen at its foot. It differs from the neighbouring fields. It is irregular of surface, and seen from above it shows where there had been a building or buildings and depressions indicating the site of a former moat. It is probable that a fortified place was there in Saxon days, but it is certain that for about two hundred years there was a Norman-built castle on that spot. Count Roger, of Poitou, who had received the royal manor of West Derby from his master, King William of Normandy, is generally credited as having been the builder. Count Roger, however, got into trouble. After his banishment the manor escheated to the Crown, and the castle went with it. In the year of Henry I.'s accession it is on record that the sum of £6 9s. 7d. was spent upon the castle, and that the men in charge of the work were Henry Travers and Henry de Walton. Among the items of service by which Theyns held land in the manor was that of making buildings and what appertained thereto for the King, so that much of the labour would be from this source, " free but compulsory."

King Richard I. held the castle in 1197, and spent two sums of money in repairing its walls—namely, £7 10s. and 100s. During his struggles with the barons King John had the castle of West Derby well garrisoned. There were ten knights and crossbowmen and 140 foot soldiers in charge, and although nothing is known of battle or skirmish, there were all the preparations for such. In studying the records of those distant days, one is impressed with the constant repairs required by the castle. Besides the before-mentioned sums, between the years 1218 and 1225 considerable costly repairs were necessary, and in the pipe roll account of Henry III., in 1227, it is stated that £4 11s. 8d. was spent upon the drawbridge and houses within the castle. The visitor to the Castle Field to-day notices that in it is a great quantity of sand. The neighbourhood is sandy; the Sandfield Estate is near to; and the beautiful parish church adjoining is on the same kind of land. The tower of the church, built as it is to hold a peal of bells, is silent but for the chimes of its clock. The architect considered that it would be unwise to have the bells, fearing the effect of the vibration upon the foundations. Perhaps the old-time castle was rendered so expensive to keep in repair by reason of its not being founded upon a rock.

FIRGROVE HOUSE AND ITS TENANTS.

Firgrove House, in Black Horse Lane, West Derby, when built, was off Black Moor, Moss Lane. In a few months' time it will be Queen's Drive. Joseph Jackson, who lived there in 1790, was a wealthy landed proprietor, whose place of business was in Callender Court, off Derby Street. The latter is now Whitechapel. In Firgrove House there is at the top of the main staircase and above the landing a glass dome. In the centre of it, represented on the glass, is a crest. It is of a dove holding an olive branch, and standing upon a serpent which appears to be in the act of striking at the dove. There is also the scroll, which in heraldry indicates the crest as different from the coat of arms. The crest is very similar to that of the Jackson family, of Bath, and would appear to establish relationship between the Lancashire and Somerset houses. He was destined to be ancestor to a notable local family. His daughter and heiress married Roger Parr, merchant, of Paradise Street, and they had a son, Joseph Parr, who succeeded to his grandfather's estate, and lived at Firgrove

House, where he died in 1820. The name Parr is world-renowned as associated with the celebrated banking concern. It is perhaps worth recording that Joseph Parr married Ellen, daughter of Matthew Lyon, of Warrington, on October 18, 1780, and they had two children, Joseph Parr, of Firgrove House, who died unmarried, June 19, 1824, and who became a banker at Warrington, the firm being Lyon and Parr, shortly after changed to Parr's Bank, as it is known to-day. The younger brother, Thomas Parr, inherited the banker's fortune. He, while living in Old Swan, took a practical interest in the Charity School, becoming a trustee. He eventually removed to Grappenhall, in Cheshire. A John Parr lived on the estate of his ancestors in Old Swan, and died at Elm House in 1736. John Parr's fourth son, Thomas, built and lived in what is now known as the Royal Institution, Colquitt Street, off Bold Street, Liverpool. Adjoining it the family name is remembered in Parr Street.

In 1828 the executors of Joseph Parr decided to sell the house and estate. It was bought by Robert Preston, founder of the noted distillery firm of Vernon Street, Liverpool. He came from Pilling, in the Fylde, and although born in a cottage, he could trace his pedigree back to a time when an ancestor owned Furness Abbey and its grounds. Robert Preston and his family were destined to make their mark upon the city His eldest sister, Jane, married a Mr. Herdman, and became the mother of William Gawin Herdman, the artist and author of " Ancient Liverpool." Robert Preston had four children—namely, Robert, Margaret, Judith and Bess. Margaret married on April 15, 1810, a noted surgeon of his day, Dr. Dawson, of Mount Pleasant, Liverpool. On retiring from the active practice of his profession, Dr. and Mrs. Dawson built Wray Castle, that well-known addition to the picturesqueness of Windermere Lake, and went to live there. Robert Preston was succeeded in the business by his nephew, William Preston, who became very wealthy, and was elected Mayor of Liverpool in 1858. He built St. Margaret's Church, Anfield, and had it dedicated to the saint which bore the same name as his wife Margaret. Robert Preston died at Firgrove House in 1833, aged 73, and was buried in the graveyard of Renshaw Street Chapel. On a tablet on one of the walls inside the chapel his character was summed up as follows :—" He was vigorous from nature and comprehensive from reflection. He was deservedly celebrated for the soundest judgment, the strictest integrity, and the most active benevolence.'' Fir-

grove House is well built, the main wall being 32 in. thick.
It has extensive cellars, which contain a well. The flooring
is of pitchpine, and the doors in the interior of the house are
made of the finest Spanish Mahogany. The walls of the
dining-hall are panelled. The house in its day has been a
beautiful family homestead.

The next owner was Mr. J. Reynolds, of Sandfield Park,
a cotton king in his day, who bought it because it adjoined
his estate. He sold it to Mr. Jeff Thwaites. Mr. Thwaites
had been a farmer in Lancashire, and saved money, and had
emigrated to U.S. America. He went in for stock raising,
but was dissatisfied with the trading methods of the country.
He found that he had but one buyer for his stock, when
ready for market, viz., "the great meat combine." He
came back to the old country and settled down in retirement at Firgrove.

The last occupant was a very different type of man, one
of the most cultured gentlemen of his day, Dr. Londini, of
the Liverpool University, who died at Firgrove in April,
1913. From the first day of the opening of University
College, in January, 1882, until six months ago, Dr. Londini
gave himself freely to the institution he loved. First as
Registrar and Librarian, and later as Bursar, and practically
throughout the whole period as Lecturer in Italian, he
worked loyally and whole-heartedly; he made many friends,
and kept their affection to the last. When illness came upon
him his chief regret was his inability to continue his work.
His was a long life and a useful one, and he has passed
away deeply regretted by his colleagues and students, to
whom his friendship will always remain as a gracious
memory.

He was a scholar in the real sense, and a graduate in
Law of the University of Siena. Apart from his University
interests Dr. Londini did good service as one of the founders
of, and a constant contributor to, the proceedings of the
Liverpool Italian Society. He also was a popular member
of the Lyceum Club, in Bold Street, and had service in the
office of president of that institution.

Dr. Londini's career had been a romantic one before he
came to Liverpool. He was, and always remained a patriotic
Italian, and had seen active service with the Italian army in
the stirring times about 1860. His services to his country
and to the study of Italian in Liverpool received recognition
from his King, when he was given, about 1895, the Order
of Knighthood, and became Cavaliére Londini.

BELLEFIELD.

Bellefield lies just outside of Sandfield Park, West Derby. In appearance to-day it is an ideal place at which to locate a Christmas Ghost Story. A long carriage drive, covered with grass and with tall trees arching overhead, leads to the house, which in its ruin is decidedly picturesque. Its many gables, its tall chimneys, its windows each surmounted with dripstone and having small leaded lights, and its shield shaped coat-of-arms over the front door give it an appearance of antiquity, to which, however, it is not entitled, the fact being that the place has been unoccupied for 27 years, and that the building is not a century old, the sham gothic and the bogus armorials show the place to some advantage in its day of decay; but the interest of the story of every house lies in its inhabitants, and it is especially so in this case, as the old Lancashire proverb has it, " There's nowt so queer as Folk." The family which claimed Bellefield as its ancestral home is that descended from Sir Edward Bates, Bart., whose great grandson, Sir Percy Bates, now owns it. Sir Edward Bates, the founder of the family, in his day held a prominent position in the commercial life of Liverpool. He was a shipowner and East Indian merchant; he was honoured by being made a Baronet, a J.P. and D.L. for Lancashire; and for many years he was M.P. for Plymouth. He was a Churchman, and owned at least one living, and in Knotty Ash Church there is a memorial tablet to his youngest son, who died of fever; it is a beautiful bit of work, and depicts an elder sister descending from heaven to welcome him to the home above. Sir Edward was fond of telling of his early struggles and how rough life was in his younger days. One story which he told against himself is typical. On one occasion he went on board one of his ships and found the crew idle, he thereupon ordered them off his ship, and tried to accelerate their movements with a few kicks, they ran, with the exception of one small man, a shipwright, who took up an axe and threatened to use it if touched. Sir Edward discharged all the men but the little shipwright, his remark was, " that he liked pluck and did not mind being faced."

The carriage drive already referred to, after being made at great expense by Sir Edward, he never used. It opened into Sandfield Park, and as he had not asked permission of the owners of that estate to come into their road, he was informed that if he used it he would be called upon to pay towards the cost and upkeep of the roads in the Park; rather than do this, Sir Edward declared that he would not use it, and the handsome gates were kept fastened, and once only after his death have they been opened.

Sir Edward Bates was the shipowner charged by Mr. Samuel Plimsoll with sending ships to sea which were unseaworthy.

Mr. S. Plimsoll's Speech on the Abandonment of the Shipping Act Amendment Bill.

"Sir," he cried in tones of the utmost excitement, "I earnestly entreat the Right Honourable Gentlemen at the head of Her Majesty's Government, not to consign some thousands of living human beings to undeserved and miserable death. There are ship owners in this country of ours who have never built a ship or bought a new one, but are simply what are called Ship Knackers." At this point the Speaker interposed and pointed out to Mr. Plimsoll that he was not in order, whereupon he passionately declared that on the Tuesday next he would put a question to the President of the Board of Trade, "I will ask the Right Honourable Gentleman whether he will inform the House as to the following ships—the *Tethys*, the *Melbourn*, the *Nora Graeme* which were all lost in 1874, with 87 lives; and the *Foundling* and *Sydney*, abandoned in the early part of this year, representing in all a tonnage of 9,000 tons, and I shall ask him whether the registered owner of these ships, Edward Bates, is the member for Plymouth, or if he is some other person of the same name. I am determined to unmask the villains who send to death and destruction—." Again the Speaker interposed amid great excitement, and said that the word villains was an unparliamentary expression, and trusted that it had not been used with reference to any member of the House. "I did, Sir," retorted Mr. Plimsoll, "and I decline to withdraw it." A scene of wild excitement followed, ultimately Mr. Plimsoll was asked to withdraw from the House. Sir Edward Bates denied the charges.

THE OLD HALL.

Midway between Old Swan and West Derby is a house which to-day is called "The Old Hall"; fifty years ago it was called "The Round House"; and two hundred years ago simply "Sandfield." The last name is remembered in Sandfield Park, which embraces the residential district around the old place. The earliest mention of Sandfield is in the list of law cases, compiled by Benjamin Ayloffe, who, while Clerk of the Duchy Court of Lancashire from 1662 to 1692, carefully indexed and arranged the records of law cases, which he had charge of. There were two cases in which a Mercer was the plaintiff. In Mercer *v.* Hallwood and Others, it was concerning a parcel of land called Sandfield, in West Derby. In Mercer *v.* Molyneux, it was concerning a messuage, nineteen and a half acres of land and a half-pennyworth of land in West Derby and Wavertree. Case was tried Eliz. 21. It is difficult to understand what the half-pennyworth of land can mean, for in Liverpool, near that time, in 1567, beer and ale were retailed at 1d. per quart. It may mean, however, a rent of $\frac{1}{2}$d. per annum. The living portion of the building is a late seventeenth-century erection, but in the wall of the old barn is a stone indicating an even earlier date—

1635.

G.S.   A.S.

In the records of Walton Church we have the marriage of George Standish and Annie Aymount, of West Derby, in April, 1628. The initials on the stone are most probably of these two. Almonds Green, in West Derby, may have been Aymounts Green, originally, and the word Almond a corruption of it.

The Standish family, of Standish, Duxbury, and Sandfield, all claim descent from Ralph Standish, who was with the Lord Mayor of London at the quelling of the rebellion in the reign of Edward I., when Wat Tyler was killed. The family was a noted one. Some members of it remained true to the old faith and took part in the Lancashire plot. Other members were strong Puritans, and in the ups and downs of that party were in turn persecuted, and anon enjoyed their period of power. In 1654 a William Standish, along with three others, all Puritans, represented Lancashire in a Cromwellian Parliament. Miles Standish, the fighting man of the Pilgrim Fathers, whose love story has been so well sung by Longfellow (who in it also immortalised John Alden and Priscilla, the Puritan maiden), came from the Lancashire family. An interesting feature of the Old Hall is that another owner of it, a Mr. Ellis Mather, was able to trace his descent from Richard Mather, who was in his day minister of the Ancient Chapel of Toxteth, who was one of the Pilgrim Fathers, and who in America founded a family which produced some of the foremost politicians and theologians of the first hundred years in the life of that great nation.

OUR VANISHING FOOTPATHS.

The public footpaths of our countryside are a source of pure pleasure for the glimpses which they afforded us of rural scenes, of green fields and hedgerow, of cottage and farm, of running brook and perchance of wild creatures, hares, rabbits, moles, and of various birds; the gradual disappearance of them as the city encroaches upon the country is mourned by many. An old gentleman living in West Derby tells of one which he used to travel upon daily when going to work as a youth. It commenced at Town Row, West Derby, and extended in almost a straight line through country via what is now Sandforth Road, Quarry Road, and across Newsham and Sheil Parks, coming out opposite to Norwood Grove Church. At the rear of the writer's house, in Old Swan, is a passage which at one time was a footpath running between Stanley and West Derby, from Green Lane to Derby Lane, and thence to Black Horse Lane and on to Eaton Road. At the present time the portion between Derby Lane and Black Horse Lane, Old Swan, is in process of change, and the path is becoming a street.

In that footpath is a small white-washed cottage, which is locally known as Maher's Cottage. The Mrs. Maher who lived there for forty years had to carry all the water required for her house from a farmhouse in Black Horse Lane. She was a strong, hard-working, and good-living woman, and when she died, although a poor woman, a special sermon was preached in St. Oswald's Catholic Church on her life. Her husband had been, in his younger days, coachman to Jenny Lind, and before he died to Mr. Reynolds, a local cotton magnate, who lived in Sandfield Park, West Derby. The firm to which Mr. Reynolds belonged became famous for a time; they were the victims of the great cotton frauds by Wilson.

DEYSBROOK.

Deysbrook Hall, West Derby, is now an institution. It was at one time kept up in grand style by members of the Blundell Hollinshead family, who were large landowners in

The Yew Tree, West Derby. (Page 18.)

Moss House, West Derby. (Page 17.)

Walton Old Grammar School. (Page 23.)

West Derby. The dining room is the largest in any local Hall, exceeding those of Croxteth and Knowsley. Its decorations were designed by Stevens.

The family of Deys is, perhaps, the most ancient in West Derby. There are records of them as far back as 1300. The brook may have fed the dam belonging to the water mill which, in 1296, Edward Plantagenet had at West Derby. In Perry's plan of the township in 1796 a field is marked as Mill Dam Hey, or if a wet ditch, the Deysbrook may have run into the one around the Castle.

The Henry Blundell family which settled at Deysbrook Hall is to be distinguished from the Ince and other families of the name. Henry was Mayor of Liverpool in 1794, and added the name Hollinshead. While Mayor, Lord Howe's great victory over the French was won, by which the greater part of the West Indies fell into the hands of the British. When the news of the capture of Guadaloupe arrived there was great rejoicing, a banquet was given by the Mayor, whose brother, Lieutanant-Colonel Blundell, had distinguished himself in the attack. The ships in the river were gaily decorated; flags were hung out everywhere; the church bells rung, and a royal salute was fired from the port.

The present owner of Deysbrook Hall is Col. Henry Blundell-Hollinshead-Blundell.

MOSS HOUSE.

Moss House, at the junction where Moss Lane merges into Queens Drive, in West Derby, has upon its leaden spouting the date 1776, and the initials P. & M. R., the latter standing for Peter and Mary Rigby. Peter Rigby was a merchant of Pool Lane, Liverpool, and became Mayor in 1774. In his day the town was growing rapidly, and two new churches were built. One on the great heath, St. John's, was at the rear of the present St. George's Hall : Mayor Peter Rigby laid the foundation stone of it. It was deemed ugly, and in recent years has been demolished.

Peter Rigby bought land from Lord Sefton and leased land from the Waste Land Commissioners. His descendants have become very wealthy. The site of the Arcade in Lord Street, and Button Street, were part of the family property.

The Hon. Sir Edward Chandos Lee, Counsel to the Speaker of the House of Commons, married Miss Rigby of Moss House.

C

A VENERABLE YEW TREE.

Standing in the grounds of Yew Tree House, now occupied by Mr. Anagnostopulos, and facing the entrance to the West Derby Golf Links, is a Yew Tree which must be of great age.

If we are to accept the legends which are so general about the antiquity of the Yew Trees of our churchyards, viz., that they are anything between 1,000 and 2,000 years old, then this must be an ancient, for surely a finer one never was seen. The fact is, however, that the age of the Yew is difficult to ascertain; there is, as yet, no reliable method of computing their age, either from their trunk or bark.

The tree suffered damage from the heavy snow storms of the winter 1911-12, and it lost some of its branches, they being broken down with the weight of snow. High up amid the remaining branches, several feet from the ground, is a summer bower where, amid the music of nature's orchestra, the song of the birds, and the sound of the wind making melody through the surrounding trees, the residents of the house and their friends can enjoy the refreshing cup of tea. The bower was made by Lawrence Heyworth, J.P., who is remembered as a noble Christian gentleman, but more particularly, that he was a teetotaller at a time when it was not fashionable to abstain from alcoholic drinks.

The Yew has been locally famous. In Jonathan Bennison's tithe plan, 1835, Yew Tree Field is marked as belonging to Mr. Torbock, and it will ever be remembered in Yew Tree Lane and Yew Tree Catholic Cemetery, to the owners of which the tree itself now belongs.

WEST DERBY WAKES.

West Derby Wakes in the 18th Century was the event of the year in the country around the village. It had been celebrated for centuries, and no other place within a long distance could boast the revelry of West Derby.

Originally it had been held on the anniversary of the dedication of the ancient Chapel of St. Mary the Virgin, the village sanctuary, and in early days the celebrations took a very different form to those of later years. In the little Chapel a service was held, the altar and pulpit were garlanded with leaves and flowers, while rushes were scattered upon the floor. In the chapel yard, tents were erected in which a liberal supply of cakes and ale could be obtained, while the people disported themselves in an adjoining field in all kinds of games and athletic exercises. All morning vehicles containing the farmers, with their wives and daughters, their sons on horseback, and the farm labourers, thronged the lanes leading to the village from Walton, Kirkby,, Simonswood, Knowsley, Huyton, and even Liverpool. They came to enjoy themselves; it was not a fair, and merriment and love-making were the features of the time. At Wakes in the South of England, Parson and Clerk attended all day to marry all who applied, and perhaps this custom was observed at West Derby.

Bye-and-bye the religious element of the festival was forgotten, and it degenerated into something like the pagan institution of the saturnalia; a legion of hawkers, showmen, and professional sports invaded West Derby. The manly exercises gave way to games of chance, with prize-fighting, dog-fights, bull-baiting, and much hard drinking. At Farnworth, about ten miles away, the township kept a bear-ward, but a feature of West Derby Wakes was a cruel exhibition called bull-baiting; the bull was fastened by a rope to a stake, which had been secured into the ground, and it was then attacked by dogs, one by one; it had free play for its horns, and beast and dog were sufferers. Bull-baiting was also carried on at Crosby, as the Crosby records show. Mr. Blundell, in his diary, records : June 15th, 1712, "I baited a large bull in ye bottom of my new marlpit. He was never baited before as I know of but played to admiration, there was I think 8 or 9 dogs played the first bait and only 2 the third bait, I think that there was not above 2 dogs but what were very ill hurt. I gave a collar to be played for, but no dog could get it fairly, so I gave it to B. Spencer of Liverpoole, being his dog best deserved it."

West Derby Wakes were discontinued about a hundred years ago. It had become intolerably rough. On one occasion a number of sailors from Liverpool, out for a bit of fun, unloosed the bull, drove it to Liverpool, and dragged it into a theatre, which was then in Williamson Square.

The Wakes were succeeded by a more praiseworthy institution, viz., Club Day, on the last Monday in July. The members of the West Derby Tradesmen's Benevolent Club had their walk, three hundred men being on an average in the procession. The sports were held in the Castle Field, in Meadow Lane. On the break-up of the Tradesmen's Club, the Oddfellows took up the institution and held their walk on the first Monday in August.

WALTON.

WALTON AND LIVERPOOL IN THE 14TH CENTURY.

The life and adventures of Richard de Winwick, Rector of Walton in 1356, takes us back to the days of the Black Prince and the English Victories in France, when it is well known that other local men distinguished themselves for wisdom in council and for valour on the battlefield, when William de la More, of Liverpool, and William Molyneux, of Sefton, received their knighthoods, the one at the Battle of Poitiers and the other at Navarette.

Richard de Winwick was brother to John de Winwick, Rector of Wigan, and we can presume that they came from the village of Winwick, near Warrington. Priest as he was, Richard had something of the adventurous spirit of the local yeomen, and with the fever which sometimes comes upon localities (and which to-day is prompting our young men to go abroad) he must needs set off to visit Pope Urban V., at Avignon, in the south of France (to which town he had removed the seat of the Papacy from Rome). Richard de Winwick was accompanied by his clerk, William Molyneux (probably a relative of the Lord of Sefton), and Thomas de Eltonhead, Canon of Penkridge, in Staffordshire. In travelling through the province of Poitiers, in the department of Vienne, the little party had been set upon, plundered and seized, and ultimately taken to the castle of Sigoyer, where they were informed they must stay until ransomed. French historians tell us something of what the English army had inflicted upon the country round Poitiers, of the robbery, outrage and devastation which had marked its progress, and one cannot be surprised at the small company of Englishmen being waylaid and detained for ransom.

There was chivalry in those days, but with it a vast amount of brigandage. It was quite usual for men of wealth or position to be so captured : had not the French king been treated in that way after the Battle of Poitiers, in 1356—the ransom fixed as the price of King John's liberty was £500,000, an enormous sum in those days, at a time when money was scarce ; when a strong horse suitable for war cost £1 ; a master carpenter earned 4d. per day ; an ordinary tradesman 2d. per day ; a plough cost 10d. ; and a gallon of wine 4d.

Richard de Winwick and his party, however, were clerics, and the demand in their case had a different significance, and instead of sending to their friends and relatives for money, an appeal was made to Pope Urban V. to procure their release. It happened at the time of this incident that there was a lively controversy going on between Edward III. and Pope Urban V. The latter had demanded of the English monarch the annual payment of 1,000 marks to the Papal treasury, as a feudal acknowledgment of the sovereignty of England and Ireland; this was resisted by the king, who was supported by a Yorkshireman, then a warden of Balliol College, John Wycliffe, a name destined to become famous in the history of the Protestant Reformation. Urban V. was a learned man, a founder of schools, and, on the whole, a good man, and it is to his credit that in the very year in which England, through its King and Parliament, refused to acknowledge the claim of the Papacy, he should have written to the Bishop of Gap, of the department of the upper Alps, and who had some authority over Sigoyer, to see to the release of the two Englishmen, Richard de Winwick and William de Molyneux, the third man of the party is not mentioned. Accordingly, they were released and allowed to return home in 1365.

Following the career of Richard de Winwick, it is recorded that in 1368 he demised the Rectory to William, son of Adam de Liverpool, for 1000 marks. Perhaps this sum of money would be required to pay debts incurred during his travels of at least 800 miles on the Continent. He became a Canon of Lincoln Cathedral about 1376, where he ministered until he died on December 12th, 1408. He was buried in the Cathedral, and, until recent years, a brass tablet on the wall recorded something of his life.

Of William, son of Adam, we know that he was Mayor of Liverpool, for he signed a deed as Mayor on April 4th, 26 Edward III., 1352, and on future dates. He was the leading spirit of the town, and was elected and re-elected almost continuously from 1351 to 1362, and, subsequently, for a further three years, a magnificent record. During his term of office, there was a visitation of plague, and, as there was no burial place nearer than Walton, a movement was started for one to be provided; Richard de Winwick, the Rector, was willing, and Bishop Stretton, of Lichfield and Coventry, issued the following Commission for the Consecration of it, also of St. Nicholas Chapel, which was contiguous thereto.

Commisio ad dedicandi capellam & cimiteriu construct in villa
de Lytherpole.
Robtus p'missione divina Coventr et Lich. Epus ditis in C'to
fit majori and burgen3 ville de Lytherpole nre dioc. saltm gra
bn : Quia multiplicate instancijs quibs apd nos p dedicacoe
capelle Sci Nichi de Lytherpole in poch de Walton ejusdem
nre dioc plurie instetistis certis de causis nob p vos expositis
favorabilitr inclinati ut p'fatm capellam ipi cu c'miteriu sibi
contiguu p quencnq' Epm Catholicu gratm sedis aptice & execucom
sui officij obtinente dedicacois munde insignire facte sepulturam
q'. ibid here libam valeat dutamen consensus vicarij dce
ecclie & alior quibs in hac p'te p'judicari pot'rit interveniat
de volutate dicti in C'to filij magri Rici de Wynewyk nuc ipi
ecclie rectoris licenciam tam vobis qm prefato Epo tenore
presenciu concedm spatem : Ita tamen qd jura & obs'vanoes
ejusdem ecclia de Walton ex hoc nullatenus minuantur. Dat
apud Heywood iij idus Februarij anno dmi millio cccmo
sexagesimo primo, et cons nro secundo21.

Translated, it reads as follows :—

Commission for dedicating the chapel and cemetery built
in the town of Liverpool.

Robert, by Divine permission Bishop of Coventry and
Lichfield, our beloved sons in Christ the mayor and burgesses
of the town of Liverpool within our diocese, saluting in grace
and peace :—

Whereas we, of certain and sundry reasons proposed by you
and known to us, are favourably inclined and do consent that
the chapel of St. Nicholas of Liverpool and the cemetery
contiguous to it in the parish of Walton within our diocese
may be dedicated by any Catholic bishop enjoying the grace
and union of the Apostolic see, and obtaining the faculty of
executing his office of sepulture ; and that he may have liberty
to constitute and appoint a burial place which you may have
entirely free in that place : with this condition, that the consent
of the vicar of the aforesaid church (and of others who as to
this matter might be prejudiced or suffer thereby) is obtained ;
and also the voluntary consent of our beloved son in Christ,
master Richard de Winwick licensed rector of the said Church.

We therefore, by these presents grant as well to you as to
the aforesaid bishop this special license ; always providing that
the rights and observances of the said church of Walton be
not in any way whatever diminished or changed by this entire
proceeding.

Given at Heywood 3 Ides of February in the year of our
Lord 1361 ; and, of our consecration, the 2nd.

William, son of Adam, left descendants who followed
in his footsteps and endeavoured to do some little for the
improvement of the town. One of them, Rector John
Crosse, bequeathed by will, dated 1515, a new common hall
to the town. William, son of Adam, lived to a venerable
old age, dying in 1383, and in his will he directed that he
should be buried before the white image of the virgin in

the chapel of Liverpool, where my sepulchre is already appointed. His gift was sometimes used as a meeting place; for wedding feasts, when 1s. 6d. was charged; for dances, when 5s. was the charge; for a court room, a gaol and a warehouse. The townsmen were very proud of it, and it went by the names of Our Lady's Hall, The Town Hall and The Praetorium.

WALTON GRAMMAR SCHOOL.

In the report of the Parliamentary Commissioners on the old School, it states, "The papers of this ancient school being destroyed in the rebellion, the foundation is unknown." It is very probable, however, that originally it was founded and endowed by a descendant of William, son of Adam, of Liverpool (who had bought the rectory of Walton), namely, Rector Crosse, in 1515, as the following item in the Port Mote II, 273, shows, in an account of the bequest of some lands near Liverpool.

> To ye fyndinge of a preste to say masse afore ye ymage of Saynt Kateryne within the chappell of Lyvrpull : (stipulating) yt ye maior and my brother Richard Crosse or his heirs after him shall order and put in a prste suche as they shall thynke best convenient : the whiche prste shall keepe g'mer scole, and take his avauntage from all ye children except those whose names be Crosse and poore chyldren yt have no sccour.

In 1548, a Walter Mildway visited Walton and gave a report upon its school, as follows :—

> A Grammar School hath been heretofore continually kept in the parish of Walton with the revenues of St. Katherine founded in the sd chapel of Liverpool, and the schoolmaster had for his wages £5 13s. 3¾d. yearly of the revenues of the sd chantry : which school is very necessary to continue as heretofore to all time used; and that Humphrey Crosse, schoolmaster there, shall be and remain in the same room and shall have for his stipend and wages yearly £5 13s. 3¾d.

At the time when this recommendation was made, the school had lost its income, the chantry having been dissolved, but Humphrey Crosse was keeping the school going at Walton Church. It was not until 1555 that the Liverpool Corporation built a school for their town. As to the present building, in the Churchyard, nothing seems to be known.

There is, however, a list yet preserved of those who found part of the money to keep it going as an educational institution. In 1613, a Thomas Harrison subscribed £120, in 1630 Alexander Molyneux gave £20, in 1690 Richard Whitfield contributed £10, and there are also others who gave various sums. In its day it did good work for the

young people of Walton and district.   Perhaps its most
remarkable Headmaster was Geronwy Owen.   He was a
Curate attached to the Church, but, besides being an
educationalist, he was a poet of no mean order, and is
regarded by some as the Burns of the Principality.   He was
born in the Parish of Llanfair, in the Island of Anglesey,
on January 13th, 1723.   His father was a tinker, somewhat
clever, but a drunkard; his mother was a woman of great
energy and of decided character, and saw to his being
educated.   He went to a circulating school.   Young
Geronwy proved an apt pupil, and was able, as a youth, to
go to the Friars School, at Bangor.   He became a pupil
teacher and took up duty at Pwllheli.   By the aid of a
friend he was enabled to leave teaching and go to Oxford,
where he matriculated on June 3rd, 1742.   He went in for
Deacon's orders, and was ordained in 1745.   It was in 1753
that he went to Walton as curate, and master of the school.
His stipend was £35 a year and £6 extra as master, also
a house in the churchyard.   He was now well off, but,
unfortunately, he inherited his father's failing and became
too fond of alcoholic drink.   In order to get away from his
evil companions in Liverpool, Rev. Geronwy Owen removed
to London, where be became Secretary to the newly formed
Cymmrodorion Society, and minister to a Welsh Church.
He had married the daughter of an ironmonger in Oswestry,
but she unfortunately also became too fond of strong drink.
In 1758 he was appointed (by the influence of some friends)
Master of a School at Williamsburg, Virginia, U.S.A.   On
the voyage across the Atlantic his wife died.   In 1760 he
lost his situation in consequence of drunken and riotous
conduct.   Another chance was, however, vouchsafed to him,
and he got an appointment as Minister of St. Andrew's
Church, Brunswick County, Virginia.   He died in 1767.
The poems and literary articles from his pen first appeared
in book form under the title " Diddanwch Tueluaidd," in
1763; a second edition was issued in 1817.   In 1860, an
account of his life and a collection of his works appeared
under the name of Gronoviana.   In recent years his poetical
works have again been issued by an admirer, the Rev.
Robert Jones.

OLD WALTON CHURCH.

A Church was at Walton at the Domesday survey, when
it appears as having an endowment of one plough land in
Bootle, probably there was also an endowment in Walton,

for there has been a considerable acreage of glebe within the township.

In 1341, from its income from the ninths of corn, wool, etc., the Church received 54 marks. In 1535 the gross income was estimated at £77 5s. 6d. At about 1720, the Walton Parsonage house and glebe of 36 acres were put down as worth £100 a year and the tithes £828 a year; Curates were kept at Kirkby, stipend £20, at Formby, stipend £20, and at West Derby, stipend £20 16s.

Prior to 1699, the Church of St. Nicholas, at Liverpool, had only been a Chapel of Ease to Walton, and the fact of the Parish Church of Liverpool being four miles away had often been commented upon. In one of the petitions which the inhabitants of Liverpool forwarded, requesting that the township should be granted a Parish, it states pathetically, "that many young men and young women when going to the Parish Church at Walton, call at a village on the way and stay there drinking"—the village would be Kirkdale.

In 1882 the Walton Vicarage Bill, promoted by the trustees of the Liverpool Bishopric Fund, received the Royal Assent. Hitherto, Walton had had a rector and a vicar with co-ordinate powers in but one Church, and many amusing tales are told of the troubles that arose in consequence of having "two captains to the one ship." This Bill enabled the trustees to purchase the vicarage advowson for £28,000, and to raise the Bishop's stipend to the maximum fixed by Act of Parliament—£4,200. Since that date, Walton has had only a Rector.

The rebuilding of the present handsome Church was completed in 1842, and a complete restoration was carried out in 1887. During Archdeacon Spooner's rectorship great progress has been made in Church extension in the large parish of Walton, and two new buildings have been erected and opened for service during the past year.

The erection of the new side chapel entailed considerable alterations to the Church. The citation authorises Canon Spooner (rector) and wardens to remove the pulpit from the north to the south side of the chancel entrance, to make alterations in choir stalls, necessitated by the removal of the organ to the north side of the chancel, and to introduce additional choir stalls.

The interior of the Church is worth seeing, the reading desk dates from the days of Charles I. There are some interesting tablets; the writer copied the following from an old carved board :—

In God the Lord put all your trust, repent your former
wicked ways.
Elizabeth our Queen most just, bless her O Lord in all
her days.
12 penny loaves to 12 poore foulkes, give every sabbath
day for aye.

WALTON HALL.

In 1199 King John confirmed Henry de Walton in his
Stewardship of the Hundred of West Derby, also as Serjeant
of the Wapentake of Salford Hundred. In those days
Henry of Walton must have been an important man, and
we may assume that he would live in a good sized house.

There were other de Waltons, at a later date, than the
Manor Lord of Walton, for in 1429 John de Walton, of
Walton, yeoman, and his sons Thomas, Nicholas and James,
with other yeomen and knaves of Walton, were indicted by
Thomas Bridges, of Fazakerley, for waylaying him at
Fazakerley, with intent to kill him and for wounding him
and his servants. Also, in 1460, a Roger Walton, of
Walton, was a defendant in a suit respecting damage to a
turbary at Aintree, belonging to Sir John Harrington.

The earliest information which we have of the Old Hall
at Walton, which we may assume stood upon the site of the
Manor Hall, is in the will, dated 1708, of Robert Breres,
when it was bequeathed to Roger, his son and heir, and who
had two children, Lawrence and Catherine; these last, in
1730, mortgaged the Old Hall to Thomas Moss, of Liverpool, and, subsequently, to Nicholas Fazakerley, but who in
1746 bought it outright.

In 1804 it was sold to Thomas Leyland. This man, in
some respects, was one of the most notable of Liverpool's
sons. He was the founder of Leyland and Bullens Bank,
and was Mayor of Liverpool three times, in 1788, 1814 and
1820. In his early days he had been partner in a provision
business, which was carried on in Water Street. He won a
large sum of money in a lottery and went into the general
merchant's business, importing Spanish and Portuguese
goods. He was not satisfied with the humdrum and slow
progress of trade, and speculated in a Privateer and a
Slaver; they turned out to be very profitable. The slaver
was a brig, which he called the " Lottery "; she made
regular trips like a modern liner, Liverpool to Lagos, Lagos
to Jamaica, Jamaica to Liverpool. In three years the brig
made Thomas Leyland a profit of £100,000. Several
families well known in Liverpool have benefited from the

fortune which Thomas Leyland, the first Liverpool million-aire, left. The two families of Arcle, one of Anfield House and the other of Edge Lane Hall, were perhaps the most fortunate in the amounts which came to them. The Naylor family also owe much to the enterprise of Thomas Leyland. When the Hall was demolished to make way for the streets of small houses which now cover its site, the remains of a former building were discovered. In 1790 some men, when excavating a garden of the Hall, found a leather bag containing coins to the value of about £1,000. They were of Charles I. and Philip and Mary.

WALTON CHURCHYARD.

In the " God's Acre " which surrounds Walton Church, there is a gravestone which bears the following epitaph :—

> Here lies the body of Thomas Marsden, B.D. About 35 years Vicar of this Parish. One of the King's Preachers for this County, and often Member of Convocation for the Diocese of Chester. Great he was, as an Happy Genius, Hard Study, an Orthodox Faith, a Heroick Piety, Much Learning and Long Experience would make him. He was a Neat Linguist, a Polite Scholar, a Profound Divine, a Good Dispu-tant, and a nice Casuist. Geneva Felt him and was afraid, and Rome trembled at his pen. He died April 25th, 1720, in the 84th year of his age.

The wording is somewhat similar to that sometimes found on mural tablets inside churches, but is unusual on a grave-stone. In his day the Rev. Thomas Marsden, B.D., was evidently looked upon as a power in Church and State ; but alas ! in 1913 it is difficult to learn anything about this man who could make Rome tremble and Geneva fear his pen. His name is not to be found in the biographical dictionaries. It is known, however, that on September 7th, 1665, he was instituted a King's Preacher. This order of preachers succeeded " The Queen's Lecturers," founded by Queen Elizabeth. They were created, first, to combat the doctrines of the old faith, and, second, to fill the pulpits of neglected churches, i.e., churches which were in the hands of illiterate clergy. There were four such lecturers sent into Lancashire. Thomas Marsden, however, was a " King's Preacher " in the days of Charles II., but twenty years after his institution, in 1685, the year of the accession of James II., he became Vicar of Walton-on-the-Hill.

Others of note buried in Walton Churchyard are John Holt, an author and antiquary. He wrote a book in 1795 on " Agriculture of Lancashire," which made him famous.

He gathered together materials for a history of Liverpool, but found he could not finish the task, so he bequeathed them to Matthew Gregson, the Antiquary, who made good use of the matter so handed on to him.

John Palmer, the Actor, and the founder of the Herculaneum Pottery, of Toxteth Park, are both buried here.

The ancestors of the writer for four or five generations are lying in the old graveyard at Walton.

OLD SWAN.

OLD SWAN PIONEERS.

Among the makers of Old Swan, as it was made in the first half of last century, Richard and Paul Barker stand in the forefront. Coming from Huyton, where their father was a builder, they realised the possibilities of this eastern outskirt of the growing town. They showed much enterprise; they were quarry owners, brick makers, and builders, owners of a large underground icehouse, had a copperas works and the water tower, all in Old Swan on the land between Prescot Road and Rock Mount and facing Derby Lane. The large quarries at Quarry Road were also worked by them. Among the places built with stone excavated from their quarries were the tower of Childwall Church, Knotty Ash Church in 1835, West Derby Parish Church in 1850, the Old Swan Police Station in 1850, Sandstone Road in Stoneycroft, &c.

They were extensive brickmakers and supplied Mr. R. Radcliffe, a solicitor, who became a very large builder, with bricks. Mr. Radcliffe built Oakhill Park, Rock Mount, and a great part of Old Swan. The icehouse, made out of a quarry at Prescot Road, was large enough to store 100 tons of ice, and in the winter, when the local ponds were frozen over, the harvest of ice was gathered and stored in it. Long processions of carts would then frequently be seen taking their turns at discharging their frosty contents into the ice chamber; the prices paid ran from 2s. to 2s. 6d. per load. When ice began to be imported from Norway the enterprise became unremunerative and the place was bricked over. However, a few years ago the top gave way and fell in, a horse and cart which had just passed over having a very narrow escape. The copperas works were alongside the water tower ; the icehouse and the builder's yard and its site is now occupied by Rock House, the residence of Miss Nancy Hoult, and the copperas tanks are now covered with the croquet lawn and garden. Where once chemicals, with their attendant ugliness reigned, is now beautiful lawn and conservatory, trees and flowers.

Paul Barker is remembered in a street in Old Swan, Barker's Row. He died in 1848.

OAK HILL HOUSE.

Oak Hill House, Old Swan, got its name from the fact that some of the oak trees of the famous Ladies' Walk, in Old Hall Street (perhaps Liverpool's earliest boulevard) were brought here, on its demolition in 1778. Oak Hill Park, adjoining, derives its name from the same source. It was built in 1773. It has had some interesting personalities among its inhabitants. Richard Watt, who came to Liverpool a poor boy from Standish, and went to the West Indies. He became a sugar planter, and came home a very rich man ; his hunting stables are still to be seen in Broad Green Road. Miss Watt, of Speke Hall, is his descendant. Sir John Tobin, Knight, who at one time was Mayor of Liverpool, and whose bust is to be seen to-day in the Art Gallery, also lived here.

In Standish Church there is a large alabaster tablet erected in memory of R. Watt, who died November 4th, 1796, aged 72 years. The sexton is very careful to show it to Liverpool visitors.

The last tenant of the Oak Hill House was Mr. Edward Chaloner, a timber merchant. He was a Catholic. He took a great interest in education and was largely instrumental in building the Schools at St. Oswald Street, Old Swan. He also helped his co-religionists in different parts of Liverpool to build schools. For his friend Father O'Reilly he bought a disused Methodist Chapel in Jordan Street, Liverpool, which he handed over fully furnished and equipped, the total cost amounting to £4,360; it was accepted by Bishop Goss on January 4th, 1859. Mr. Chaloner, during the time that he resided at Oak Hill House, at his own expense, brought the children to his grounds and entertained them year by year.

In later years this school was demolished, and the new schools erected in place of it were called Chaloner Schools, thus handing down to posterity the name of one of the good men of Old Swan.

Mr. Chaloner gave the land upon which the fine church
(from a design by Welby Pugin) was afterwards built in
St. Oswald Street, Old Swan.

Oak Hill House has been demolished and its site is now
occupied by numerous houses and a laundry.

THE STORY OF HIGHFIELD.

Highfield, at Old Swan, near Liverpool, has as romantic
a history as the New York House, the story of which has
been so well told by H. C. Brunner. It was built in 1763
on the site of an older house, by a Mr. Wakefield, described
in his day as a Liverpool sugar baker. It next became the
home of Charlotte, Dowager Duchess of Atholl, Baroness
Strange and Lady of Man in her own right as heiress of her
great great grandfather James, seventh Earl of Derby. For
a neighbour, at the adjoining township of Wavertree, she
had a relative in Lord Henry Murray, who was brother to
the Duke of Atholl. He lived at Eton House.

In 1775 she bought Highfield House and estate. She
enjoyed the salubrious air of the neighbourhood, and was
delighted with the extensive views from the windows on all
sides. In one of her letters, preserved at Blair Castle, she
speaks of being able to see five parish churches from the
upper windows of her new home. It is interesting to be
reminded of the parishes represented by the spires and
towers which existed in her day, for it must be remembered
that the country was then but thinly populated. They
would be those of Walton-on-the-Hill, Huyton, Prescot,
Childwall, and Melling (in Halsall parish). The Duchess,
in 1779, sold her house and lands, commonly known as
Highfield, to her son John, Duke of Atholl, who in turn sold
them to Mr. Parke, a Liverpool merchant, who became the
founder of a famous family, the most eminent member of
which was James Parke, in his day a famous lawyer and
judge. He was knighted in 1828, and made baron in 1856,
and helped to make national history, for it was he who was
objected to by the Members of the House of Lords, who
declined to allow him, as Lord Wensleydale, to sit in their
House, on the ground that his peerage was a life peerage,
and they (the Lords) insisted, at " that time," upon all new
members of that august House being made hereditary.
E. A. Freeman, the historian, writing about the incident,
says : " I refer to the peerage granted to Lord Wensleydale. That eminent lawyer was, according to a crowd of
ancient precedents, created a peer for life only. He had no

sons, so that the question was not a practical one; it was simply that this occasion was chosen to assert an ancient and wholesome principle. But with matchless impudence the hereditary peers, in defiance of precedent, in defiance of law, in gross contempt of the lawful authority of the Crown, refused to let Lord Wensleydale take his seat in the House.'' The Crown yielded its ancient and undoubted right; Lord Wensleydale, lawfully summoned to Parliament, was shut out from his seat till the new patent was granted securing the seat after him to the descendants who were not in being. He had, however, three daughters who married and had offspring : they were (1) Cecilia Anne, who married on 21st September, 1841, Sir Matthew White Ridley, fourth Baronet, and had a son, the first Viscount Ridley, who died 28th November, 1904; (2) Mary, who married the Hon. Charles Wentworth George Howard, son of the sixth Earl of Carlisle; her son, born in 1843, is George James, ninth Earl of Carlisle; (3) Charlotte Alice, who married in 1853, the Hon. William Lowther, brother of the third Earl of Lonsdale, and her son, born in 1855, is the present Speaker of the House of Commons, who still wears the gold watch given to him by Grandfather Parke.

After Lord Wensleydale, who, by the way, was born at Highfield, the occupants of the house were a series of merchants and lawyers, each in their day people of standing belonging to Liverpool, perhaps the most notable of whom was Thomas Littledale, who was Mayor of Liverpool in 1826. His son, likewise named Thomas, succeeded to Highfield, and he, too, took an interest in civic affairs, while still a young man being elected a member of the Town Council; he represented Exchange Ward. Thomas Littledale was Commodore of the Mersey Yacht Club, and during one of his cruises he came across a burning emigrant ship '' The Ocean Monarch,'' it was off the coast of Wales. He at once, in the most gallant manner, went to the rescue and was able to save a large number of the unfortunate emigrants. His conduct was much commended, and in 1851 he was elected, without opposition, to fill the Civic Chair. He died in 1861 at the early age of 42. There was a large gathering to the funeral, his partners, H. Littledale and John Torr (afterwards M.P. for Liverpool), his wife, with three daughters and two sons, St. George Littledale and Alfred Littledale. He was buried in the churchyard at Knotty Ash.

Born at Highfield House, C. St. George Littledale, having the means to gratify his tastes, became a great traveller and sportsman, the latter in the sense of being a veritable Nimrod. Despising the ease, comforts and luxury of home, he traversed the dreariest and most inhospitable of countries. He received the Royal Geographical Society's Medal for information collected in a journey across the Pamirs in 1890. The Pamirs are called by the Chinese, " The half-way house to Heaven " : it lies between China, Russian Turkistan, Afghanistan and Kaffiristan, and its climate is said to be nine months of winter and three months cold. In 1893 St. George Littledale travelled from Kokhan to Peking, collecting a vast amount of information and having remarkable adventures. His most famous exploit as an explorer was in Tibet, and here he had to endure hardships enough to discourage a less intrepid explorer. He was accompanied by his wife, Mr. W. A. L. Fletcher, of Allerton, and a dog. In crossing the Tibetan plateau, which lies 2,000 feet above the Pamirs, he recorded that as they mounted above timber height, the trees and bushes were found dwarfed, none being higher than an umbrella or walking stick. Water and grass were scarce and the animals which carried the luggage of the little party died off one by one; all had to walk and carry stores, and eventually had to abandon specimens, goods, and all impedimenta. On nearing civilisation the little party found that they were in a hostile country, false information was given and all kinds of hindrances were placed in their way, and threats were used towards them if they persevered in their attempt to reach Lhassa. To make progress it became necessary to travel by night and dodge all human beings. Eventually, when this plan became impossible, officials came and pleaded with them, begging them to return, as they (the officials) feared to lose their heads if they allowed foreigners to go through their provinces towards the capital. The little party, however, kept on and tried to make progress towards their goal. The Tibetans were apparently anxious not to injure Mr. Littledale and party, and yet they desired to prevent their progress; the bridges in front of them were destroyed and soldiers gathered in their path. At this critical time Mr. Littledale was taken ill, and the little cavalcade were compelled to return to a more hospitable country.

At a later date Mr. Littledale and party again made an attempt to penetrate the Hermit Kingdom. He took another route and travelled across it from north to south and west to Ladak. On this journey they were for four weeks at a

A 14th Century Document relating to Walton and Liverpool. (Page 20.)

Old Walton Church, now demolished.　(Page 24.)

Scandinavian Font, Walton.　(Page 24.)

Walton Hall, now demolished. (Page 26.)

Oak Hill, Old Swan, now demolished. (Page 29.)

Wesley Chapel, Old Swan, now Catholic Club. (Page 35.)

height of 17,000 feet, and so intense was the cold that everything was frozen; bread had to kept near the body to keep
it soft, and in the morning their hair would be found frozen
to the pillow on which the head had reposed during the
night. Particulars of this journey of exploration can be
found in the Geographical Journal, dated May, 1906.
In connection with the Philosophical and Literary Society
of Liverpool, Mr. Littledale gave an exhibition in January,
1890, at St. George's Hall, of his trophies of the chase, they
numbered fifty and consisted of full-sized stuffed animals and
mounted heads and necks, the most striking were what are
called Marco Polos sheep; these wild animals were shot on the
Pamir, 15,000 feet high, in 1888, and they are as large as
an English calf or a Kerry cow. There were many rare
specimens, viz., Olland stags, bear, chamois, deer, coral
scrow, ibex of the goat family, and wild sheep called Bharal
of the Altai mountains, Asia. Most of these are now on
view to the public at the Museum, William Brown Street,
Liverpool.

Among the most remarkable tenants of Highfield was
F. W. Sandford and his followers, at one time numbering
sixty. They were missionaries from a new religious sect
who had their headquarters at Shiloh, Maine, U.S.A.
Sandford and his followers were known as Holy Ghosters
by the profane, from the prominence which they gave to their
belief in the third person of the Trinity. Sandford himself
claimed to be the reincarnation of Elijah. They were very
harmless while at Highfield, they paid all their tradesmen,
and there was no scandal about their morals. One boy who
went there on a message from Old Swan came back very
frightened. He said that a black man had tried to convert
him. The mission was a failure. They took a chapel in
Edge Hill, but eventually, after spending a lot of money,
the enterprise of converting England was abandoned.

Sandford next visited Palestine, giving it out that he had
a mission to evangelise the Holy Land. He then purchased
a yacht called the Coronet, and his party set out on the
strange quest of a search for the promised land,
and he held out alluring hopes to his followers. The vessel
visited ports in Egypt and elsewhere, and wandered
about the ocean for months, in almost aimless fashion,
many times being provisioned by passing ships, which were
attracted by a signal of distress. The boat was quite
unseaworthy, and nearly everybody on board was ill from
scurvy, while many could not walk. Sandford was arrested

D

on the charge of retaining the fortunes of some of his followers, who put money into the scheme, but could not withdraw it. There were fifty-five survivors of the voyage out of between sixty and seventy who started, and Sandford is now in an American prison.

Highfield is now in possession of the Liverpool Select Vestry, and is used as a hospital for epileptic and other patients.

In the garden of Highfield was a sundial, on the plate is engraved " Liverpool Lat. 53-13, Egerton Smith, Facit." The engraver is to be remembered as the founder of the great newspaper " The Liverpool Mercury." In his day he carried on the various businesses and professions of Writing Master, Printer, Mathematical Instrument Maker, and Publisher. On the dial plate is engraved a ducal coronet over a large capital " A " for Atholl, and below it, in smaller type, " S " for Strange, all now hardly legible. The sundial has been removed to the garden of Mr. Fletcher (whose wife had been a Miss Littledale), at Allerton.

EARLY OLD SWAN POSTAL ARRANGEMENTS.

It may be of local interest to know how the letters were distributed in the eastern outskirts in 1840. The post office was in the Old Swan Inn, then a stopping place for the coaches. The writer's grandfather was the proprietor of the inn, and it was part of the duties of his wife to look after the post office. There was one postman, and his name was Wright. His duties commenced at six o'clock in the morning, when he had to clean boots and do odd jobs about the inn until eight o'clock, when he took out his bag of letters. Between eight o'clock and twelve o'clock noon he had to deliver letters all over Broadgreen, as far as Court Hey, then to Knotty Ash, as far as Dovecot House, also a portion of West Derby. In the afternoon he had to continue delivering his letters, and took the districts of Old Swan, Edge Lane, Fairfield, Stanley, and Green Lane. Village Postman Wright received six shillings a week wages and his food. For some years the old man, on his day out from the workhouse, of which he had became an inmate, called upon the writer for a small dole of tobacco, which he was glad to give him in memory of the old times. His last call was about six years ago, when he complained of feeling ill. It is more than probable that he is now dead.

OLD SWAN AND ITS METHODISM.

The first meeting of the people called Wesleyan Methodists in Old Swan was in a shed, in the back garden of a large house in Broadgreen Road, called May Place (now a Catholic Reformatory), the entrance being from Mill Lane, and the date 1838.

Earnest men were attached to the cause from the beginning, and members were won so rapidly that in 1841 the largest room obtainable in the neighbourhood was taken, it was in St. Oswald Street, over a Mrs. Murphy's shop, now a clothier's, and occupied by Miss Beer. On removing here, the South Liverpool Circuit took the young society under its care, and provided preachers for its Sunday Services.

Progress was maintained, and in a very few years, in 1845, a real chapel (called Wesley Chapel), which had been erected on a piece of waste land bought from the late Lord Salisbury, was opened amidst great rejoicings; it was situated on the opposite side of St. Oswald Street to the meeting place, and is yet to be seen.

The Circuit, which took over the Chapel on erection, was a large one, consisting as it did of eight places of worship, scattered over a considerable tract of country in and near Liverpool; they were Pitt Street, Mount Pleasant, Wesley, Wavertree, Windsor, Woolton, Aigburth and Garston. There were four itinerant ministers, and about a score of local preachers, who in turn occupied the pulpits.

The Superintendent of the Circuit, at the time of the opening of the Old Swan Chapel, was the Rev. Wm. Wood Stamp.

The gentleman, however, who laid the foundation stone, and afterwards formally opened the building, was a Mr. Spence, of May Place, who had previously bought the land and given it to be the site of the Chapel. The little place was christened Wesley Chapel, after the founder of the Society, and at once entered upon a period of prosperity. People of influence in the neighbourhood joined and became officers and leaders, among whom were Mr. Hurst, who built Hurst Street, and who was the manager of Jackson's Ropery; Mr. Austin, of Valentine's Farm, Stoneycroft; the foreman of the Glass Works, Mr. Standard, the first Superintendent of the Sunday School, and a local preacher; and a Mr. Fraser, the leading grocer and baker of the district, having shops in Old Swan and Grey Horse. The services from the beginning were well attended, and the sittings in demand. The most eminent ministers in the Connexion on special occasions occupied the pulpit, and crowds flocked to hear men like the Rev. R. Newton, D.D., four times President of the Conference; Squire Brook, the noted Yorkshire orator, and others equally renowned in their day.

Although deeply in debt, the building having been erected in faith, the leaders and stewards felt that the need of more sitting accommodation was pressing, and a scheme was originated for adding a gallery at the west end of the Chapel. The choir and the lovers of music in the congregation also claimed that an organ was a necessity, and money was raised towards the cost of both, but again there was a deficiency, the result being that when the gallery was erected and the organ bought, the debt had reached alarming proportions.

Whether the extra expenses were justified or not may be realised by a statement of the income for the year 1854 :—

Collections, Class & ticket money—March Quarter,	£1	15	6
,, ,, ,, June ,,	5	17	5
,, ,, ,, Sept. ,,	3	9	4
,, ,, ,, Decr. ,,	3	12	9
	£14	15	9

In that year the Vestry expenses were : for Coals £3 6s. ; for Gas 4s. 8d. ; for Wine £1 3s. 6d. ; and Refreshments 3s. 6d. The respective amounts are very curious— only 4s. 8d. for gas, and the amount of £1 3s. 6d. for wine, being especially so. The organ was put in, and the first organist was a local genius, who was appointed to the position when only 11 years of age. His name was Mr. Sam Fraser, who afterwards took his degree of Mus. Bac. At the age of 15 he left, and became organist at St. Bridget's Church, Liverpool, afterwards at the Parish Church, Holmfirth, Yorkshire, at Queen's Park Parish Church, and at Elder Park Parish Church, both of Glasgow. When he died, the Glasgow papers gave great prominence to the matter, and published accounts of his career. A very serious blow to the Chapel was the closing of the glass works, which were near to the Chapel.

The day of adversity had arrived with a vengeance and at last the trustees had to face the awkward position of not being able to meet the liabilities of the Chapel. At this crisis, Mr. Stewart, who was Treasurer of the Trust, Poor and Society Steward, and Superintendent of the Sunday School, volunteered to buy the place and let it back to the Society at a yearly rent of £25. This was agreed to.

For a time things looked up again, but, unfortunately, Mr. Stewart failed, and the Chapel building, being an asset, was offered for sale. The highest bidders were the agents for the Roman Catholic Church, which adjoined the Chapel, and so, in 1866, they became the owners of the place. It is now used as the meeting place of the Catholic Young Men's Society, and is furnished with billiard and card tables, etc.

Methodism, however, was not dead in Old Swan, and at once plans were prepared for another start; generous friends appeared on the scene, and land was bought in Greenfield Road; it was a better position in every way, and a building was erected in 1868, called St. Paul's, at a cost of £3,500.

The income for the year 1869, beginning at March Quarter, was as follows :—

Collection, Class & ticket, March,	£32	14	0
	June,	32	2	6
	Sept.	24	13	4
	Decr.	37	7	8
	Total............	£136	17	7

Not reckoning Connexional Fund Collections, or Pew Rents, this financial statement was quite satisfactory. The families then associated with the new Chapel were Mr. Edward Hutchinson, Mr. Edwin Green, Mr. Wm. Potter and Mr. L. P. Brooke, to be followed with the Ashcrofts, Iveys, Warnocks, Fieldings, Nyes, Hoults, Porters, etc. Prosperity has attended the cause at Greenfield Road. Among the ministers have been the Rev. W. H. Dallinger, John Hornabrook, C. E. Dove, H. H. M'Cullagh, B.A., and Rev. L. Waterhouse.

SUNDAY SCHOOL.

The earliest date recorded in the Sunday School minute book of an organised school is 1850, but the record of teachers' meetings begins on February 7th, 1858. Fortunately for us, in our search after knowledge of our beginnings, a report of the " state of the school " appears; it was read at a public meeting held after a tea meeting. The meeting took place in the schoolroom under the Chapel.

The report tells of the school having been closed and of a state of things which must have disheartened the most loyal and enthusiastic of teachers. It tells of an ill-ventilated room with a low ceiling, and so dark that gaslight was required even at day time to allow of reading; the walls were damp, and the floor in such a state of bad repair and rot, that only portions of it would bear walking over; but as a climax to the discomfort of this school, we are told, that on the Sunday previous to closing, that every square pane of glass on the side adjoining the Roman Catholic Chapel was broken, and that the floor was covered with stones, many of them 7 lbs. in weight.

The attendance of scholars had dropped to the dimensions of a single class, the number present being 20, viz., 12 girls and 8 boys.

Mr. T. Standard, who had been Superintendent and Secretary combined, tells of a certain Sunday afternoon when only one scholar turned up (a girl named Stubley), and he, feeling it was his duty to teach her, devoted the afternoon to her instruction. The report is very frank, and the Secretary must have been a man of courage, for he mentions that in the school there are two drawbacks to success, one, lack of funds, the school having had an income for the previous eight years of less than 35s. a year, and the other (what a hero to state it), the inefficiency of the teachers; one is glad to find that the word inefficiency was used by someone in those days.

A library had been part of the school equipment from an early date, for the report says that out of 140 volumes in it, 60 have been found useless, partly the result of the damp schoolroom and partly from wear and tear. It is noteworthy that Mr. W. Potter, afterwards well known as a librarian in the City, was deputed to buy books, and to use his discretion in the choice of them. At that time, 1858, books were more valued than now, scholars paid 1d. per month and teachers 2d. per month for the privilege of being members of the library.

There is a sentence in the report which reads as follows, viz. : " Things were in such a state that school and chapel were all but passing into the hands of our next door neighbours, had not Divine Providence raised up a kind friend who came to the rescue and saved the place." Does it not read strange to us who in these days can see the old place daily, as part of the Roman Catholic Church premises?

However, for a few years the officers, teachers and

scholars were able to meet for mutual help and religious service in an improved and comparatively commodious schoolroom, thanks to the anonymous friend of the Sunday school. The first Sunday School Anniversary Sermons were preached on Whit Sunday, May 28th, 1858, by the Rev. George Curnock, known in his day as the Precentor of the Conference; the services were in every way a success, and a new era began for the school. The collections amounted to £7 10s. 4d.

The Sunday School at Greenfield Road has turned out a number of successful men; among them an ex-Lord Mayor of Liverpool, S. M. Hutchinson, Esq., J.P., Sir C. C. Wakefield, J.P., Alderman of the City of London, the late Professor John Ivey, of Sacramento, Mr. Wm. Potter, of Moor Hall, each of whom were teachers and officers in the School.

Mr. Standard, an early Superintendent of the old school, had, although but a working man, won the affections of a lady, the daughter of a British Admiral. Her father, angry at the marriage which took place, disowned her, and the couple found it expedient to leave Portsmouth, their previous home, and seek the seclusion of this part of the country. She, on Sundays, appeared in Chapel, resplendent in old fashioned silks and satins which she had saved from the days of her prosperity. In old age, husband and wife came to poverty, and the Chapel took charge of them, various members contributing to their support; they received 15s. a week.

MAY PLACE.

May Place was built before 1768; it is a large, red brick house, and is now a Catholic Reformatory for Girls; it is directed by Sisters of Charity, and is doing good work. In its time it has had many owners and. tenants. There is a legend to the effect that its builder was an African slave merchant, who also traded to India for silks, and who married an Indian Princess. But in recent years it has been the home of Mr. Papayanni, a Liverpool shipowner; a Mr. Spence, who favoured the Methodists, and allowed them to hold meetings in an out-house in the garden; a Mr. Austin who was said to have had 20 children; and a Rev. Mr. Wilson, who was Chaplain to Lord Derby, and who had here a large and flourishing School. The drowning of a boy (who was the son of a wealthy gentleman from the south of England) in a pond near the School, was a serious blow to the School, and it declined from the date of that tragedy. A Mr. Walker, a wholesale grocer, of Liverpool, also lived here, he is remembered as having been an epicure, and building for his French cook the square cottage at the bottom of the hill at Oak Vale. The Right Hon. Augustine Birrell, when a boy living at Wavertree, went to May Place to school, when Rev. Wilson was headmaster.

A LESSON FROM AN OLD CHARITY SCHOOL.

THE PURPOSE OF EDUCATION.

The Head Constable's report, which brings out the painful fact that juvenile crime has increased from 944 cases in 1906 to 2,402 cases in 1912, has prompted me to moralise on juveniles and morality from my study, as an antiquary, of Old Swan Charity School, and as an educationist connected with a modern Corporation school.

Herbert Spencer says that " education has for its object the formation of character." Character, therefore, is the first consideration, according to him.

A little over a century ago, four Liverpool citizens met together and agreed to erect a charity school at Old Swan, and in the memorandum of association it states that the chief object of the subscribers is " to promote decency of behaviour, and by having the children taught to read, to instil into their minds more effectually the principles of religion and a proper sense of moral duty." These gentlemen—Messrs. T. Staniforth, J. Jackson, R. Watt, and T. Parke—were leading merchants of the town, and they considered that " decency of behaviour and a proper sense of moral duty " were the most important things to teach children. The subscribers, or governors, of the Old Swan School, which, by the way, was built in 1792, had very crude ideas with regard to the education of young people, and just as we agree with them in their first proposition, so we differ with them with regard to others. For instance, the head master was instructed " that he shall not on any pretence whatever presume to teach any of the boys to write or to understand arithmetic without the special orders of the Governors." Evidently, the idea in the minds of these educationists was that the children were not to be taught too much ; that they were to be trained to be labourers (as their parents had been), and not to aspire to learning or culture, as these accomplishments were for their so-called betters.

These thoughts were general among the well-to-do of

Highfield, Old Swan.   (Page 30.)

Old Swan Charity School. (Page 40.)

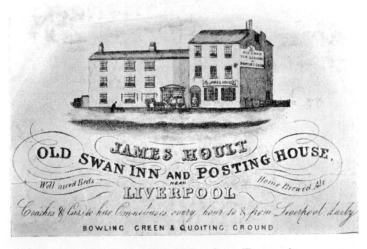

Old Swan Bill-head in 1842. (Page 45.)

that time. At a neighbouring Church school, at a somewhat later date, at Knotty Ash, the wife of the rich man who built the school, on one occasion brought a hairdresser to the school and instructed him to cut short the hair of those girls who had long tresses. This was done to impress their young minds with the fact that they belonged to a lower order of society, and that only the girls of gentry families were privileged to make full use of this " glory of womanhood." If at the same school a little daughter of Eve wore coloured ribbons about hair or neck, she was reprimanded and the ribbon was confiscated.

It is interesting to notice the point of view of educationists of a hundred years ago. They considered children as young savages, and the need was to civilise them ; they were heathen and wanted enlightenment. Throughout the minute book of Old Swan School one cannot but notice the important place given to religious instruction, the necessity for the scholars to go to church, and the instruction as to their behaviour when there. For example, the Governors rented a pew in Wavertree Church for them, for which they paid £3 2s. 6d. for two and a half years' rent. This was on November 16, 1800. They engaged a singing master, so that the young people could be instructed in psalm singing. It is significant that they engaged no other outside teachers. On one occasion the Governors passed the following resolution : " That the children do stand while the Psalms are sung, and not suffered to lean carelessly on the side of the pew, or on one another, but stand upright with their hands before them and clasped, this will contribute greatly to decency of behaviour." We can picture to our- selves the scene on a Sunday morning in old Wavertree Church, with its double-decker pulpit, and these children, naturally restless from the young life within them, having to stand so stiff and, with hands together, take part in the service.

The time of Confirmation was the event of the school year. Although the school was in West Derby Township, this religious ceremony took place at the nearest parish church, which happened to be Childwall. An old lady, recently dead, described to the writer how she, as a girl, went to be confirmed from this school. The maidens dressed in white and the boys in black clothes formed a little procession, headed by the master, and marched from the school, via Score Lane, to Childwall. Other boys went before and prepared the way, laying leaves and straw upon muddy places. They were confirmed by the Bishop of Chester, in whose diocese Childwall then was.

Just as the founders of our old charity schools required instruction on the importance of giving the children a good all-round education, and preparing them to make the best of life by training their intelligence and fittng them to become more useful members of the community, so in our day we, perhaps, want reminding that the building up of a good character is the most important item in early education, and we may well ask ourselves if we are doing all that we might to train the scholars in our schools to be " decently behaved " in moral conduct.

" In my class, and it is a large one," said a teacher the other day, " there is not one girl who would not on the slightest pressure tell a lie." The writer, who has taken into his employment numbers of boys fresh from school, has been startled at the way in which some of these boys will lie, often when no object could possibly be served by so doing. The fear of the policeman and the disgrace of falling into his hands is strong to-day, but where minor dishonesties can be perpetrated they are alarmingly common. Tradesmen also tell of young married people habitually trying to get into debt, and then in various ways endeavouring to avoid payment—a sure sign of low moral fibre.

In the code of regulations issued by the Board of Education for the use of managers and school officials we find in the introduction that it states : " The purpose of the public elementary school is to form and strengthen the character and develop the intelligence of the children entrusted to it." To form and strengthen the character takes the first place. At headquarters they are sound on the subject, as the following extract proves :—

Moral instruction should form an important part of the curriculum of every elementary school. Such instruction may either (1) be incidental, occasional, and given as fitting opportunity arises in the ordinary routine of lessons, or (2) be given systematically and as a course of graduated instruction.

The instruction should be specially directed to the inculcation of courage; truthfulness; cleanliness of mind, body, and speech;. the love of fair play; consideration and respect for others; gentleness to the weaker; kindness to animals; self-control and temperance; self-denial; love of one's country; and appreciation of beauty in nature and art.

The teaching should be brought home to the children by reference to their actual surroundings in town or country, and should be illustrated as vividly as possible by stories, poems, quotations, proverbs, and examples drawn from history and biography.

The object of such instruction being the formation of character and habits of life and thought, an appeal should be made to the feelings and the personalities of the children. Unless the natural moral responsiveness of the child is stirred, no moral instruction is likely to be fruitful.

Amid the crowd of subjects being taught in our schools to-day, can it be honestly said that a proper importance is given to character formation? In one school (Corporation) is hung in a conspicuous place the legend, " Honour is our motto." Would that in every school this noblest of our words were understood, and that more of honour in its relation to conduct was taught to, and practised by, the rising generation ! The need of the hour is that every head master and mistress, and every teacher, in our schools should take it as a serious responsibility to follow in the spirit and in the letter the instructions received from the Board of Education on moral training.

GLASS-MAKING.

Travelling towards Old Swan from any direction, the huge cone of the old glassworks is to be seen on the top of the hill. Started in 1825, when glass, like most other things, was taxed, the proprietors had to face a restricted home market. The business having to depend largely upon export trade, and to compete with French and Italian glass in the world's market, it was necessary that the latest and best methods of glass manufacture should be adopted. The old English sheet of glass was made round, and always had in the centre, an unsightly knob. The French method did away with this, and made the glass in large, even, clear, square sheets. With commendable enterprise the Old Swan firm imported forty French glass-makers, and adopted their improved methods. They quickly built up a large and profitable trade ; a new cone was built ; men's wages rose to £3 10s. a week; the works had a brass band ; some of the men were noted athletes ; and it looked at one time as if Old Swan were to become a great glass manufacturing centre. Liverpool itself became a good customer. The sheet-glass for the Custom House, price 1s. 9½d. per foot, and the plate-glass in the Royal Insurance Buildings, at 7s. 6d. per foot, came from the works. However, the end came, the wrong-doing of one man causing the disaster. The Government allowed a rebate of 80 per cent. off the tax on glass exported. The proprietor, or some official from the works, got access to the Revenue export books, and on several occasions altered the items by adding the decimal figure, making 30 cases of glass exported into 300 cases, and so on. The fraud was at last discovered; a great trial ensued in London. The grandfather of the writer had to go up (by stage coach) as a witness, and the result was the closing of the works. Many of the Frenchmen had married English wives. Some settled down in their new country, but others went back, taking their wives with them. The name of the manager was Tipton. He lived in the top house in Edge Lane, on the north side of the Lane. At one time there were three glass houses, with cones. Mr. Lancaster, the Chief Librarian of St. Helens, has an excellent water colour of " A View in Old Swan," in which two cones are shown and a church in the background; the church would be St. Oswald R.C. Church, which was built from a design by Pugin, and is a beautiful building.

SWAN HILL FARM.

In 1768 there was no road between Wavertree Lane, Wavertree, and Old Swan, excepting Mill Lane. Within the memory of inhabitants still living, the present wide, handsome Rathbone Road was a lane leading to a farm from the Wavertree side. There was also a lane to the same farm from the Old Swan side. The farm was called Swan Hill Farm, and passing it from west to east was a footpath which was a relic of the old pack-horse track. The farmer, John Clifford Etches, was also a cattle dealer. His land extended from Edge Lane Hall, Fairfield, to Cunningham's Nursery, Broadgreen. He was a pioneer in exporting cattle to America; he also imported from Spain. He, at one time, owned the Liverpool Abattoir, and was a large shareholder in the Stanley Cattle Market, which was opened in 1830.

He was succeeded by George Roddick, also a large cattle dealer, and he imported cattle from America. Geo. Roddick was a public man and was well known for his interest in Education. He was a Governor of the Old Swan Charity School, living to a good old age, in his latter years in retirement in Rock Ferry, Cheshire, where he died in 1911.

OLD SWAN BAPTISTS.

The first Baptist Meetings in Old Swan were commenced in 1839 by Mr. Geo. Cunningham, of the Broadgreen Nursery, and his father, both of whom were members of Lime Street Baptist Church, the minister of which was

Rev. J. Lister. For a few years they were carried on, at first with success, but afterwards languished. The little company of Baptists then joined their friends, the Congregationalists, who were worshipping in a hayloft in Green Lane, and helped to build their first Chapel (it is now used as a School). They remained together for some years and then, in consequence of a disagreement concerning Baptism, they parted company, the Baptists hiring the Old Swan Assembly Room, in Salisbury Street. Here they held their services for twelve years. A member, Mr. Lascells, contributed £50 a year for most of the time, to pay for the services of students from Spurgeon's College. A fair amount of prosperity was experienced, and in 1873 Rev. Daniel Jones was invited to become Pastor, and accepted. At once a movement was started for the building of a Chapel, Mr. Geo. Cunningham being the moving spirit and most generous contributor, and in 1878 the present Chapel in St. Oswald Street was opened. It is noteworthy that it has a very handsome marble baptistry, said to be the finest in Liverpool. The cause has fluctuated considerably, at times the Chapel being crowded, and keeping its own minister, but of late years it has fallen upon evil times and has attached itself to another Baptist Church, by which it is supplied with lay preachers.

THE NAME OLD SWAN.

Old Swan, which is now the most rapidly growing suburb of Liverpool, takes its name from the hotel of that name. It has been the custom from time immemorial for inn proprietors to take for their sign the coat-of-arms or crest of the local aristocratic family. In the early eighteenth century the family of Waltons, of Walton Hall, were the great landowners of Old Swan neighbourhood, which then was moss and moorland of little value. The coat-of-arms of the Walton family had on it three white swans on a blue shield. On an old map there stood on the site of the present hotel an inn named the Three Swans. Two more inns in course of time (as traffic increased on the turnpike road) were erected, and each claimed the name. The writer remembers, as a boy, their designations as the Old Swan, Middle Swan, and Lower Swan. The centre one (the new red brick house) was the site of the old original inn. It consisted in the coaching days of a long, low-built, straw-thatched wayside hostelry, built upon the rock which could be seen at its base. It had a mounting stone for horse travellers in front, and a spacious yard at the rear. It is easy to imagine the slight change of name from the Three Swans to the Old Swan, especially as the "old original" was the stopping place for the coaches and also the post office for the district.

COCK PITS.

The most popular of all sports one hundred years ago in Old Swan was cock fighting. At the rear of the original Old Swan Inn was a cockpit, much patronised by men of the cocking fraternity. Being almost equi-distant from Liverpool, Knowsley, and Prescot, it was a good centre for battles between the champion cocks of these places. While the patrons of the sport among the nobility were contesting their cocks in the noted pits of Winwick and Aintree, exciting themselves over the champion cocks of Lancashire, and matching them against the champions of Yorkshire and Cheshire, the local farmers and tradesmen were doing the same at Old Swan. A main between Knowsley and Liverpool would bring a crowd of sportsmen to see the contest, and a full account of it would appear in "Bell's Life." Lancashire was famous for its breed of cocks, and for the love of the sport among all classes. The most famous patron was the 12th Earl of Derby, who had cocking in his bedroom during his last illness. His feeder, "Potter," was esteemed the best trainer of cocks in England. His method was to teach them to spar and to fight while they had pads on their heels, these pads being like miniature boxing gloves. At the recent Royal Agricultural Show the old English gamecocks were to be seen to perfection, strong of leg, broad in chest, quick of eye, and with the most dangerous looking beak. It was plainly to be seen that they had been bred for war.

OLD SWAN BRIDEWELL.

"West Derby Bridewell, 1803," was the legend inscribed on the small lock-up which stood a few years ago on the site of the present branch of the Bank of Liverpool, Old Swan. It is a singular fact that the stocks were at West Derby Village, and the lock-up in Old Swan. It is said that it was erected at a time when highway robbery and sheep-stealing were too prevalent in the neighbourhood. Both crimes were then deemed so serious as to be ranked as equal to murder in the eyes of the law, and were punishable by hanging. The furniture consisted of a stone seat, and chains riveted to the wall, to which prisoners were handcuffed if violent. The building was made of blocks of sandstone, and originally was very strong. After thirty-five years, however, it began to show signs of decay, and the last prisoners broke through the roof and escaped. Through the crevices between the blocks of stone, where the mortar had been, friends outside could communicate with those inside. On occasions a long or churchwarden's pipe would be passed through. Beer was poured into the bowl outside, and the prisoners imbibed it from the mouthpiece of the stem inside. It came about on a number of occasions that prisoners were put in sober and came out drunk.

STORY OF AN OLD SWAN CONSTABLE.

Old Swan, interesting as most places of a century or so old are, has its special spots, and one of them is Black Horse, a hamlet consisting of a group of cottages, an inn, a wheelwright's and a blacksmith's shop. Mr. Davies, the proprietor of the blacksmith's shop, is proud of the fact that the business has been in the family for considerably over 100 years ; the anvil now in use is over ninety years old. It was in this smithy that a local parish constable (so the story goes) sold his wife. It appears that he was gossiping with the smith and a soldier home on furlough, when the wife of the constable, a buxom woman of about forty, came to call her husband to come home to dinner. The soldier noticed her, and casually remarked " that she was a fine-looking woman." " If you think so," said the careless husband, " you can have her ; I am open to sell." " If she will agree," said the gallant soldier, " I will take her." The matter was put to the wife, and after a little bitter thinking she said, " Well, if he (her husband) thinks so little of me, I will go." Two gallons of ale was the price fixed upon. The bargain was completed, and she, gathering up a few of her belongings into a bag, went off with her new master. So recently as 60 years ago, it was commonly believed that a man could legally sell his wife, if she was agreeable to the transaction, and willing to wear a halter while for sale, in the same way that a horse wore one while in the market. An old gentleman told the writer that he had seen a woman standing in the market place at Farnworth, near Widnes, with the halter over her head.

Here are other authenticated cases :—

The following is an extract from the " Wolverhampton

Chronicle and Staffordshire Advertiser " of February 10th,
1790 :—

> " At Burton Fair, last Tuesday, there was a sale of a young
> woman of the parish of Swadlincote, whose husband some time
> since absconded, and left her chargeable on that parish.
> " She was put up in the Market Place by the parish officer,
> and sold to a man of Greasley for the sum of two shillings,
> deducting the price of the halter in which she was delivered.
> " This last transaction was entered in the Toll Book, and all
> parties went home well pleased."
> Says the Rev. S. Baring-Gould in "A Quiet Village,"
> "there lived a publican some miles off whom I knew very well.
> Indeed, he was a namesake of a first cousin to a carpenter in
> my constant employ.
> " He bought his wife for a stone two-gallon jar of Plymouth
> gin, if I was informed rightly.
> " She had belonged to a stonecutter; but, as he was dis-
> satisfied with her, he had put up a notice in several public-
> houses to this effect :
> " ' Notice.—This here be to inform the publick as how
> G—— C—— be disposed to sell his wife by auction. They be
> a dacent, clanely woman, and be of age 25 years. The sale be
> to take place in the — — Inn, Thursday next, at 7 o'clock.' "

ROCK HOUSE, OLD SWAN.

Mr. Joseph Hoult, J.P., of Thornton Hough, Cheshire,
lived at Rock House, Old Swan, in his younger days. He is
a shipowner, and as a public man has served in Parliament as
M.P. for Wirral, and when on the City Council of Liverpool,
he was elected to the important position of Chairman of the
Watch Committee; in late years he has given generously
towards aviation schemes and towards the movement for
fighting cancer.

THE FIRST OMNIBUS.

The first omnibus in Liverpool was put on the road
about 1833—in which year it is said that one was started
in London. It plied between the Turk's Head, Knotty Ash,
and the Town Hall, Liverpool. The pioneer was a Mr. Dell,
followed by a Mr. Bullen, and perhaps others, all finding
it unprofitable. In 1840, however, Mr. James Hoult, grandfather of the writer, took up the enterprise, and made it a
success. In those days the outside fare all the way was 6d.,
and inside 10d. The inside passengers had luxuries in the
shape of rugs to cover their knees, and straw for the feet.
There were also looking-glasses to ornament the rather
confined apartment. The time occupied on the journey was
about 1½ hours, the 'bus stopping at most of the public-

Bridewell, Old Swan, now demolished. (Page 46.)

Historic Blacksmith's Shop, Old Swan. (Page 47.)

Pre-historic Urn, Wavertree. (Page 51.)

A Lawrence and Catherine Davis Jug. (Page 47.)

Urns, Scraper, and Arrow Head from Wavertree. (Page 51.)

Urn found at Wavertree. (Page 51.)

Gates of Wavertree Hall   (Page 53.)

Wavertree Lock-up, 1840. (Page 54.)

houses en route. The local aristocracy, "those who lived in the big houses," were especially well catered for, the driver blowing his horn to advise his coming, and then driving up to the house door for his passengers. It was possible to book seats beforehand, and one gentleman, who lived at Oak Hill House, regularly booked two seats for his wife, so that she should not be squeezed by the other passengers.

OLD SWAN WATER TOWER.

The Old Swan water tower, that tall square stone building which is so prominent by the tram terminus, was built by Messrs. Richard and Paul Barker, builders and quarry owners. Originally it was two storeys higher than at present, and had at the top an enormous tank, into which the water was pumped from a well beneath. It supplied Messrs. Barker's tenants and any other inhabitants of Old Swan who were willing to pay the water rate which they charged. On the whole, the enterprise was not profitable, for in 1845 the Liverpool Corporation sank their very large well at Green Lane, which was on lower ground and eighty yards deep, and tapped their underground reservoir. The water tower became almost useless, but not quite, for the well was found to be able to take the liquid contents of the drains of the adjoining property, and for some years it acted as a sewer outlet. It is now, however, filled up. The water supply in the subterranean sandstone of the neighbourhood is marvellous. The Green Lane well has pumped as much as 22,000,000 gallons of water a week, and if the pumps are running slack, other wells in the neighbourhood begin to fill up. Previous to 1845, the great Fir Grove delph had several feet "in depth" of water, which teemed with fish, the water, however, disappeared when pumping began at Green Lane. Paul Barker died in 1848 and the business was continued by his brother, Richard.

AN OLD SWAN SUNDAY SCHOOL.

Literary and debating societies are often credited with having had much to do with the making of some of our public men. Sunday schools, however, have done much in Liverpool. It is doubtful if the record of the Methodist Sunday School at Old Swan can be beaten in the quality of men who, as young men, were trained to speak in it.

E

Among many others who have " got on " and " made their mark " are a late Lord Mayor, Mr. S. M. Hutchinson, J.P., who was secretary of it, and whose wife was a teacher of a class of young ladies. The writer heard him give his first Sunday school address, which he was not able to complete, but on a subsequent occasion, trying again, he did very well. Then there was Charles C. Wakefield, a teacher of small boys, now Sir C. C. Wakefield, Alderman of the City of London and an ex-Sheriff of the Empire City, and who in the near future is destined to be Lord Mayor. Among those who have passed away are Professor John Ivey, of Sacramento, U.S.A., whose paintings were, a few years ago, exhibited in Liverpool, some of them—namely, " Scenes in the Yosemite Valley," being much admired and commented upon. The late William Potter, of Moor Hall, Aughton, was librarian of the small library of the school, and his declining years were lived in one of the most stately homes of Lancashire.

ST. OSWALD'S CHURCH.

In August, 1842, the Church was formally opened by the Catholic Vicar Apostolic. The spire was the gift of Mr. Michael Gibson, of West Derby, and the whole architecture is of a very fine order, reminding one of the churches built in early mediæval days. The land had been bought from Lord Salisbury by a loyal member of the church, Mr. Ed. Chaloner, and given to the Benedictines, and it was by this Order that the work was carried through. The bells were the means of stirring up a little bigotry, and a formal protest was made by some local Protestants, they being under the impression that only the Established Church of the land had a right to call people to service by the ringing of bells.

In the same month on which St. Oswald's Church was opened, Daniel O'Connell, then Lord Mayor of Dublin, and in the height of his power and fame as an agitator, spoke at the Liverpool Amphitheatre and there made the acquaintance of Mr. E. Chaloner, they became friends, and in the following year Daniel O'Connell came and stayed at his house at Oak Hill, Old Swan.

WAVERTREE.

ANTIQUITY OF WAVERTREE.

The question is sometimes asked " Is Wavertree very ancient?" and the answer has to be, "What is meant by ancient, and what is meant by Wavertree?" If we understand the latter to mean a settlement of people on the spot now known as Wavertree, then Wavertree goes back to remote antiquity, further than any other place in S.W. Lancashire, for the Olive Mount Cemetery, with the sun baked urns, arrow heads, and flint scrapers, takes us to the earliest race of people to inhabit our countryside. The so-called " Calderstones " were originally in the old Township and also indicate a people of the stone age who carved on stone with a flint instrument and mallet. If the place known by the name of Wavertree is intended, then again it can be said " that Wavertree is as old as any other place in the country," for it had its manor in the days of the Saxons and was in the Parish of Childwall of the Diocese of Lichfield. In Edward the Confessor's time the manor was held by one named Leving, after the Conquest it was added to the royal manor of West Derby. The spelling of the name is interesting. In Domesday book it is Wauretree, in 1329 Wavertree, in 1381 Wartre, and later it varies between Wartre, as pronounced locally, and Wavertree which has been for centuries the correct and official name of the place. The manor was revived in the 12th century, and in 1189 Henry de Walton held the whole 16 oxgangs of land which constituted the manor; he rendered for it 2 marks and 100s., also a palfrey (a small horse led by the bridle on state occasions). In 1205-6 the manor estate was in the hands of the king, and according to the pipe roll, the sheriff was allowed 70s. from corn produced in Wavertree. In 1346 it was in the hands of Henry, Earl of Lancaster, and it is recorded that free tenants paid 4d. and other tenants £4 10s., and that the turbary or turf lands were valued at £6 13s. 4d.

Numerous cases are recorded in the Law Courts in mediæval days in which Wavertree inhabitants were interested. In 1329 a Thomas de Warrington was charged with the murder of Robert de Wavertree, at the Hallmote Court at West Derby. It was a long trial : it was found that the wrong man had been charged and the verdict was that another Thomas, a shoemaker, was the guilty party.

In the days of Queen Elizabeth there was a dispute

between Richard Latham and the inhabitants of Wavertree regarding the rights of the latter to 50 acres of common.

In 1592 the Bishop of Chester visited these parts and caught James Claighton pipeing in Wavertree on the Sabbath day. He was so indignant at the man's levity that he excommunicated him. From the record of the visitation of Warrington deanery of this time, it would appear as if the majority of the worshippers at Childwall Church had come from Wavertree and some of them got into trouble, for instance, Thomas Greaves, of Wavertree, for talking in the Church at sermon time, was ordered to confess his fault in the Parish Church on the 22nd instant. A William Ather, of Wavertree, was excommunicated for being in the ale-house at time of Divine Service.

Charles I., in 1628, sold the manor of West Derby to some London citizens. The purchasers contended that their bargain included Wavertree, but the tenants at Wavertree refused to acknowledge the new claimants for their rent. There was litigation over the matter which lasted ten years, eventually the tenants had to give in. When the dispute was settled, in 1639, the manor was sold to Lord Strange who became Earl of Derby. It was sold again in 1717 to Isaac Green, the ancestor of Lord Salisbury who is the present owner.

From Gregson's Fragments we find that Wavertree township contained, in 1731, fifty houses out of which only three were untenanted.

In the reign of George III. the people of Wavertree lost their Common or Green, a most valuable estate, by Act of Parliament.

In 1849, Mr. Hugh Hornby in the Chair, the Select Vestry of Wavertree, took in hand the proper sewering of the village.

In 1851 Wavertree became a Local Government district, familiarly known as a Local Board.

In 1894 Wavertree was made into an Urban District Council, and in 1895 it was incorporated with Liverpool and is now part of that great city.

The Chapel of Ease in Church Road, now the Parish Church, was opened along with the burial ground which surrounded it, in 1794.

The Congregationalists formed a Church at Wavertree in 1836 and opened the present Chapel in 1839.

The Wesleyans built their Church in Victoria Park in 1872.

The Catholic Church is strong in Wavertree, the most famous being that of the Redemptionists at Bishop Eton in Woolton Road. The designs of the Chapel were by Pugin. It was built in 1851. In the grounds is a fine Calvary, a most unusual object of reverence in England.

WAVERTREE HALL.

Wavertree Hall does not now exist, and the sole reminder of the Hall of the Township is the beautiful wrought iron gate, which, from its design, the late Bishop Stubbs used to say reminded him of his College Gates at Cambridge. When the building was being demolished portions of an earlier building were found, with rough hewn timbers fastened with wooden pegs and indications of a straw thatched roof.

The earliest record which the writer has of the occupants of Wavertree Hall is derived from Greyson : He mentions Richard Percival as living in poverty at Wavertree Hall, about 1760. The Percivals were a county family and boasted a pedigree, from which they traced their descent from Harfrestus the Dane. They had been among the local landed aristocracy, being Lords of Allerton, different members marrying into the families of Norres of Speke, Lloyd of Bryn and the Gregge's and Radcliffe's. An ancestor was bailiff of Liverpool and an Alderman of the Town. The Richard Percival mentioned was a man of strict integrity and denied himself the comforts of life at Wavertree Hall, so that he might pay off debts incurred by his father, and also to increase his mother's slender means.

The next occupant of the Hall was John Blackburne. He was Mayor of Liverpool in 1788. He erected a mansion on the east side of Hope Street, called Blackburne House (now a Young Ladies' School), but removed subsequently to Wavertree.

More recent occupiers of the Hall have been a Mr. Harvey, John Smith, a wealthy Drysalter, and Bishop Stubbs of Truro, during the time that he was Vicar of Wavertree.

MEANS OF COMMUNICATION AT WAVERTREE.

Omnibuses and Railway Trains came almost together in point of time; it appeared as if people had suddenly begun to realise that there was need of quicker and more frequent communication between the towns and villages.

In 1835 the Directors of the Liverpool and Manchester Railway Company sent a letter to the Select Vestry of Wavertree requesting permission to place gates and make a level crossing at Wavertree lane. This the Company were allowed to do, and a sort of station was made there, a man was placed in charge of the crossing and to hurry people over, also to stop the trains if there were passengers.

An Omnibus was placed upon the road about the same time, starting from the Lamb Inn in High Street, John Bland being the pioneer. The fare was 1s. 6d. inside and 1s. outside. The earliest journey to town was made at 9 o'clock. Passengers could be called for at their houses. It was usual to stop at the principal public houses on the line of route; the horses were put up during the middle of the day, morning and evening being the times when the conveyance was in demand. In those days seats could be booked and two local magnates, Hugh Hornby, of Sandown, and Henry Royds, of Elm House, had seats regularly reserved, if necessary the omnibus would call for them at their offices.

The next enterprise was undertaken by James Redish, of Woolton, who started coaches which ran hourly between Woolton and Liverpool, via Wavertree. Mr. Redish did well at the business and was able to retire to Brighton. Others succeeded him and the coaches were popular, old George and Adam being still remembered, while the blowing of the horn always awakened the sleepy of Wavertree village. The coachmen wore white hats in fine weather and black if the rain should be falling. Although the coaches were strong vehicles there were occasional mishaps, once a back seat full of passengers came down and caused injuries to some of them.

There was a time when Wavertree become quite a resort for Liverpool people, the "Old Thatch," recently pulled down having pleasure grounds at the rear. The Coffee House and the "Lamb Inn" both laid themselves out for afternoon visitors. With increasing demand came increasing competition and rival Omnibuses began to run, it was Dilworth or Matterson, and the fare dropped to 6d. inside or out, and then to 4d.

THE CONSTABLE AND HIS DUTIES.

With the 19th century came fresh duties for the Constable. The authorities at London wanted to know a lot of things about the country, and who could get the desired information better than the Constable. Among other items

which our Wavertree official was asked to furnish were
(1) in 1801 to give an account of the number of bridges
between Wavertree and Prescot. (Road-making schemes
were at the time being much discussed.) For this information he charged 1s.; (2) In 1803 he had to supply a list of
all live and dead stock in the Township. We can imagine
that among the farmers and tradesmen there would be some
resentment at this inquisition and that some difficulties
would be put in his way, and that, having filled up the
schedule correctly, he would feel that he had earned the 3
guineas which was his fee; (3) In the some year he supplied
what was called " a return for the Army of Reserve,"
presumably a list of able-bodied men of the township—for
this he only charged 10s. 6d.; (4) In 1811 he had to take
a census of the entire population of his township. The book
which he bought to record the names in cost 5s., his labour
in the matter 12s. 6d., total 17s. 6d.

The Constable's burden of work and responsibility,
added to by the Government, had a further load added to it
by the Church. It happened that on February 11th, 1810,
the tower of St. Nicholas' Church, Liverpool, fell, killing
22 people. Other Church towers and spires were then
examined as to their stability, among them that of Childwall,
and it was condemned as being unsafe. As Wavertree was
of the parish of Childwall the call came upon the township.
It was ordered that the expense of pulling down the tower,
and the re-building of it, was to be met by an assessment
and a lay which the Constable had to look after. In July,
1810, the first call was made and realised £427 12s. 1d.,
and in 1811 the second collection was taken, which realised
£432 9s. 6d. In going through the books dealing with the
matter, we notice that Bamber Gascoyne, Lord of the Manor,
M.P. and J.P., was the largest landowner and that he had
14 tenants who each had to pay the amount to which they
were assessed.

RURAL WAVERTREE.

Life in a rural township in the 18th century was not
very different from life in the country to-day. The cultivation of the land in field and garden and the care of live stock
were and are the main business, but in Wavertree the change
has ever been from rural to urban; it is noticeable how
thoroughly rural it was 150 years ago. We can get some
particulars from the township records. To us it is passing
strange to read that a man could earn as much as £9 16s. 3d.

in a year for catching moles, and this is the amount that
was actually paid in one year to Richard Knaggs. The mole
is an insect feeding reptile, and to get at the worms which
it prefers it is in the habit of burrowing through the soil,
forcing to the surface small piles of loose earth, so making
the field look extremely untidy. The farmer looked upon the
mole as an enemy.

On December 21st, 1780, the following item appears in
the Constable's book : " By Cash received for Atkin killing
a Patridge (Partridge) £2 10s." The farmer was willing to
put the township to the expense of destroying moles, which
probably did his land more good than harm, but killing a
partridge was another matter, and here we have a reminder
of one of the great evils of those days ; game was strictly
protected for the sport of the Landlord and his friends, the
farmer had to submit to partridges feeding in his fields, and
severe was his punishment if he killed one, as Atkin found
out.

Dogs were kept by nearly everybody, but farmers and
labourers found them almost indispensable, they even
accompanied them to Church. At Childwall the Church-
wardens appointed a Dogwhipper to keep the dogs in order,
while in Church. The Overseers at one time considered that
owning a dog was a luxury and passed a resolution to the
effect that " A poor person must not be allowed relief if he
or she kept a dog."

WAVERTREE CHAPEL.

The earliest record we have of a Church or Chapel at
Wavertree is to be found in a will, that of Thomas Gylee,
of Liverpool, dated February 3rd, 1525, wherein certain
copyhold and burgage lands are given to the Chapel of
Wavertree, " Chappell of Wavetre."

On a map in the possession of the writer, from a survey
taken of Lancashire in the days of Charles II., Wavertree
is marked as having a Chapel. Nothing is known of the
old place of worship other than that a street has been called
from time immemorial Chapel Street. It would probably be
a small straw-thatched wooden building, had it been otherwise some remains of its foundation, its altar, its font, or
its communion vessels would have been found.

The present Parish Church (Holy Trinity) was built in
1794, to be a Chapel of Ease to the Church of Childwall.
In 1825 it had, as perpetual Curate, Rev. W. L. Hutching
Clark, M.A. It was well attended from the opening, the

inhabitants of Old Swan went there, it being nearer than their Chapel at West Derby, or their Parish Church $3\frac{1}{2}$ miles away at Walton.

As an indication of how the new Church supplied a need to the entire district, the list of those who bought graves in the Churchyard tells its own tale. In 1798 John Tarleton, of Wavertree; in 1798 Charles Eyes, of Wavertree; in 1804 William Ewart, of Broad Green; in 1805 James Swan, of Wavertree; in 1808 C. Clements, Jr., of Broad Green; in 1811, James Gildart, of Knotty Ash; in 1819 Thomas Parke, of Old Swan. Those who lived outside Wavertree had to pay a higher price than local people for graves.

Wavertree was made into a Parish in 1828, and the Rev. Wm. Badnall, M.A., was the first vicar. He had been domestic Chaplain to the Duke of Cambridge; he is remembered as having been a good elocutionist, and able to read the lessons and prayers in a most impressive manner. He entered into all the life of the village and became very popular. He became Chairman of the Select Vestry, when it was formed to look over the local government of the Township.

The Church is of Doric architecture, and, as modernised, is a beautiful building, both in its exterior and interior. It is remembered by old worshippers as being very different inside, and they like to think of when it had a three-decker pulpit, and when Mr. Morgan, the Clerk, occupied the lower one. There are many interesting memorial tablets on the walls.

Among the Ministers, the late Bishop Stubbs was perhaps the most famous. The present Vicar is the Rev. J. L. Mitchell, M.A., B.D.

Wavertree had no Grammar School like the neighbouring townships of Walton and Liverpool. There was, however, early in the 19th century, an Academy and a Common School, but little is known of either. There was a Charity School in Mill Lane, but in Old Swan, which admitted Wavertree boys and girls, and on Sundays the Scholars had to attend Wavertree Church. On November 16th, 1800, the subscribers paid £3 2s. 6d. rent of a pew in the Church for $2\frac{1}{2}$ years for them. On one occasion the Subscribers or Governors decided that " The children do stand while the Psalms are sung and not allowed to lean carelessly on the side of the Pew, or on one another, but stand upright with their hands before them clasped.'' Then follows the comment, " This will contribute greatly to decency of behaviour." This latter being more important in the minds of the subscribers, who, in building the school, stated that "the chief object of which School shall be to promote decency of behaviour, and by teaching the children to read, to instil into their minds more effectually the principles of religion and a proper sense of moral duty."

EARLY LOCAL ADMINISTRATION.

Wavertree township in the 18th Century, in common with other townships in Lancashire, had three departments of local organisation to attend to, viz., the care of the poor, the upkeep of the highways, and the safety and peace of the community; for the latter there was an official, "the Constable." The cost of administration was usually met by a lay or levy of 1d. in the £ for the poor, 2d. in the £ for the highways, and 1d. in the £ for the Constable; the total in 1768 came to £76 19s. 6d. The Constable, in 1767 to 1770, was supervisor of the roads, and kept the books for the Overseers of the Poor. He was the important official of the township. Among other duties, he summoned Juries to look over water cosies (presumably the streams, ponds and mosses); to look after boundary stones (which were sometimes missing) and to periodically ride the liberties of the township (as was done in Liverpool and elsewhere), the Constable heading the procession and finishing, as usual, with a dinner at the public cost—the usual charge was 10s. 3d. He frequently had to kill mad dogs, for which he received 1s. He it was who summoned town's meetings to appoint land tax sessors, and fix the number of ale houses for the township. He also had to do with the surveying of windows for the windows tax, also with the levying of the lays, or what in these days we call rates.

Annually, on November 5th, the constable saw to the making of a bonfire, which cost from 5s. 6d. to 10s. 6d. a time.

The exciting topic of the fate of the common required that he should call meetings about it (the Wavertree enclosure was passed in 1768).

Crime was rare in the township, and when in May, 1768, the constable had to make an arrest for a sessions case, it was an event in his life. He took into custody a certain Betty Conley for felony. He engaged a series of men to guard her for eight days and eight nights (preparatory to her trial) at a cost of 9s. 4d. He then hired a man and horse and cart

to take her to be tried at Preston, at a cost of £1 12s. 2d.;
the following month he had to appear with her at Wigan;
eventually, Betty Conley was discharged. Stealing in those
days was looked upon as a terrible crime and was punishable by hanging. When the next town's meeting was held,
and the constable's accounts were looked into, there was
great complaining about the expense of the case, and he
was told that he must be more careful and economical in
future. Matters of assault, drunks, and bastards, the
constable took before Bamber Gascoyne, J.P., of Childwall
Hall.

Cases of drowning and sudden death were expensive to
the township. The jury invariably cost 4s. in ordinary
cases, but there were times when foul play had been
suspected, and expenses ran up to a guinea. At other times
the constable had to buy a coffin, and see to the interment,
when the items were : Burial 4s. 6d., Coffin 4s. to 10s.,
Church Dues 2s.

POOR RELIEF.

Arising out of the dissolution of the monasteries, the
problem of poor relief was first considered by Parliament
in the days of Henry VIII., in 1531, when it was ordered
that the churchwardens and the parish constables were to be
responsible for the welfare of the poor of the parish. It was
all right in theory, but in practice it did not work in the
majority of parishes. The townships eventually came to
looking after their own poor.

The overseers of Wavertree township, in the last half
of the 18th Century, had the care of but few poor, but these
were conscientiously looked after in times of frost, sickness
and death, fuel and clothing being freely distributed to
necessitous cases. Old people and widows were also relieved
with grants of money ; young women who could work had
work found for them ; at the death of a poor person the
overseers paid the cost of their burial. The food and drink
for the sick was not too generous ; on October, 1767, it
appears, from the Overseer's book, that 3s. 10d. was paid
for ale and bread for W. Worthington during his sickness.
In January, 1768, the parents of children were allowed 1s. 6d.
per week for each child, during the frost. It is interesting
to notice the various items of clothing provided by the
Overseers for different people in need, also the spelling
and the cost of them, viz., check handkerchiefs 11d. each,
pettycoats 3s. 6d. each, bedgowns 2s. 6d. each, stayes 2s. 6d.

each, shifts 2s. 6d. each, a yard of cloth 1s. 6d., clogs 6d.
per pair, leather britches 2s. per pair, blankets 7s. each, etc.
Coals were provided and sometimes part of the rent was
paid.

Some of the poor gave great anxiety, for instance, there
was the case of Ann Whitstone, who first came upon the lay-
payers in May, 1767. She seems to have been a bad lot, for
in 1769 she is again costing money, and there appears the
item of £1 7s. 1d. for laying out and burying Ann
Whitstone's bastard child (the word illegitimate does not
appear in the Overseer's book until 1825). In July, 1769,
the Overseers were paying her board wages, 3 weeks at
1s. 6d. per week, total 4s. 6d. At the end of the month
we have it recorded, "Troubled with Ann Whitstone, she
being out of her senses, extra expenses 2s. 6d." There is
a dramatic element here and one wishes that one could know
more about the erring and unfortunate Magdalen. Another
case was that of Kitty Kirkham, who was a heavy charge
on the little township; eventually, the sum of £6 8s. 4d.
was paid to her on condition that she asked the township
for no more relief. There was also a case of a man being
paid to marry a woman and take her off the rates. In 1774
a system came into vogue of apprenticing boys of poor
parents; a representative item in the accounts reads, "Paid
two indentures to bind Lyon's boy 5s."

NOTABLE WAVERTREE TOWNSMEN.

In looking into the way in which Wavertree township
was governed, especially in its local administration, a little
over a century ago, one is impressed with the fact that the
best men of the district were looking after things.

Among the signatures in the Constable's, Overseers',
and Road Supervisor's Books, we note those of (1) Bamber
Gascoyne, J.P. and M.P. for Liverpool. He was the son
of Bamber Gascoyne, M.P. for Truro, who had married
Mary, co-heiress of Isaac Green, and who became Lord of
the Manors of West Derby, Childwall, Wavertree, etc.;
Lord Salisbury is descended from the same ancestor. The
constable frequently reports that he took prisoners before
B. Gascoyne, Esq., at Childwall, and (2) Edward Falkner,
at Fairfield. In 1797 the national outlook was very gloomy.
Invasion from France was anticipated and rebellion had
broken out in Ireland. Our people of S.W. Lancashire at
once prepared for war—Wavertree had the honour of being
first to provide a Volunteer Regiment. Mr. E. Falkner

raised and commanded it, *i.e.*, a troop of light horse. He was a J.P., and, in 1788, High Sheriff of the County. He married a Miss Tarleton, of Wavertree. The Tarleton family were large local landowners, the part of Old Swan now known as Stoneycroft belonging to them. E. Falkner built Fairfield Hall, which is still standing. In 1803 there were again war alarms and we find that Major-Commandant Edward Falkner was to the fore, and commanded " The Liverpool Light Horse." (3) Thomas Earle was Mayor of Liverpool in 1787. He had, in his early days, lived at Brook Farmhouse. In 1797 he commanded a regiment of volunteers. About the year 1803 he built Spekelands, a large square building of white stone between Wavertree and Edge Hill, where he resided until his decease in 1822. In 1810 he signed the accounts relating to the re-building of Childwall Church steeple and the assessment of the township.

(4) James Clarke was Recorder of Liverpool. He was a great student of books, but he also studied men and was noted for his shrewdness and knowledge of the world. He was renowned for the justice of his decisions; an " old stager," however, records an incident in which he did not shine. A huge sailor and a small boy were being tried for stealing an immense piece of cable. The sailor threw the blame upon the boy, and the Recorder, who believed him, was charging the jury to the same effect, when one of them, rising, commenced, " But, Mr. Recorder "; the Recorder was full of indignation at being interrupted and he tried to silence the intrepid juryman. There was an excited time in the court; the man would not sit down. The Recorder made another attempt, and exclaimed, " From the evidence the boy must have been the culprit, the law says so and I say so." The juryman was not done, however, and insisted upon having his say : " But, Mr. Recorder, I say that commonsense tells me that that boy could not even lift that piece of cable from the ground, much less run away with it." This was a poser with a vengeance. There was a laugh in the court which nothing could check. The poor Recorder was nonplussed, and the jury acquitted the boy without a moment's hesitation. James Clarke signed the Wavertree township accounts as a Magistrate in 1809.

(5) Joseph Birch, afterwards Sir Joseph, has been described as a noble-looking specimen of the merchant prince and old English gentleman. He was engaged in the West India trade. In politics he was a Whig and became M.P. for Nottingham. He found time, however, to oversee the

affairs of the poor of Wavertree, especially in the year 1799. About the year 1803 he bought the estate of the Red Hazels, which lies between Wavertree and Prescot.

(6) Nicholas Ashton's name appears very frequently in the old books of Wavertree township, at one time as magistrate, at another time as making a special contribution towards the supervisor's fund for the repair of a road. Once he is mentioned in connection with the arrest of some men who had assaulted him on the high road. He was, in 1770, High Sheriff of the County of Lancaster, and required the constable to attend on him. John Ashton, the father of Nicholas, had been an important man in his day. He had been Bailiff of Liverpool, and became rich from his connection with the Sankey navigation. Nicholas was very popular and on one occasion was escorted all the way to Lancaster by a large body of gentlemen on horseback. Nicholas Ashton did not aspire for Parliamentary or Municipal honours, but lived an active, useful and benevolent life at Woolton Hall, which he greatly improved and adorned with lead statues.

(7) Charles Eyes was engaged, professionally, by the township to survey their boundaries, which he did in 1795, preparing a plan, etc., for which he charged £1 11s. 6d. He resided in Wavertree, but was at one time Surveyor to the Town of Liverpool. He owned a field in Wavertree known by the name of Edge field, which he bought from Matthew Gregson. He also owned a seat or pew in Trinity Church, Wavertree; it would require to be full size for he had eleven children. Chas. Eyes will be remembered for many generations to come for the excellent plans and maps which he prepared of Liverpool and district.

The signatures in the old books are in their penmanship extremely varied, as is usual with writers of to-day. There are specimens of caligraphy which could not be excelled, and going to the other extreme there are a few who, not being able to write, signed with a cross.

Among other names which appear, and which have not been forgotten by the oldest inhabitants of Wavertree, are William Carr, who went to London, made his fortune in New Bond Street, came back to Wavertree, died there and was buried in the churchyard of Trinity Church; of James Swan, of Olive Mount, who died in 1829 aged 81 years; of Thomas Plumbe, of the old house nearest to the lock-up, and whose ancestors were known there 250 years ago; Mr. Lance, who gave the name to Lance Lane; and John

Dunbabin, farmer, whose name is handed down to us in the thoroughfare named after him.

WAVERTREE CONSTABLES.

In 1784 there were two constables for Wavertree Township, Sam Dutton and John Wainwright (blacksmith), the latter being the deputy. In those days the Township or Parish Constable was subordinate to the High Constable, who had jurisdiction over the Hundred : hence it came about that the Wavertree Constable was called upon by the Chief to look after Courts and Inquests outside of the Township. From his accounts we find that he had to look after Inquests at Toxteth Park, Old Swan, Woodside (between Knotty Ash and Croxteth), and at Derby Chapel (the old Chapel of Ease of Walton in West Derby); the most numerous cases were in Toxteth Park. From his accounts we also find that he summoned Juries of thirteen men for West Derby Court at a cost of £1 19s. od., and that he attended at the Manor or Copyhold Court of West Derby (this latter court house is still to be seen). Bamber Gascoyne, M.P., J.P., etc., was Lord both of West Derby and Wavertree Manors. West Derby had a Constable of its own.

The Wavertree Constable attended Quarter and Petty Sessions at Lancaster, Preston, Wigan, Ormskirk, and Prescot, so that at times he would be away from his own township and a deputy was necessary. The deputy was usually a tradesman, J. Brown (a baker), etc., but in 1791 a Rev. Thomas Dannes was appointed, his remuneration to be house rent free.

Constables in some parts of England may have been stout, elderly men who wore a cocked hat, cut-away coat, and knee breeches, and were more ornamental than useful ; but here, in South-west Lancashire, they were strong, intelligent men in the prime of life, and were respected for their office. At Ormskirk Church there used to be the Constable's Pew, adjoining the Churchwarden's Pew. There was a close connection between the Constable and the Churchwardens; for many years it was a condition of the Constable's office that it should be followed by a Churchwardenship. At Ormskirk, the Constable had a staff 5 feet 6 inches high, of heavy wood, with a massive silver knob, but at Wavertree he carried a truncheon. It was called the Town's Truncheon, and in 1784 it was decorated at a cost of 1s. 6d. He carried also handcuffs and a whistle.

There were times when our Wavertree Constable had brighter duties than attending to prisoners, Inquests, and Manor Courts : he had something to do with the recreations of the Township. We find that in 1794, Thomas Leech, the Constable, had engaged Morris Dancers (under instructions from Mr. Ed. Falkner, a Magistrate) to dance upon the Green at Wavertree Wakes. The usual festivities, the Bull Baiting, Boxing Matches, Running and Wrestling Competitions, and the attractions of the show and refreshment booths, had not been sufficient, and the Morris Dancers were engaged as a special attraction. Their bill of expenses, however, of £1 19s. 6d., caused trouble, and at first the Township refused to pay, and for eighteen months the Morris Dancers were unable to get their charges ; eventually on December 16th, 1795, it was agreed that the Constable should settle the claim.

Originally the Court Leet (practically the Saxon Township) had appointed the Constable, the householders who had constituted the meeting gathering at an inn. The earliest inn mentioned in the Wavertree records is the " Thatched House Tavern." At a later date, before the Town Hall was built, the Township Meetings were held alternately at " The Sign of the Lamb " in High Street, and the " Coffee House " in Church Road.

WAVERTREE LOCK-UP.

The inhabitants of Wavertree in 1793 were waking up to the fact that they had responsibilities with regard to law and order, and there was much talk about the necessity of providing a Lock-up for the use of John Leach, the Constable, his prisoners having to be entertained and guarded in his dwelling-house. In his list of expenses, presented to the town's meeting, were items like the following :

" For assistance to take care of a man who shot a man, 2/-."

On April 12th, a town's meeting was called at a cost of 3/8, but nothing was done, and things dragged on for three years. On June 24th, 1796, a large and influential gathering of the inhabitants of Wavertree, forming a town's meeting, decided that a Lock-up house should be built ; that it was to be erected on the vacant land facing the village pond, and that a Mr. Hind was to prepare plans and get the work in hand. There was opposition to the site chosen from Mr. John Myers (one of the magnates of Wavertree), who lived at Monkswell House, he contending that the suggestion to build the Lock-up on land which was in front of his house showed a desire to annoy him. However, peace prevailed, and at the conclusion of the meeting he agreed to sign along with the others. Among the signatures are those of James Swan, of Olive Mount (he died in 1821, aged 81 years, and was buried in Wavertree Churchyard), of William Rigg, father of John Rigg, who is still remembered as the first Postmaster of Wavertree, which position he held for 55 years; also of Robert Parke, John Leech, E. Ditchfield, and other representatives of the influential families of the Township.

In the Constable's accounts are many items of expenses for the Lock-up, such as ½ cwt. Coals 3½d., Meat for Prisoner 4d., Bread and Milk for 3 boys for 2 nights 2/1, Straw 1d. The building was badly built, and frequently required repairs to door and roof. One old Wavertree resident tells of seeing two men escape through the old flat roof, and get away up Olive Mount.

At holiday times the little Lock-up was often quite full. Wavertree 70 to 80 years ago was a popular pleasure resort for Liverpool people, and the " Coffee House " and the " Lamb " and other inns catering for the visitors. At times the Constable engaged a cart to go round and collect drunks of both sexes, and when full the load was upkecked at the Lock-up.

During the dismal time known as the Potato Famine, thousands of Irish families landed at Liverpool, and there was a difficulty in finding shelter for them. A number were sent to Wavertree, and found cramped lodging in the Lock-up.

The little round house, as seen to-day, was beautified on the recommendation of Sir J. A. Picton, who, as an Antiquary, was interested in it.

A FREE QUARRY.

Wavertree Township has a free quarry, and, just as the householders had a right to water from the town pump, and to play upon the green, so they had the right of helping themselves to stone from the quarry. It is still to be seen by the old wind-mill. The privilege was used to the full, and it became very deep. On March 21st, 1837, it was decided by the Select Vestry, which had authority over the quarry, that as it had become dangerous, posts and rails were to be placed round it. This was done, but the next year, in 1838, the posts were reported broken (during a fog), and

F

again the Surveyor had to attend to the matter and make the quarry safe. It happened at this time that an Act of Parliament dealng with Pounds and Strays (Act of 5 & 6 Wm. 4th, Chap. 50, Sec. 70) came into force, and a pound had to be provided at Wavertree. The Surveyor was now instructed to make the town quarry into the town pound, and he was told that in future persons were to be prevented from getting stone from the quarry. The town pump has gone, the village green is useless, and the quarry is no longer used for delving out stone for the people. The times have changed. and the people have changed with them. In mediæval days a common pound was enclosed for every Township for stray cattle and other beasts. It was a source of profit to those who erected the pound, as the owners of stray cattle had to pay to redeem their stock, but it was also compulsory for the Impounder to feed the cattle while in the pound. In West Derby, the site of the ancient pound is to be seen by the tram terminus,. the village stocks are upon it, and a tablet commemorates both interesting relics of the past.

THE TOWN'S-WELL.

Wavertree Well, commonly called Monkswell, was the public well of the township, and it is undoubtedly very ancient. It was in close proximity to the British Burial Ground where six cinerary urns were found. The date 1414, which used to be upon a slab over it, has been a mystery to many Antiquaries, the prevailing opinion being of scepticism. It is worth recording, however, that in 1386, the Abbey of Whalley held land at Wavertree. Descriptions of the well differ considerably, the earliest stating that the source of the water was under the lawn of Monkswell House, and that a passage led to it. A later account tells of its being about 100 feet deep, and that buckets brought up the water, the motive power coming from a hand-turned windlass; as one bucket went down empty, another came up full. In 1798 it is mentioned in the Constable's book as the Towns-well.

In 1828 the Township was converted into a Select Vestry for local administrative purposes, and under the Chairmanship of the Vicar, Rev. Wm. Badnal, M.A., they decided to erect at the well an iron pump and at the same time to enlarge the reservoir; this was done in 1834, and the bill came to £40 2s. 9d. The Constable, Wm. Andrews, was instructed to keep the pump fastened up with lock and

key during service time on Sundays : it had been found that
women met at the well when drawing water, and stayed
gossiping there.

The well was never known to run dry, and in times of
drought, water from it used to be hawked round the neighbouring villages of Old Swan, Childwall, etc., the rate
being 1d. per lading can.

WAVERTREE ROADS.

In the last quarter of the 18th Century, great interest
was manifested by the Authorities in the public roads. It
was a time of trade expansion, manufacturing industries
were taking the place of the spinning wheel and loom in the
home of the worker, and the foundry was superseding the
village blacksmith. Traders were now demanding something
better than pack-tracks for their heavily-laden waggons, and
the mail carrier and traveller asked for a better surface of
the road, so that the stage coaches might travel with
greater speed and safety.

In the book of accounts which William Claughton
(Supervisor of Roads for the Township of Wavertree) kept,
there are some interesting items of this date. The Township had numerous roads, the two principal being the one
from Liverpool to Warrington, along High Street, and the
other from Garston and the south along Church Road and
Olive Mount to West Derby and the north.

Road repair is costly work, but in 1771 labour was
cheap, as the payments in the Supervisor's book prove, viz. :

" Edward Justus, for 34 days' labour at 14d. per day,
£1 19s. 8d.

Edward Jones, for 15 days' labour at 15d. per day,
17s. 6d.

J. Septon, for 54¾ days' labour at 16d. per day,
£3 15s. 0d."

Presumably the latter would be skilled workmen. Loads of
stones were carted for 2d. per load ; paving stones are put
down as costing 1s. per load.

It was for the public good that the roads should be
made as perfect as possible, and all co-operated in the work.
Twenty-six farmers worked on the roads with their teams,
eighty-nine workmen worked with their spades ; this labour
was accounted as equivalent to the lay. There were forty-
one householders who preferred to pay in money, their total
was £11 18s. 0d., the lay was 2d. in the £. There is an
item of £1 1s. 2d. for carting stones from the old cause-

way. The pity is that we are not informed as to the whereabouts of the old causeway. At Warrington an old causeway is remembered in the name of the road which succeeded it; there it ran between the Roman camp at Wilderspool and the town; here, at Wavertree, it would probably lead to the Well or Windmill.

Other items in the Supervisor's accounts indicate something of the rural character of the neighbourhood, viz., the erection of a guide-post, laying flat stones on the moss, ditching through the moss-lands to Broad Green, and sending warning to keep ye cattle off ye common highway, cost 1/-.

In the Wavertree Chest in the Town Clerk's Office is a plan showing the Moss at Wavertree, and what used to be the Common, drawn by John Eyes in 1769.

WAVERTREE SELECT VESTRY AND ITS MEMBERS.

Among the many forms of local government which have been tried is that of the Select Vestry. That of Wavertree was formed in 1828. A Town's meeting had been called at the house of John Bibby, called the Sign of the Lamb. After a stormy meeting, the minority being very strong, it was agreed that the old Township should adopt the different system of local government known as the Select Vestry. The Chairman was Rev. Wm. Badnal, M.A., and the meetings, instead of being held in the various inns, were held in the District Church of Holy Trinity, presumably the School. The Constable, instead of being appointed, was now only nominated. The Vestry was remarkable as having so large a number of first rate men associated with it. The following are the names of some of the local gentlemen present at a meeting :—Messrs. Hugh Hornby, J. S. Leigh, T. B. Bartley, T. S. Gladstone, Wm. Rathbone, James Bourne, P. W. Branckner, J. A. Picton. A short sketch of these men may be of interest.

Hugh Hornby lived at Sandown Hall and was the founder of a notable Liverpool family. He was Mayor in 1838. The name will ever be remembered in our city by the Hornby Dock, named after Thomas Dyson Hornby, who was Chairman of the Dock Board, and the Hornby Library, a noble bequest of valuable books and a building to house them, made to the city by Mr. H. L. Hornby.

Mr. John Shaw Leigh was an Attorney of the city, who owned much property in the centre of Liverpool and the north end by Bootle, and became very rich. Leigh Street,

off Whitechapel, is named after his father. He lived at
Edge Lane Hall.

Mr. T. B. Bartley was a magistrate, and seemed to
have had special authority in Wavertree, many prisoners
being taken before him at his house, Wavertree Lodge.
This house, by the way, is very old, and there is a legend to
the effect that it was originally a lodge or hunting seat
belonging to the Royal Park of Toxteth, which it is now
known included at one time the whole of Wavertree.

Mr. T. S. Gladstone was an ardent politician, and is
chiefly remembered for the active part which he took in the
agitation for the passing of the Reform Bill in 1831.

Major James Bourne succeeded his father, Peter
Bourne. At Heathfield, on March 22nd, he exhibited his
newly formed corps of Artillery Volunteers, said to be the
first, and was much complimented for his patriotic spirit.
Major J. Bourne took a keen interest in Wavertree affairs.
He leased the mill (the ancient windmill), and turned out
the miller (Foster) and accepted Charles Taylor as tenant,
during whose tenancy of the mill a son of Sir James
Bourne's coachman was killed by the sails, as they revolved,
striking the boy on the head.

William Rathbone lived at Greenbank, where he spent
a life of more than sixty years in going about doing good.
He was a zealous advocate of every cause which was in any
way calculated to add to the happiness of mankind, and
innumerable were his acts of benevolence. He was elected
Mayor of Liverpool in 1837. When he died, in 1868, over
a thousand people attended his funeral.

Sir J. A. Picton, F.S.A., was born in Wavertree, and
very proud are the inhabitants of the old township to
remember the fact. His name will go down to posterity as
the Historian of Liverpool. He was one of the founders of
the Free Library, Museum, and Art Gallery. The circular
reading-room was called after him. When it was opened
on October 8th, 1879, a banquet was given in his honour
which was presided over by Lord Derby. Sir J. A. Picton
lived towards the end of his life at Sandy Knowe, Olive
Mount, Wavertree.

BIRTHPLACE OF AUGUSTINE BIRRELL.

The Right Hon. Augustine Birrell, Chief Secretary to
the Lord-Lieutenant of Ireland, is usually spoken of as a
" Liverpool man." His father was for thirty-six years
minister of Pembroke Chapel, and it was during this period,

on January 19, 1850, that Augustine was born. The house
in which the event occurred is called " Rooklands," and is
No. 4, Olive Lane, Wavertree. The house was newly built,
and at that time was quite in the country. Its situation
would be what the eminent Baptist minister and his bright
and sharp-witted wife would desire. When Charles M.
Birrell died, Professor W. Graham, D.D., wrote thus on the
occasion :—" On the evening of the day in which he was
buried in the Norwood Cemetery, of London, and not far off,
the marvellous genius that created ' Adam Bede ' and
' Romola ' passed away from us, and not many weeks afterwards Thomas Carlyle was carried back, like an old patriarch,
to lie with the dust of his father and mother in the village
churchyard of Ecclefechan. Charles Birrell has left in many
memories and hearts, if not the marks of a nature so original,
so passionate, and powerful, yet the memory of at least
one work of holy art—a life more disciplined, of serener
purity, and more spiritual elevation than that of either of
these great contemporaries. His wife was the daughter of
the Rev. Dr. Henry Grey, of Edinburgh. Augustine was a
younger child." On Sundays his father usually preached
at Pembroke, taking the elder children with him to chapel.
The nurse (who married a young plumber who came to work
at the house) is still living in Wavertree, and tells of Master
Augustine standing upon a chair and playing at being a
preacher practising at home on a Sunday evening. His first
school was at Old Swan. It was a boarding and day school
kept by the Rev. T. Wilson, Chaplain to Lord Derby, at
May Place. The distance from the house to the school
would be about a quarter of a mile.

GEORGE BROWN AND THE BLUECOAT SCHOOL.

George Brown was a Bluecoat School boy, and tells how
that as an orphan " they took me in. I was naked, and
they clothed me ; I was hungry, and they fed me." In the
year 1765, friendless and alone, at the tender age of eight
years, he brought papers to the institution, and with his
own tiny hands adduced proofs of his parents' marriage, his
own baptism, his orphan condition, together with proofs of
his being a Liverpool boy, as required under the charter,
and although without recommendation, he was admitted.
On leaving the school, at the age of fourteen, he chose his
late father's profession—the sea. Before, however, he had
taken one voyage, his legs got entangled in a rope, crushing
them both. For twelve long months he was compelled to lie

on his back and be in a sick chamber. Truly, he seemed
to be a very child of misfortune, but a brighter day awaited
him. Having recovered from his accident, he determinedly
continued to follow the sea, and ere he was twenty years
old became the captain of his ship. While he was yet thirty
years old he was owner of a small fleet, and in process of
time became a merchant prince of his native town. But,
better still, he was known as one of the most exemplary of
Christian men. The introduction to the old chapel hymn-
book used by the children has this testimony to his high
character : " He was no less distinguished for his commercial integrity than for his unaffected piety and Christian
benevolence in his private life." In 1809 George Brown
was elected treasurer to the Bluecoat School, and thus
became at the head of it. He worked very hard for the
charity, and gave very liberally of his own means, so that,
as he put it, " he could do for other orphans what had been
done for him."

VILLAGE GREENS.

A survey taken in the year 1768 of the township of
West Derby shows the following village greens as then
existing : Almonds Green, Dwerryhouse Green, Norris
Green, Honeys Green, and Mount Vernon Green, while just
outside of it were the extensive open public spaces of Broad
Green and Wavertree Green. The patriotic and public-
spirited officials and politicians of the day did not view these
open spaces with the admiration that the same classes do
to-day. They were distressed at seeing good land wasting,
being used only for the children to play on, and for the
cottagers' hens, or pigs, or donkey to feed upon, and considered that if brought into the hands of private owners it
would be better cultivated. They acquiesced in owners of
adjoining land extending their boundaries and taking in the
greens. In the case of the larger ones, however, this easy
way of acquiring property could not be encouraged. In the
matter of the Wavertree Green, which extended from the
Monk's Well to Wavertree Nook in one direction, and to Elm
Hall in another, and was, therefore, rather extensive, the
matter was arranged between the Lord of the Manor, Bamber
Gascoyne, M.P. for Liverpool, and his tenants that they
should acquire the lands between them, he to have the largest
share. He thereupon brought the matter before Parliament,
and the Wavertree Enclosure Act, 8 Geo. III., c. 51, was
passed. The Commissioners for executing the Act were

Joseph Jackson, of West Derby, Caryl Fleetwood, and John
Eyes (a noted surveyor), of Liverpool, and the Lord of the
Manor of Wavertree, Bamber Gascoyne. The largest green
in the West Derby township was Mount Vernon Green, at
Edge Hill, and the smallest Dwerryhouse Green, which was
little more than a double-width of the road passing through
a hamlet.

In the neighbourhood of Aughton and Ormskirk are
numerous places named after village greens, and, strange to
say, the majority of them have names which indicate some
personal interest in the green, viz., Bates Green, Hollin
Green, Brook's Green, Holmer Green, and Bennison Green;
among others are Town Green and Hall Green.

BROAD GREEN.

ORIGIN OF SCORE LANE, BROAD GREEN.

Score Lane lies between Childwall and Broad Green.
It is part of one of the oldest roads in the outskirts of Liverpool. In a plan map of the environs of Liverpol, prepared
from an actual survey made in 1758, by William Yates and
George Perry, this lane is shown as a clear and open road
and a means of communication between Speke, Woolton,
Gateacre, etc., on the one side, to Old Swan, West Derby,
Walton, etc., on the other. To-day it is a favourite lovers'
walk and much used by cyclists, but otherwise it is a closed
road, gates are across it, and it is marked as private. The
Childwall end of the lane gives a panorama of delightful views
of the countryside and embraces Broadgreen, Roby, Huyton,
and the range of hills which have Rainhill and Pex Hill as
highest points. Now that the Garden Suburb has Score
Lane as a boundary, the time has perhaps come when this
ancient thoroughfare should again become the property of
the public. Street names can teach much, and especially so
in Liverpool, where we have Castle Street, Church Street
and Water Street, indicating their connection with castle,
church and waterside, with many other examples.

Score Lane very probably derived its name from score,
an old Lancashire name for a public pasture, the lane either
leading to such a common field, or it might be derived from
the fact that there used to be a strip of common grazing land
alongside of the roadway. An old man, when speaking to
the writer, once used the word score in the latter sense in

relation to a strip of land which he had enclosed from a road
between Childwall and Wavertree. He said: "We brought
up the hedge and enclosed the score." In Wright's
"Dictionary of English Dialects" it is stated that at
Frodsham, Cheshire, the part of Frodsham Marsh upon
which farmers have a right to graze their cattle is called
Frodsham Score.

Score Lane has been a public highway for centuries.
The oldest plans and maps of the district show it as clearly
as any other road. There are no indications of it being only
a footpath. The late Canon Hume, who was president of
the Lancashire and Cheshire Historic Society, always claimed
the roads as public, and the editors of the Victorian County
History of Lancashire take the same view. There was a
time when Garston, Hale, Farnworth, and Little Woolton
(now called Gateacre) were fairly populous, and a considerable amount of traffic passed along the roads (now closed)
to and from West Derby, Kirkby, and Walton, also places
of some importance.

Free and open communication between towns and
villages is vital, and hindrances are not to be tolerated.
Another aspect of the question is that of the cruelty imposed
upon the horses, who are compelled to drag their loads up
Gateacre Brow, as they have now, if travelling south to north
via Childwall, the most direct and level way. It is quite
probable that Lord Salisbury will claim rights to the roads,
and demand monetary compensation for surrender of these
rights. The time has come, however, for the authorities
to face the matter, and in some way or other to get the
ancient thoroughfares restored to the public.

EARLY PIGS FROM CHINA.

Once upon a time, in fact within the memory of people
still living, an enterprising Liverpool stock-raiser brought
home from China a few pigs. They were small, had short,
chubby heads, and would keep fat on the smallest and poorest
of diet. Mr. James Lee, the importer, found a demand for
the pigs, and started, at Broad Green, a regular Chinese
pig farm, and sold hundreds of the little porkers. His
salesman was an Irishman, called Pat. When showing buyers
the pigs, Lee invariably called to Pat and enquired if the
pigs had been fed, and asked, at the same time, how much
they had had. The reply was: "Yes, sir; a bucketful of
swill." Lee would then appear to get into a temper, and tell

him that half-a-bucketful a day was the proper amount to keep them in condition. Buyers were impressed with the economy of this kind of feeding, and the size of the pigs indicating small butcher's joints, they sold readily. The writer occasionally comes across small pigs, plump, but very short of lean, and although Lea's Piggeries has been given up for 20 or 30 years, he thinks that the descendants of the little pigs from the land of the Celestials are still with us.

ASH HOUSE AND DR. CHRISTY.

At Broad Green, in the midst of a good class, residential district, a veritable villadom, is a margarine factory, the only works of any kind in the neighbourhood. The land upon which it stands was formerly part of the grounds of Ash House, which was the home of a member of one of the great local families—i.e., Molyneux. The most notable occupant of recent years was the late Dr. T. W. Christy, who went to live there in 1848. Although holding medical degrees, he had a strong preference for matters theological. He, as a married man, went to Cambridge, and took his degree of B.A. He became influenced with the wave of Evangelicalism which was passing over the country, and would, "despite the protest of the dons," preach in his cap and gown in the open streets of Cambridge. He also took part in a rather bitter controversy with members of the Ritualistic party, the cause being the prosecution and imprisonment of an Evangelical clergyman named the Rev. M. Shore, whose offence was described in the writ "as publicly performing ecclesiastical duties in a certain unconsecrated chapel or building without licence or authority for so doing."

Dr. Christy was presented to the living of All Hallows', in Cumberland, but although he had passed the Bishop's examination he declined to be ordained, preferring to be free. He became a Dissenter. He converted a barn, part of his premises at Ash House, into a meeting-house, and fitted it up with pulpit and seats. He preached himself, had his own doctrines (which he expounded in sermons of two hours' duration). He allowed no singing, and never took a collection. His delight was in controversy, and at different times attacked Wesleyanism, calling John Wesley the "Antichrist of the Revelations"; the temperance movement, calling teetotalers "dry drunkards"; and the Rev. Hugh Stowell Brown for claiming the Gospel as for all people, Dr. Christy teaching "that it was for the elect few only." Dr. Christy died in 1892, and was buried in St. James's Cemetery, where his tomb is one of the most prominent in that beautiful resting place of our city's dead.

The religious excitement of the house was too much for the Doctor's housekeeper, who was found dead in a Bathroom, having committed suicide.

Among other occupants of Ash House have been Mr. Bolton Littledale, he was a noted athlete in his day and loved to run and jump in the fields adjoining the house, in the scantiest of clothing, viz., his underpants. His genteel neighbours accounted him a madman. Then, as tenant, came a Mr. Witherington. Mr. Watts, afterwards Alderman Watts, of Compton House, also lived at Ash House for a time.

STAPLANDS.

Staplands, Broad Green, was a home of the Molyneux family of Newsham. Edward Molyneux had gone to live at Sandhills and removed to Staplands. It used to be the family boast that it had at one time been possible to walk from Newsham to Town Green, near Aughton, on their family land. There is a Molyneux window at Knotty Ash Church.

The most noted member of the family was Mr. Horatio Nelson Crichlow Molyneux. With a nautical name he had nautical tastes. He is said to have designed and built a yacht. In the grounds of Staplands were two brass cannon, said to have been captured from the French, and on special occasions, such as a wedding in his family, or at a neighbour's, they were fired; they were also fired at the opening of the Manchester to Liverpool Railway.

One daughter, Miss Ellen Molyneux, once broke her leg, having fallen off a rockery in the garden. She was attended to by a young local doctor, and they became attached to each other. However, on the doctor wishing to marry her, one of her brothers became so angry with the doctor that he got hold of him, and, being a big, strong man, dropped him into a waterbutt.

One son, who lived at Ash House, was very rich, and from a peculiarity in spending habits was called " Ready Money John."

The last of the family, Mr. Edward Molyneux, now lives at Barmouth.

THINGWALL HALL.

Thingwall Hall can be seen from the railway line near to Broad Green Station, on the northern side of the line. Like most of the halls of a century or so old, it has its story.

In 1824 a Mr. Thomas Crowther, a Liverpool merchant, lived there and he gave it the name of Summerhill. Perhaps he thought that there was nothing, either of history or romance, in the name Thingwall, and that Summerhill sounded nicer.

There is a legend connected with the house which the writer has heard on two occasions, and once told by a gentleman who is usually a good authority. It is to the effect that an occupier of the Hall died while insolvent, and that as the custom was, in the first quarter of the 10th Century in such cases, the creditors tried to seize the body for the purpose of selling it to surgeons, hoping thereby to make their loss a little less. The relatives of the insolvent corpse, however took the body and buried it at midnight, and so thwarted the creditors. As names and dates are not furnished, the legend must be taken for what it is worth.

Thingwall Hall has, in recent years, been the home of one of Liverpool's most distinguished and philanthropic families. The head of the family was Samuel Henry Thompson, of Heywood's Bank. He married Anna Maria Yates, of the Dingle, and their children have so lived their lives as to leave to posterity names which will be fragrant of their good deeds. They are as follows : Henry Yates Thompson, proprietor of the Pall Mall Gazette (Mr. W. T. Stead was at one time his Editor), and who gave the splendid Palm Houses to Sefton and Stanley Parks ; Samuel Ashton Thompson (afterwards changed to Thompson Yates), who presented the Physical Laboratory to Liverpool University College ; Anna Marie Thompson, who gave to Knotty Ash the Art Schools, Forge, etc., and Cricket Ground ; and Edward P. Thompson, who built the row of Model Cottages overlooking the recreation ground. As a family, they gave to Knotty Ash the Village Hall and Gardens, and have handsomely endowed the Church.

The Hall and Estate were bought from Mr. Thompson by Sir David Radcliffe. It was anticipated at the time that he would live there and keep on the old servants, but it turned out that the transaction was merely a business speculation, and that he was open to sell again at a profit.

At the present time Thingwall Hall is occupied by " The Brothers of Charity," a religious and philanthropic order. They have built alongside of it a number of large buildings in which are housed about three hundred boys— they are waifs and strays of our cities, and are mostly orphans.

THINGWALL.

The hamlet of Thingwall, lying between Knotty Ash and Broadgreen, near Liverpool, was for centuries "extra-parochial," which means that its owners paid no rates, but against this they had to repair their own roads and supply their own needs for water and drains.

It belonged, however, ecclesiastically to Childwall, to the rector and vicar respectively of which parish its tithes were paid. The freedom from local taxation is said to have been granted to the Lord of the Manor in consideration of a payment which the Manor of Thingwall made towards the Order of the Knights of St. John of Jerusalem, the military religious Order which, in mediæval days, kept open the roads and protected the pilgrims on their journey to the Holy Land. The hamlet is now attached to Huyton township; this was brought about by a Local Government Board Order in 1877.

There has been some scepticism as to the antiquity of our local Thingwall as compared with the Tynwald of Manxland, and the Thingwalls of Cheshire, and of other places in the North. They all, however, come from "Thing-vollr," the name given to the Scandinavian meeting, from Thing-Parliament and Vollr-field, the place where councillors or elders deliberated upon the affairs of their people and then legislated for them. The "Thing," however, as an institution, is earlier than the Dane in this country. Thorpe, in his "Ancient Laws and Institutes," states that it is mentioned in the seventh century. Among the Domes of Eadric we have the following : "If one man make pleint against another in a suit, and he citeth the man to a Methel or to a Thing, let the man always give "borh" to the other, and do him such right as the judges prescribe to him." The word methel is Celtic, and means a concourse (our word meeting was probably derived from it). The thing or methel here mentioned was a gathering of people for the settlement of disputes, on the principle of a large jury, and was apparently a Continental custom.

The hardy Northman from the Norwegian fiords, and Frisian sandbanks, with his piracy, murder, and conquest, brought to us a system of government and ideas of law and order for which in later days English people had reason to be grateful. The "Thing" was at the root of legal and legislative administration. They were of various kinds. The Thing-moot was summoned in times of war, or threatened war; and just as further north it was usual to summon the clan or tribe by arming the runner with a symbol of authority for the clansmen—a wooden cross which had been scorched with fire and then smeared with goat's blood—the summons to the Thing-moot was also by a runner, who, on production of an arrow (his symbol of authority), could call upon the landholders to leave all duties of farm, field, or forge, and come prepared for service under his lord, and to meet him at the Thing-moot. The Althing was another institution for the trial of criminals, and was presided over by what was called a law-speaker. There also they fixed the feasts and festivals for the year. The hill of Thingwall rises to 166 feet. This is not high, but it is the highest thereabout. We have no proof of its having been used as an open-air Parliament, or even Wapentake, but we know that in our South-West Lancashire the settlers were of the old Norse fighting breed, and that it was wont to be said that a summer without a fight or a raid was a wasted season.

The names of the landholders at the time of the Domesday survey indicate their nationality. Among them are Orm and Ulf, both at Melling; a Dot at Huyton and at Tarbock; a Godiva, widow of Leofric; Uctred, Chetal, Wilbert, and a Ughtred, who held the Manor of Aughton.

The Norse settlement in South-West Lancashire and Wirral had been very complete; the Vikings had sailed up the Dee, the Alt, and the Douglas, had conquered the British-Angle inhabitants, and had established their own systems of government and laws. After the Norman conquest it was noted in the survey report, dealing with West Derby Hundred, how that the assessment for the geld was made in caracutes, i.e., a Danish ploughland. In other parts it was in the older English hide (it is calculated that one English hide of land equalled six Danish caracutes). It is significant that at the treaty of peace made in 878, known as "Alfred and Guthrum's Peace," the Danish invaders were recognised, and they were allowed to hold (at that early date) almost the whole of Lancashire, where they were to be independent dwellers, with their own laws and institutions. At Harkirk, in the parish of Sefton, large numbers of coins have been found, some of Saxon King Alfred and others of Danish Gulfrith, who became King of Northumbria in 883. Imagination is not going beyond its function when it pictures the gathering together of the man of the coast and of the countryside, the rough, tar-smelling sailor, the fighting man, the farmer who had become peace-loving, and who desired only to be allowed to cultivate his land and build his byres, the smith who followed his calling at the village forge, the fisherman and hunter who garnered their harvest from stream and wood, and all who had homes, with wives and daughters to ply at spinning-wheel or loom, or to care for beast or bird. Theirs was a civilised society, rude it may be, but they knew that progress could only be made by good government, just laws, and an organised people, and these were to be attained by their " Things."

That Thingwall is linked to the distant past is undoubted, for it was a manor in the Royal demesne of West Derby in 1177. There is an account in the Lancashire pipe rolls of a transaction in which King John gave the manor to one Richard, son of Thurston. The descent of the de Thingwall family of later years has not been traced. In the thirteenth century, a Hugh de Thingwall was Lord of the Manor, his son, Richard, in 1250 held three ox-gangs of land within his father's manor, one ox-gang in Walton, and other land in Knowsley. He gave his estate to Roger, his son, who married Alice de Aigburth. In 1298 William, the son of Roger, held the whole of the manor of Thingwall, namely, eight ox-gangs of land.

From an account of a law case tried in 1339 we get a glimpse of a township which has gone, and left little trace of its existence. In the plea, Margery, widow of Roger, son and heir of Robert Thingwall, and wife of Henry, son of John de Blackburn, claimed her dower in messuages, mill, &c., at Thingwall. The mill has passed away, none of the houses remain, and the old farmhouse now demolished (Mr. Peter Ashcroft's) was certainly not over 200 years old. The only remains of the past are two or three wells, one of which, in extra-parochial days, became a receptacle for sewage, and the other relic of the past is the road which leads from Thomas Lane, Knotty Ash, to the Thingwall Farm; more than that, tradition claims that it was one of the earliest roads out of Liverpool, the pack horse track which ran between the Castle and Prescot and Warrington.

EARLY RAILWAY MEMORIES.

Very like ancient history reads the account of the earliest local railway and its management, i.e., the Manchester and Liverpool Company's line, afterwards the London and North-Western. The terminus was at Edge Hill, and the first stopping place a level crossing at

Wavertree Lane, where the company had built a cottage for a big Scotchman whose duty it was to look after the line, and where, armed with a long whip, he hurried people across the rails. Then there was a watchman at the entrance to the Olive Mount cutting, which was then only about 27 feet wide for about 700 yards. There were no stations, and it was customary for trains to stop to take up or let down passengers at any place where required; but at all points where a road crossed the rails, and known as level crossing, the trains were supposed to stop, and at all of these the company placed gates and erected cottages for the gatemen to live in. These cottages were the first beginnings in the process of evolution which ultimately produced the railway station as we know it to-day. But there were no platforms, no tickets, and no signals to stop the train. Consequently the drivers had to be prepared to stop at any moment. For tickets the guard used to have a card about the size of a playing card, and he pricked them according to the number of shillings and pence collected. The carriages were of two kinds : the first class, painted yellow and made to look as much like a stage coach as possible (the name coach still survives), and the second class, something like a cattle truck and painted blue. Then there was the mail box, 4 feet 6 inches long, 3 feet wide, and 2 feet deep, which was fixed at the rear of the second-class carriage. This was in charge of an official called the mail guard, who wore a top hat with " Royal Mail " painted on it, and an oilskin cape, which was lettered " R.M., V.R.," and in this costume he had to ride on top, in all weathers. Truly, since September 15th, 1830, when the line was opened, great progress has been made. In 1840 the Tunnel Hotel was opened in what is now Tunnel Road. It was described as a convenient resort for the passengers proceeding by the quarter past three train, morning, and grand junction train which leaves at half past three, morning, suitable refreshments and every comfort and accommodation being in constant readiness. Omnibuses also proceed eight times daily between the hotel and the Town Hall, Liverpool.

A FORGOTTEN STATION.

At Broad Green the station is not the original railway station, neither is the Rocket Hotel the original inn commemorating the coming of the famous old engine to that neighbourhood. The long, low, straw-thatched cottage occupied by Mr. Skinkfield was a wayside inn long before

Wavertree Church. (Page 56.)

Sandown Hall, Wavertree. (Page 68.)

Entrance to Thingwall. (Page 77.)

First Rocket Inn, Broad Green. (Page 80.)

House in Oak Vale Nursery. (Page 81.)

Dove-cote, now demolished. (Page 89.)

The first Irish Yew. (Page 82.)

the navvies came to delve out the cutting, and it was to curry favour with them that it was named the Rocket. The first station was a stone's throw from it, and for position would then be superior to the site afterwards chosen, and removed to. From Dennison's map of the neighbourhood, published in 1835, it appears an admirable centre. There was the direct road to Stanley Cattle Market, 1½ miles off, for which it brought cattle and sheep ; a road to Roby and Huyton, another which led to Wavertree and Garston, and the road (now claimed as a private road) was then open for traffic to and from Childwall and Woolton. The station was but small, though at times very busy, and a siding had to be provided for its use. What is now the St. Helens main line at Broad Green was then the siding. Edge Hill Station was the Liverpool terminus. The Queen's Drive from Waver-tree to Broad Green is practically completed to the site of the old station, the hewn-out slope and steps of which can be seen at both sides of the bridge at Childwall Priory Road. Adjoining the station at that time was the famous nursery known as Cunningham's, and Mr. George Cunningham and Mr. George Stephenson had many a serious talk about the anticipated effect of the vibration and smoke from the latter's engines upon the tree and plant life of the nursery. Mr. Cunningham, knowing the effect of smoke upon roses, was alarmed for his other cultivated flowers. He was assured, however, that the amount of vibration and smoke would not be sufficient to do any damage. They became great friends, and when the railway was formally opened, Mr. Cunningham decorated the bridge with thousands of scarlet dahlias, then quite a new flower in the country. Special comment was made in the London " Times " on the brilliant show.

A FAMOUS NURSERY.

Old Swan has lost within the last few years a nursery (Oak Vale Nursery) which deserves keeping in remembrance. It was famous in Wales, Cheshire, Ireland, and America 120 years ago. To the latter country many hundreds of thousands of apple and pear stocks were exported, the fruit of which comes back to us now in large quantities. Great numbers of gooseberry and raspberry bushes, also straw-berry plants, were forwarded, the gooseberry being the only failure. The proprietor, Mr. Cunningham, was one of the first to introduce the brown beech into this country. His son, Mr. George Cunningham, was in his day one of the first

G

to introduce the scarlet dahlia, then the only kind of that popular flower. When the Liverpool and Manchester Railway was opened he decorated the bridge which crossed the line in his nursery with a brilliant show of these scarlet flowers.

Visitors to the Principality and to the sister island, enjoying the spring beauty of the trees, would, if hailing from our city, perhaps be surprised to learn that in some of the most charming spots of both countries the original trees had journeyed from Old Swan nursery. The following is a list of estates in Wales and Ireland afforested from this famous old nursery: in Wales, most of the estates from Towyn to Carnarvon, on the Carnarvon and Cardigan coast, including those of the Marquis of Anglesey and of Lord Mostyn; also the estates of Coed Coch, Kinmel Park, Mainwaring, Llanbedr Hall, and Nannau. In Ireland, those of the Vice-regal Lodge and Phœnix Park; also those of the Earl of Caledon, Marquis of Kildare, Marquis of Drogheda, Lord Dufferin, Lord de Vesci, Duke of Leinster, Sir John Leslie, and numerous other small parks and gardens of lesser fame and importance. Truly, if a thing of beauty is a joy for ever, the old nursery which has now passed away, and the firm of Cunningham, which is not now in existence, deserve to be remembered with gratitude by those among our Liverpool holiday-makers who are privileged to see nature's lovely landscapes, so much enhanced by the varied tints and graceful forms of the trees.

THE FIRST IRISH YEW.

Whence came the first oak; when did beech, birch, ash, and elm, and the other so-called British trees first appear on our soil? The story will, perhaps, be told some day by the geologist, who will read it in the stones of a prehistoric age. When written, the romance and interest of it will be great. The above thoughts were prompted by the contemplation of the first of a new order of tree, the tree from which has sprung all the others of the same species. The tree referred to is the Irish yew, which is to be found to-day in gardens all over the world. The discovery was made about the year 1780, when a Mr. Willis, a tenant farmer under Lord Enniskillen, observed two trees on the side of a mountain overlooking the estate of Florence-court, County Fermanagh, belonging to his landlord, these trees being different to any seen by him before; and, being a man of wide knowledge of his native flora, he drew the attention of Lord Enniskillen to them. It was agreed that they should take one each and plant them in their respective gardens. This was done. That, however, belonging to Mr. Willis died, and so it came about that Lord Enniskillen became possessed of this, the first Irish yew, for it was a conifer, but strikingly different to any other of that order. It was an evergreen, and beautifully adapted for garden decorations : it attains a height of about twenty feet, but its superiority over the yews of our countryside and church-yards lies in having its branches growing erectly after the manner of a Lombardy poplar, and in the leaves being scattered over the branchlets, instead of the usual two regular rows. The man, however, who popularised the tree was the late Mr. George Cunningham, of Oak Vale Nursery, Liverpool, a once famous tree cultivator (the nursery is now covered with streets and houses). Mr. Cunningham's father, the founder of the firm, when over in Ireland, " where, by the way, he did a large business," " afforesting the estates of the Marquis of Kildare, Marquis of Drogheda, Lord Dufferin, Lord de Vesci, Duke of Leinster, Sir John Leslie, also of the Vice-regal Lodge and Phœnix Park," came across this tree and obtained cuttings from it. These he cultivated, and after he died his son was able to do a very large business in it. In the early Victorian years it was the fashion to cultivate dark leaved and evergreen trees in the garden, the holly, the box, the juniper, the yew, and the rhododendron being favourites. Between the years 1835-45 Mr. George Cunningham was selling annually over 3,000 Florencecourt or Irish yews, and sending the majority of them abroad. The name Florencecourt was given to it out of compliment to Lord Enniskillen. Mr. Cunningham cultivated a rhododendron which he christened the Cunningham rhodo-dendron, and which he claimed grew the greatest number of perfect flowers of any tree or bush of that order.

BROAD GREEN HALL.

At Broad Green, a stone's throw from the station, stands Broad Green Hall, architecturally one of the most beautiful halls in the neighbourhood, Childwall Hall being its near rival. On the well-kept grass lawn, facing the dining-room, is a sundial, upon which a few years ago was the following inscription :—

S.S.
1800.
Ut Hora Sic Vita.
Life is as an hour.

The above is now effaced. The initials are those of Mr. Samuel Staniforth, who resided at Broad Green Hall at that time, and who had succeeded his father, Mr. Thomas Staniforth. The family was one of the best-known and most highly respected in the district, Mr. Thomas Staniforth himself being a very admirable character. He was one of the founders of the Old Swan Charity School, the building of which still exists in Mill Lane. He, with three others, all neighbours—Messrs. Thomas Parke, Richard Watt, and Joseph Jackson—built in 1791 the little schoolhouse, and also agreed to pay the salary of a schoolmaster, so that the children of Old Swan cottagers should be educated free. Human sympathy was evidently alive in this care for the children.

Mr. Staniforth filled the mayoral chair in 1790. It was a time when the poor of the old town found life very hard; food was dear and wages were low, while the laws were most severe. As an instance of how cheap life was held, it is recorded that in that year two men were hanged for mutiny, the alleged insubordination taking place on the Liverpool ship Gregson; also, two men, Edward Robin and John Clarke, were hanged for stealing a boat. Human sympathy was evidently dormant at that time for transgressors. Mr. Thomas Staniforth was a man of wealth, and had his town residence, as well as his country house at Broad Green. It was in Ranelagh Street, and eventually it became the Waterloo Hotel, but generally known as Lynn's. Its exact situation is now part of the main entrance to the Cheshire Lines Railway Station. The Staniforth family have had some useful and distinguished members, among them the Rev. Thomas Staniforth, who was stroke in the Oxford Eight in the first University Boat race between Oxford and Cambridge, which was rowed in 1829, and which was an easy win for Oxford. He afterwards resided at Storrs Hall, Windermere. The present representative of the old Liverpool family is the Squire of Kirk Hammerton, Yorkshire.

Dr. BRANDRETH.

Broad Green Hall, after providing a home for the Staniforth family, came into the possession of another Liverpool worthy, who in his day was noted far and near

as a physician and surgeon. In 1845 Joseph Pilkington
Brandreth, M.D., retired from his profession, which from
1835 he had carried on at No. 67, and afterwards at
45, Rodney Street, Liverpool, and came to reside at Broad
Green Hall. He made considerable alterations in it, and
left his mark on the name-stone on the front of the house.
As is usual in these initials, that of the surname was above
those of the christened names of husband and wife, in this
case the names being Joseph and Alice. Famous as
Dr. Brandreth was when he retired, he had not come into
the fame of his father, who is likely to be remembered for
many generations yet from the fact that his life is given in
the Dictionary of National Biography. His was a national
reputation. Dr. Joseph Brandreth, Senr., was of a Cheshire
county family, and came from Stublach. He was born in
1745, and died in 1815. His memorial is the Liverpool
Dispensary, which he established, and which has been of
untold service to thousands of our city's ailing poor. In
1847, Dr. J. P. Brandreth is described in the Directory as
gentleman; in 1849, however, he dropped the retired title,
and again appears as M.D., and this continues in the
Directories of 1851, 1853, and 1855. The fact was that he
became medical adviser to Lord Derby, to whom he was
also a friend. He also prescribed for the local poor, but
from whom he would receive no pay. He won a great
reputation for a surgical operation on a man's nose. After
curing the disease he transferred skin from another part of
the man's body to the nasal organ, and the skin growing
on its new basis, gave to the man's face the appearance of
having a new nose. The grateful patient was often taken
by the doctor to Knowsley, and to other places, and exhibited
as a wonderful example of how nature aided his skill.

Mr. Samuel C. Hignett, of the Imperial Tobacco Co., is
the present occupant of Broad Green Hall.

KNOTTY ASH.

DOVECOT AND DOVECOT HOUSE.

Dovecot House stands in spacious grounds on the
south side of the tramway terminus of Knotty Ash. Like
so many of our local halls it has become an institution
devoted to philanthropy. It is now a horticultural school
for girls. Its story is interesting. It was built in 1829 by

John Torbock. The Torbocks of Torbock, in their day, were among the great families of South Lancashire, and were connected by marriage with those of Knowsley and Croxteth. John Torbock inherited the estate, upon a portion of which he built his house, from his second cousin Margaret Molyneux. The family at one time had a private chapel. It was on Torbock Green, in the Parish of Huyton. It is on record that in 1558 William Torbock appointed a priest there, with a stipend of £4 a year. The chapel does not now exist. The most notable occupier of Dovecot House was Adam Dugdale, a wealthy East Lancashire cotton spinner—a man who, with little education and with many disadvantages, rose to be a Lancashire cotton king. Many stories are told of his shrewdness, his ability, and his philanthropy. He helped the Royal Infirmary and other Hospitals in Manchester with generous gifts, and to Knotty Ash he gave a farm, the land of which was to be used for a church, a vicarage, and a schoolhouse. The present vicarage is built on the site of the orchard. Towards the cost of the church building he and his friends contributed the sum of £4,000, and when, on June 26, 1834, the foundation-stone was laid, Adam Dugdale was honoured by being called upon to perform the ceremony.

It is of passing interest to know that the cost of the church fabric exceeded expectations, and that as a means of raising more money the pews were sold to leading local families. These were Molyneux, of Staplands; Littledale, of Highfield; Worrall, of Knotty Ash House; Molyneux, of Alder Hey, and, of course, Dugdale, of Dovecot House. Adam Dugdale loved the church, and when he died, at his own request was buried within the sacred building. The Dugdale hatchments are now in the church tower, and memorial tablets are preserved in the church and also in the little village school. Following Adam Dugdale, Dovecot House was occupied by Charles M'Iver, of early steamship and Cunard fame. It is remembered of him that on the occasion of his daughter's wedding he gave the sum of £500 to the vicar of Knotty Ash to be spent partly on decorations of the village and church and partly for the poor of the locality, while for a fortnight the festivities were kept up at the house

" T.S." writes—In his interesting notice of Dovecot House, Knotty Ash, Mr. James Hoult is, I venture respectfully to suggest, in error as to Dovecot House being built by Squire Torbock in 1829. Gregson locates Squire Torbock as living at Finch House, Finch Lane, West Derby, still a fine example of Georgian architecture. It is hardly reasonable to suppose that Torbock built in 1829, and that Adam Dugdale was at Dovecot in 1834 holding high festival over the foundation of Knotty Ash Church. Adverting to the history of the Torbock family (with its races, cockpits, and chantries), I should like Mr. Hoult to indicate through your column the exact location of the Torbock Green in Huyton. It might incidentally throw some light on an old and useful building in Huyton long devoted to parochial purposes, the origin of which no man knoweth.

"J. H." in reply writes—" T. S." wishes me to give further information about the Torbocks, about Torbock green, about an old parochial building in Huyton, and suggests that I am wrong in stating that Squire Torbock built Dovecot House in 1829, " T. S." giving as his authority Gregson. I am well acquainted with the last edition of Gregson's " Fragments," and cannot find the reference. Perhaps " T. S." will oblige with further particulars. It is, however, not improbable that Squire Torbock would be staying at Finch House while his own house was being built, Finch House being near to it. About the old parochial building at Huyton, Bishop Francis Gastrell, in 1719, made certain notes on Huyton Church and parish. In them he refers to the Grammar School there, and states that its foundation is unknown; also that he does not know if it is a free school or not; that it is repaired at the expense of the parish, and that the church-wardens appoint the master and generally look after it. Probably this old school-house is the building referred to by " T. S." The bishop also notices the size of Huyton parish, which included the three townships of Knowsley, Huyton-cum-Roby, and Tarbock, the latter being at the extreme south end. The position of the Hall and green at Tarbock is easily located on Bacon's Road Map of Liverpool and district. It is difficult for us to realise the fact that on Torbock Green, in the fourteenth century, a market was regularly held, with all its busy excitement; and that there was a chapel on it, noted for its beautiful carved woodwork. There is a significant statement, however, about the chapel in William Torbock's will, dated 1557. When arranging for Masses and other Divine service on behalf of his soul and the souls of his ancestors, he names Sir George Robinson, a priest, to serve during his natural life at the chapel that stands upon Torbock Green, " if the said chapel be not builded up at the time of my decease." It would appear as if the chapel structure had been showing signs of decay, and was perhaps dangerous, and that instead of building it up it had been demolished. Torbock Hall had until recently a private chapel in it.

" J. H. K." writes:—I have read with interest Mr. Hoult's communications re Dovecot House, and " T. S.'s " intervention. I waited for Mr. Hoult's reply to " T. S." Clearly, Dovecote was built before 1829, because Gregson (" Fragments," first edition, page 232, 1817), speaking of a brass seal of Sir William Torbock, who had in ages bygone married Margery, sister of Sir James Stanley, says: " It is now the property of John Torbock, of Dove Cote, late of Finch Lane, both of West Derby." It may also interest Mr. Hoult to know that in the Liverpool Directory for 1829 Adam Dugdale is given as the resident at Dove Cote. Dugdale had then bought the property.

" J. H." writes :—In reply to " J. H. K." In my two items in the column of " News, Notes, and Queries " I gave some information about Dovecot House. " J. H. K." however, writes about Dovecote. Now Dovecot House and Dovecote are two different buildings altogether. " J. H. K." says: " Clearly Dovecote was built before 1829, etc., refer Gregson's ' Fragments,' page 232." I should think that it was; from its mullioned windows, its dripstones, and general appearance, I should say that it was there in 1729. It stood, until pulled down a few years ago, facing Finch Lane, on the side of the Liverpool-Prescot Road. Gregson evidently located it as being as near as possible to Finch Lane. " T. S." states that Gregson locates Squire Torbock as living at Finch House, Finch Lane, still a fine example of Georgian architecture. " J. H. K." disproves this and gives the true statement made by Gregson. Gregson does not associate the Torbocks with Finch House at all. Finch House was built by a Mr. Gildart in 1776, on land which he had bought from Lord Sefton, and it was in the possession of his family until 1821, the last owner-occupant being the Rev. James Gildart, who became Rector of High Wickham, Bucks. It was bought by the Mather family of Mount Pleasant; it now belongs to Lord Derby, it having been bought by his uncle. From the pedigree of the Molyneux-Torbock-Graham family, I find that Margaret Molyneux died at Dovecot in 1829 and left her estate of Dovecot, with Boltons (the old Accers Millers house and grounds in Finch Lane), to her second cousin, John Torbock, her nearest living relative, who immediately afterwards sold it to Adam

Dugdale. This indicates Adam Dugdale as the owner of the estate. The present house, whether built by Torbock or Dugdale, was always distinguished from the old homestead. It was Dovecot House, the old place Dovecote.
"J. H. K." writes:—I wish to add a few words as to Dovecot House, Knotty Ash. But first I must thank Mr. James Hoult for pointing out the distinction between Dovecot and Dovecote House. I must confess I did not know of the former and older house. When I wrote that Adam Dugdale was in possession of Dovecote House in 1829 I had referred to the Liverpool Directories for 1825 and 1827; and having found no "Adam Dugdale" mentioned, had concluded that he only arrived in 1829. But further investigation shows that as early as 1821 "Adam Dugdale, manufacturer, Dove Coat (sic) House, West Derby," was in residence. In the Directory for 1823 he is given as "gentleman," of the same address. Evidently, therefore, there was a Dove Cote House in existence as early as 1821. Equally evident is it that John Torbock did not build the house in 1829, when, according to Mr. Hoult, he inherited the estate from his cousin, Margaret Molyneux. As to the silence of the Directories for 1825 and 1827, may I throw out a suggestion? Is it not probable that several years prior to 1829 Adam Dugdale had purchased this portion of the property from Margaret Molyneux, and had proceeded to demolish the old, presumably small, house, and erect for himself the present building?
I would remind Mr. Hoult (continues "J. K. H.") of the distinction between Dovecot and Dovecote House. Torbock might well succeed to Dovecote in 1829, whilst Dugdale was in possession of Dovecote House. It may, perhaps, explain the wide gap that appears between 1823 and 1829 if it is stated that the Directories only appeared at intervals of two years. Hence, at the end of 1824 Dugdale may have commenced the demolition of the old house, so that in 1825 and 1827 the place would be left unrecorded. By the end of 1826 the place would be nearing completion, and would find no place in the Directory of 1827; but Dugdale would, as already recorded, be duly noted as resident in that of 1829. That Dugdale built the place is, perhaps, verified by the anecdote that Messrs. Bennett Bros. preserved. They had a free hand in the fireplaces, kitchen-ranges, and general sanitary work, and, said Dugdale, "They ca' me Owd Stink o' Brass; see to it thou mak'st the place worthy of the name."

FINCH HOUSE.

Finch House, Finch Lane, Knotty Ash, was built by Richard Gildart about 1776, on land which he had bought from Lord Sefton. He had represented the Borough of Liverpool in Parliament from 1734 to 1754. He came from an old and respected Liverpool family. Quite a number of Gildarts took turns at being Mayor of the old town in the 18th Century. Francis Gildart, brother of the Member, filled the office of Town Clerk for 38 years, from 1742 to 1780. The last representative of the family was Rev. James Gildart, who was curate of St. Nicholas Church from 1808 to 1813.

The next owner and occupant of Finch House was Ellis Mather, who married Blanche, daughter of Lawrence Heyworth, of Yew Tree. Mr. Mather sold the house and estate to Lord Derby. At one time Mr. Brammall, of the Shakespeare and other theatres, and later a manufacturer of Dry Soap, lived there.

The house was remarkably well built, with a special hand-moulded brick of superior quality, the size of which was 9½ins. by 2¾ins. It is said, locally, that it took seven years to build. Everything about the building was of the best, all doors were made of mahogany, and the shelves and drawers were of walnut; the cornices and panels were removed to Knowsley to adorn the Hall, and the bricks went to the estate yard for further use. Finch House was demolished in March, 1912.

CORPORAL SHAW.

Not to believe everything that one is told is an adage ever to be remembered by the student of local history. The writer was once informed by an elderly gentleman " that Corporal Shaw, the Life Guardsman who so distinguished himself in the Battle of Waterloo," was a native of Old Swan. He was quite sure about it; knew the family, and so forth; telling of his capture of the French eagle, of the attempt to retake it by six men of the Imperial Guard, four of whom he killed outright, but falling at last to the remaining two; and even spoke of the family likeness as seen in the famous painting, where Corporal Shaw is represented as having seized the eagle in the struggle. On investigation, however, it was found that two men from Old Swan—one named Davies, brother or son of the local blacksmith, and a John Shaw, son of the proprietor of the Black Horse Inn—had enlisted, and had both fought in

1.Prescot Road, showing Hoult's corner, 1938.

2. West Derby village, 1858.

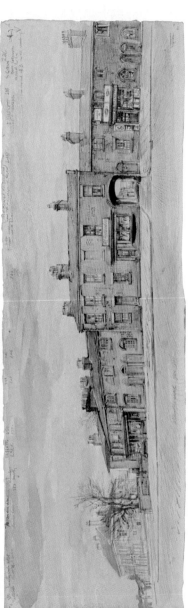

3. East Prescot Road, 1950.

4. St. Oswald Street, Old Swan, 1938.

5. Prescot Road, 1911

6. Swan Row, Prescot Road, Old Swan, 1911.

7. Black Horse lane, 1912.

8. View from New Hall Lane, Clubmoor, 1909.

9. Wavertree Green, 1910.

10. Wavertree Mill, 1884.

the Battle of Waterloo. Corporal John Shaw, the hero, however, was evidently not a Liverpool man, for the "Liverpool Mercury," in giving its account of the battle at the time, describing it in detail and mentioning the incident, did not allude to his having any local connection, which it certainly would have done had there been any. Also, Corporal Shaw's skull was taken to the Royal United Service Institution, Whitehall, where it is yet to be seen in the museum; while the body was interred in a country church-yard in Nottinghamshire with a Richard Waplington, who had fallen in the same battle. So far as can be traced, "the" Corporal Shaw had no connection with Liverpool.

MONUMENT AT SPRINGFIELD.

Springfield Park, Knotty Ash, one of the most recent acquisitions of the Liverpool Corporation, has in the centre of one of its grass plots a monument about 40 feet high, upon which are inscribed the following words : " Sacred to the memory of the illustrious Nelson, who gloriously fell in defence of his country, and to whose skill and valour Britons are indebted for domestic security and the tranquil enjoy-ment of their industry." The writer is informed that after the Battle of Trafalgar there was much discussion in Liverpool about the advisability or otherwise of erecting a monument to the memory of Nelson. The owner of Spring-field, " a wealthy gentleman," offered to the Town Council to " at his own expense " erect a suitable monument. The offer was favourably considered, but full particulars as to size, design, &c:, were asked for. In the meantime the would-be donor had ordered the obelisk which to-day is to be seen in Springfield Park. The members of the Town Council, however, on receiving the particulars of " dimen-sions, &c.," considered that the monument was too small and unworthy of the town, and declined it " with thanks." Lord Nelson's admirer thereupon had the monument delivered at his own park at Knotty Ash, where it was erected and has remained to this day.

KNOTTY ASH CHURCH AND ITS BELL.

In the belfry of Knotty Ash Church is a bell having the motto " God save the Church and Queen : A.D. 1707," upon it. The Queen referred to was Queen Anne, and the bell was said to have been cast from cannon taken from the French. John Churchill, Duke of Marlborough, was then winning his battles ; Blenheim was fought in 1704, and he probably forwarded cannon home among his other trophies won in the war. The bell, however, has silver in it, and it is renowned for the mellow sweetness of its tone as it rings out Sunday by Sunday its call to the people of Knotty Ash. It was hung originally in the tower of St. Peter's Church, Church Street, where it remained until 1830, when, a peal of bells having been purchased, it was sold to the wardens of Knotty Ash Church. The churchyard is worth a visit, for in it are buried many of the illustrious dead of the locality. It has been said that there are more former Mayors of Liverpool lying in its peaceful acre than in any other churchyard in or about the city. It also contains the dead taken from the portion of the churchyard of St. Nicholas's Church which was cut off at the time when the road to the Landing Stage was widened. The very handsome lychgate was made from oak beams taken from Accers, a famous local old building, the home of the miller who had charge of the " King's Mill," which adjoined it. The house and mill were occupied and in use in 1342. An immense amount of labour was put into the carving of the archway over the gate, and its cost to Mr. R. D. Radcliffe, M.A., F.S.A., who defrayed the expense, was £400.

MEMORIES OF ASHFIELD.

In Knotty Ash, at the junction of the old lane which leads from Thingwall and joins Thomas Lane, is a stone pillar, and on it is the date 1776, with the legend on one side " To Thingwall," and on another side " To Broad Green," also the initials " J.C." Exactly opposite to it is the main entrance to Ashfield, now the home of Mr. Allan H. Bright, J.P., and the garden which has been made famous by a charming little book entitled " A Year in a Lancashire Garden," from the pen of Mr. Henry Bright, father of the present owner. The " J.C." of the pillar is James Clemens, who built Ashfield and who laid out the wonderful garden, which has been such a pleasure to all who have seen it since his day. James Clemens came originally from the Isle of Man, made a fortune, became a country J.P., and in 1775-6 was Mayor of Liverpool. Perhaps he was a builder, for he had a considerable amount of property in Knotty Ash and Broad Green, and much of the property is distinguished with an uncommon shape of window, the style being a kind of Gothic. They are to be seen in the stables at Ashfield and in many cottages in Prescot Road, Knotty Ash, and at Ash House.

James Clemens lived in exciting times, for it is recorded in Lacey's " History of Liverpool " that in 1775 an attempt having been made to reduce the sailors' wages, serious riots took place, the men attacking the Town Hall with cannon. They established mob law and seized all the arms and ammunition in the town. They looted the offending ship-owners' houses and did enormous damage until the arrival of soldiers put an end to the disturbance. Mr. James Clemens died on April 3rd, 1796, and was interred in the burial ground of St. Nicholas's Church, in which a tablet was placed to his memory, and also of his son, who was the last of the race. The son, Thomas Crowden Clemens, was a worthy son of a worthy father, for he left his property to be divided between the following Liverpool charities :— The Lunatic Hospital and Asylum, the School for the Deaf and Dumb, and the School for the Blind. He evidently had great sympathy for the unfortunate ones who had not the common senses of sight, hearing, speech, and intelligence.

Mr. Clarke Aspinall, in his " Liverpool a few years since," tells that in his day John Clarke, brother to the Recorder of Liverpool, lived at a mansion called Ashfield. He was a town councillor and had been Mayor. He was a peculiarly good looking little man, was always well dressed, rode a good horse and drove a neat carriage.

Mr. John Clarke had two daughters ; one of them married a Mr. Heatherington, and for some years lived at 14, Greenfield Road, Old Swan.

SOUTH-WEST LANCASHIRE.

EDGE LANE HALL.

Edge Lane Hall, built partly of local sandstone, partly of brick, with all its windows surmounted with drip-stones, and some of them mullioned, "that is, having upright stone divisions between the windows," from its general structure would appear to be a 17th century house. Little seems to be known about its early history.

In Perry's Map, dated 1768, it is marked as the only building on the south side of Edge Lane. The following references to it are from Gore's Directory :

1825 and 1827—John Shaw-Leigh, attorney, Edge Lane, West Derby.
1829 to 1835—John Shaw-Leigh, attorney, Edge Lane Hall.

1837 to 1857—Francis Haywood, Edge Lane Hall.
1859—Mrs. Francis Haywood, Edge Lane Hall.
1860—Peter P. Rodocanachi, Edge Lane Hall.
1862 to 1885—Benjamin Arkle, banker, Edge Lane Hall.

John Shaw Leigh was son of the well-known lawyer, John Leigh, of Sandhills. Mr. John Leigh came from Appleton, near Widnes, in 1752; he did well at his profession and invested money in houses and land in the centre of the city, and at the north end of Liverpool, particularly in the neighbourhood of the docks, and as the town extended to Bootle, his land increased enormously in value. In 1810 he bought the advowson of Walton Church. Returning to the Hall and its occupier, Mr. John Shaw Leigh inherited a large fortune from his father, and was able to keep up Edge Lane Hall in good style. He also at one time lived at Childwall Hall. Leigh Street, which runs between Whitechapel and Parker Street, was named after him. His tastes were, however, for a country life; he bought an estate in Luton, to which he retired, and where he died in 1871.

The following is extracted from the pages of the " Liverpool Post and Mercury," and relates to Edge Lane Hall :—

" Curious " writes :—Your "News, Notes, and Queries" column is always interesting, and particularly so when it embraces a topographical contribution from your kindly correspondent, Mr. James Hoult. For years I have been curious as to the history of the old house in Edge Lane. Who built it? When? What was it like in its prime? Who have occupied it? Like the late Sir James Picton, Mr. Hoult has frequently described land and buildings close to it, north and (in Mr. Hoult's case) east, but has not touched it. There are people on the ground who tell you a wonderful tale of haunted rooms and secret passages, and a drive right to Wavertree Lane, and lodge gates at the top of Deane Road, and they will tell you of the room in which Queen Victoria slept, etc. I wonder if Mr. Hoult would favour us with these interesting particulars.

In reply to "Curious," the old house referred to is, I presume, Edge Lane Hall. The queries are numerous, and cannot all be answered in one reply. Queen Victoria never slept there when in Liverpool. Her Majesty slept at Newsham House. The lodge gates would hardly be at the top of Deane Road. Any lodge and gates there would belong to Fairfield Hall. Nor do I think that a carriage drive would come out at Wavertree Lane, for Edge Lane

Hall is quite close to Edge Lane, which is itself a leading thoroughfare. With regard to the secret passages and the haunted rooms, there are plenty of legends about them, and perhaps the stories told by the family of Mr. John De Nash, who lived there as caretaker for the Corporation for thirteen years, from 1888, are as interesting as any. Mr. John de Nash had been a member of the Royal Irish Constabulary, and at a time of agrarian agitation in Ireland had been shot in the hand by moon-lighters. He came to Liverpool with his family, and by-and-bye became caretaker of the hall. He was nervous since being shot, and so always slept with door and windows fastened. He tells of mysterious noises heard by himself and the whole family one night, as of someone chopping wood in the kitchen. In the morning, however, there were no chips found, and nothing had been disturbed. On another occasion, between two and three o'clock in the morning, a noise as of someone in heavy boots coming upstairs was heard, and Mr. de Nash's dog began whining and yelping in evident terror. When, later in the morning, the bedroom door was opened, it was found crouching on the floor and trembling violently. While at Edge Lane Hall Mr. de Nash had a visit from an old gentleman, who asked if he could be allowed to look round the place, stating that he used to live there as coachman, thirty years previously. He stated that in his time mysterious sounds were sometimes heard in the butler's pantry. With regard to the underground passage and the hidden room, a hunt was once undertaken for both by a Corporation official and Mr. de Nash, but without success. The hall has very large cellars and seventeen bedrooms, is rather gloomy in appearance, and the wind, as it blows through and around it, has a mournful sound. " Curious " will perhaps be able to put two and two together.

Mr. M. O'Reilly writes:—I have seen in Saturday's edition of " News, Notes and Queries," where Mr. James Hoult writes about Edge Lane Hall. As one who lived there for a number of years with my uncle, John de Nash, and has heard all sorts of sounds at night, the following may interest some of your readers. The night which Mr. Hoult refers to about the dog happened this way : I was awake on that occasion. The dog ran upstairs to the bedroom where I was, yelping. There was a sound downstairs like as if someone had a piece of wood on an axe. It came from the kitchen into the hall and stopped opposite my uncle's door. My uncle got up and lit a candle, took a revolver and searched the house upstairs and down, but could find nothing. I never knew him to be nervous. He was just the opposite. It was nothing new to hear all sorts of noises at night. There is a long passage under the Hall which goes down towards the Botanic Gardens. There was also a drive known as Queen's Drive. That will be the drive referred to by the other inquirer. There could always be a room more found outside than inside. It is the back of the hall—that is, towards Edge Lane. The front faces the Dogs' Home. My uncle was a sergeant pensioner from the R.I.C., and if he was a nervous man when eight men attacked him in County Sligo, he would not have got away, as there was no one with him. They fired several shots at him and he was wounded. All the fingers of the left hand were shattered. He is still alive and living in Ireland.—The new portion of Wavertree Park belonged to the hall, it was opened in 1893; that is where the Queen's Drive was.

The Queen's Drive was made by the Liverpool Corporation when the Exhibition (Shipperies) buildings were being erected.

Edge Lane Hall was demolished in April, 1913, to make way for a front entrance to the Exhibition of that year.

GILL MOSS.

Gill Moss and Page Moss are outside the city boundary, the former beyond West Derby, and the latter beyond Knotty Ash, but both are within Bootle Parliamentary Division. Both names remind us of the bog lands which used to be a characteristic of South Lancashire. At Gill Moss is an old house, the living portion of which is tenanted by a Mr. Valentine. In the roof is a hidden Roman Catholic Chapel. The entrance to it is through what looks like a stable door; then up three flights of stairs, and through another roughly-made door. The services were held here in the days of the penal laws against Catholics, the members of the Molyneux family and their Catholic tenants being the worshippers. Adjoining the house of Mr. Valentine is now the Roman Catholic Chapel of St. Swithin, which was built immediately the times of persecution had passed. The interior is very beautiful, and has recently been redecorated, the cost being defrayed by a legacy left by Mr. Michael Burns, a cattle dealer, of Stanley. The altar, of pink and white marble, came from France; and the pictures were from the private chapel of Croxteth Hall. There is one seat in the chapel which always has a cushion upon it, and it is known as the King of France's seat. It derived this title from the fact that in 1812 M. d'Artois—the name by which he was known during his exile—sat in it, when staying at Croxteth Hall; he came regularly to prayers in the chapel. For more than two centuries, in defiance of the intolerant laws then in force, a chaplain was maintained at Croxteth, ministering to its residents, and to Catholics in the surrounding district. While the fires of persecution burnt fiercely, the priests lived and officiated at the Hall, going thence in secret, as opportunity offered, to administer the sacraments, and to give succour and consolation to the distressed members of the little community.

It is only from the beginning of the eighteenth century that we are able to record the names of the chaplains. In 1700, Father Albert Babthorpe was the priest in charge. He died in 1720, aged 74 years, and was succeeded by Father Richard Billinge, S.J. On his death in 1733 the Rev. William Molyneux, S.J., who became Viscount Molyneux in 1745, was priest.

The first Protestant member of the Molyneux family was Charles William, created first Earl of Sefton in 1771. His father, the Hon. Thomas Molyneux, died in 1756, and he became ninth Viscount Molyneux on the death of his uncle, the Rev. the Viscount Molyneux, S.J., in 1759. He was at this time only eleven years of age. It has frequently been asserted that he " embraced " Protestantism, and he has been stigmatised as an " apostate," but as his father had left him under the guardianship of the Protestant Duke of Beaufort and others without any stipulation as to religion, it is highly improbable that he had any opportunities of being brought up a Roman Catholic. At the age of 20, he publicly read a " Renunciation of the Errors of the Church of Rome " before the Curate and Clerk of St. Martin's-in-the-Fields, London, on March 5th, 1769. This curious document is now in the Muniment Room at Croxteth. He married Isabella Stanhope, daughter of the Earl of Harrington.

At Gill Moss the mission was placed in the charge of the Rev. Father Emmott, S.J., who states in one of the registers that he came there on April 10th, 1773. During his ministration, some distinguished worshippers attended the hallowed sanctuary, as is shown by the following record, written on the fly-leaf of one of the baptismal registers either by him or his successor, Father Coupe, S.J. :—

H

During the month of September, 1812, Mons. Le Comte de Artois, with his attendants, the Baron de Rolles and the Duc de Berri, paid his customary annual visit to Croxteth Hall, and, as usual, regularly came to prayers at Gill Moss. His seat in the chapel, known by the name of the King of France's seat, is the one nearest the Gospel side of the altar, afterwards occupied by Mr. James Morton.

The Comte d'Artois became Charles X. of France in 1824, his elder brother, the Comte de Provence, ascending the French throne in 1814 as Louis XVIII. Both were brothers of the ill-fated Louis XVI., who was guillotined during the Revolution.

The Duc de Berri, son of Comte d'Artois, and father of the Comte de Chambord (the last of the elder branch of the Bourbons), was assassinated by Louvel in 1820.

On a recent Sunday evening, the writer visited the chapel; the congregation came from Knowsley, Kirkby, Simonswood, and Croxteth; they were in good numbers. Many children were present, and they took part in a procession. It is quite evident that the old faith still lives at Gill Moss.

KING JOHN AND SOUTH-WEST LANCASHIRE.

If in Liverpool the citizens observed Founders' Day, as is the custom in Oxford, the name honoured would be that of King John, but that King John was ever in West Derby Hundred has yet to be proved ; there are, however, certain evidences which indicate that he had been hereabouts, and was familiar with West Derby, Liverpool, and Toxteth Park, and was acquainted with local families. His actions indicate a knowledge of the then lovely S.W. Lancashire and its people. He it was who started Liverpool on its career. He made the hamlet into a free town, granting such privileges as to induce 160 heads of families to settle within its borders. He built the castle, a considerable work in his day, and attached the park of Toxteth to it as its demesne, and for the use of its Governor, both for sporting purposes and for profit. He also added to the estate of Toxteth the adjoining estate or manor of Smithdown, persuading the owner Richard, son of Thurston, to accept that of Thingwall in exchange. Contemporary writers speak of the transaction feelingly for the owner, styling him " poor man."

It is very probable that, as a large part of Smithdown was peat land, smiths and other workers in iron had founded a colony there, hence the name Esmedune, as Smithstown would be pronounced by the Norman French clerk of the day. These people would be undesirable neighbours, perhaps given to poaching, also the peat cutters were usually rough and lawless men, and the King desired to protect his parks from them.

The park was enclosed with a wall; part of the wall was in existence at one side of Parliament Street as recently as the days of Queen Anne.

The Smithdown demesne included the whole of Wavertree—its boundaries being Wavertree Nook, Elm Hall (now demolished), to the waterfall at Otterspool, on the eastern and southern sides, and the Moss Pits adjoining the boundary of the old West Derby township, on the north.

On February 26th, 1206, King John was at Lancaster, and at Chester two days after; perhaps he stayed a night at Liverpool when travelling between the two places. On August 28th, 1207, he granted his famous charter to Liverpool, and in 1208 the Wapentake Court was removed from the Castle of West Derby to Liverpool.

John, while acting as Regent during his brother's absence in Palestine, appeared to have acquired some knowledge of S.W. Lancashire, for in 1199 he confirmed Henry-de-Walton as steward of the Hundreds of West Derby and Salford, and as serjeant of the Wapentake Court of West Derby, and, as soon as he became King, he expended large sums of money on his castle at West Derby. His friendship with William Ferrers, Earl of Derby, is also significant. King John made him a present of a large house in the City of London, which had belonged to Isaac, the Jew of Norwich, the consideration being "That the Earl should serve at the King's table at all annual feasts with his head uncovered and bound with a garland, the breadth of his little finger." It is almost incredible that King John should go to the extreme of cruelty to his Villains on the new Smithdown Manor, of laying the Vill waste, had he not been there hunting personally, and knew the place. In the succeeding reign of Henry III., a letter was sent to the Sheriff of Lancashire, which reads as follows : "The King to the Sheriff of Lancashire, greeting. We command that without delay you enquire diligently by discreet and legal men of your county what is the value of the Vill of Smethdon, which our Lord, King John, our father laid waste for a Haia of Toxteth." The answer was as follows : "In the waste of the Vill of Smethdon, which King John laid waste for a Haia of Toxteth 13s. 4d." It is of passing interest to remember that we got our words " Village " and " Villain " from " Vill," which, freely translated, meant a country village owned by the King. The lot of the villani or villains was a hard one. They were chattels and belonged to the land, and were usually disposed of with the farm at which they worked. The villain was at the mercy of his lord who could chastise him, but not to the extent of maiming him; he could also take of the goods and chattels of the villain at his will. He also claimed a right over his daughters, and also could dispossess the man of his cottage and cultivated ground. It would be a sad day for the smiths, peat cutters, and farmers, whether free men or villains, when King John began to interfere with S.W. Lancashire. However, there is another aspect of his interest in our county, and it is right that he should get the credit for a deed which was a truly great reform, he abolished the Forest Laws as affecting Lancashire. In his day there were large areas of land under these laws; locally, there was a wood at West Derby, four and a half miles long. These laws dated from Saxon times, and were extremely harsh. For instance, if any freeman offered violence to one of the Verderers (or officials) he lost his freedom and all that he was possessed of, while for the same offence a villain had his right hand cut off, and for a second offence, either a freeman or villain was put to death. For chasing or killing any wild beast of the forest, for the first offence the freeman got off with a fine, but a bondsman was to lose his skin. Freemen were allowed to keep greyhounds, but unless they were kept at least ten miles from a royal park or forest their knees were to be cut. A Royal Park was a chase enclosed by walls or strong hedge. A forest was not necessarily all wood, it might include farms, on which all animals (wild by nature) were not to be molested except by the King or his servants. The farmer held the land for cultivation, and the King held the same land for his sport.

There would be great rejoicing at the abolition of the Forest Laws by the King.

The Royal Park at Toxteth was kept up for centuries at considerable expense. In the book of accounts, or close roll of Henry III., we find that a master huntsman, 49 men, 10 horses, 2 packs of dogs, and 52 spaniels were kept there; there were also 2,000 handnetts; but with all the care of the Verderers, poaching was carried on, and occasionally the game stealers were caught. In 1337, reign of Edward III., William Bassett and Robert de Hungerford were charged with concealing themselves in bushes and shooting deer, that they had killed two does and taken them away at night.

Ranulph de Dacre, Parson, of Prescot, was charged with a similar offence. The Park was disforested in 1596, in the days of Elizabeth.

The character of King John was not good. It was undoubtedly very mixed; he was able, a great worker, and a statesman, but in general conduct he was wicked to a degree. A contemporary, writing of him said, " Foul as it is, Hell would be defiled by the fouler presence of John." J. N. Green says of him : " He united into one mass the wickedness, the insolence, the selfishness, the unbridled lust, the cruelty and tyranny, and the cynical indifference to honour and truth of the Angevin family, from which he was descended." His treatment of the Jews illustrates some of his ways. In 1210 he ordered that all the Jews in England were to be imprisoned until they gave up to him all their possessions. One unfortunate Jew at Bristol had a tooth extracted daily until the King had extorted from him 10,000 marks. His rule was so bad that the Barons, with the nation at their back, demanded from the King what is known as the " Great Charter," and forced him to sign it. In it the Englishman is recognised as having a right to freedom. He is not to be seized, or imprisoned, or outlawed, or in any way brought to ruin, save by legal judgment of his peers or by the law of the land. He is in future to have justice, security of his person and property, and, generally speaking, good government. John resisted it to the last, and after signing the Charter, did his best to destroy it, going so far as to persuade the Pope to annul it.

After the lapse of a few centuries, there is a tendency to look back at the past and see the events in a dim and misty light, and to weave around them a garland of romance. In this atmosphere a King becomes a hero or a saint. This is so in the case of King John. Even our sane and reliable historian, the late Sir J. A. Picton, confessed to having " rather a sneaking sort of regard for him."

EARLY ENGLISH HOUSES.

Mr. James Hoult writes in answer to the query by " Curious." In Seebohm's " English Village Community " there is an account of how the early English house was built. It was built of trees newly cut from the forest. A long straight pole is selected for the roof-tree ; six well-grown trees, with suitable branches reaching over to meet one another, and about the same size as the roof-tree, are stuck upright in the ground at even distances on two parallel rows, three in each row. Their extremities bending over form a Gothic arch, and, crossing at the top, each pair makes a fork, upon which the roof-tree is fixed. These trees supporting the roof-trees are called gavaels, forks, or columns, and they form the nave of the house. Low walls of stakes and wattle shut in the aisles of the house, and over all is the roof of branches and rough thatch, while at the ends were the wattle doors of entrance. Giraldus Cambrensis, a British historian, who died about the end of the twelfth century, gives a similar description. There are houses built in the above manner still existing in Lancashire and Cheshire. The best preserved specimens near Liverpool are the old portion of Rainhill Hall, and a cottage near the Church at Farnworth.

LOCAL FAMILIES.

Old Swan and neighbourhood have place and street names which in many cases indicate something of interest to the observant traveller. The local families are remembered in Stanley, and Derby Lane and Derby Street, of the lords of Knowsley. In Gascoyne Street and Salisbury Street of the Childwall Hall family, owners of much land in Old Swan, and which family gave Liverpool two M.P.'s—the Gascoignes, father and son—and Britain a Prime Minister in Lord Salisbury. Brookland Road tells of a famous Rector of Liverpool who formerly owned the land upon which it was built. The physical features are remembered in Moss Lane, Moss House, Moss Farm, Moss Cottage, and Black Moss Lane, of late, vulgarised into Black Horse Lane, telling of the time when the district was moss and bog in character. Blackmoor, a hall belonging to Mr. R. R. Heap, tells of the ancient Blackmoor Moss, which existed 150 years ago. Rock Mount, Rock Street, and Rock House recall the famous quarries of Old Swan, the stone facing of the George's Dock, built in 1771, and the stone in many of Liverpool's churches and buildings of the eighteenth century, coming from them. The local occupations and industries are remembered in Mill Lane, one of the oldest thoroughfares, and which leads to the old King's Mill (wind), which had a right of soke or milling monopoly over the manor lands. There is documentary proof of its existence in 1475. Nursery Lane tells of the famous Nursery. Hurst Street and Bibby Street are names of bygone rope makers. Maddocks Street, of the first Catholic priest sent to Old Swan, the saintly Canon Maddocks, pioneer of a religion which afterwards built the stately church dedicated to St. Oswald.

EARLY INLAND TRAFFIC.

Inland traffic has always been of vital interest to Liverpool, and it is passing strange that so little is known of an era extending over centuries, when the commerce of the port was fed from the Lancashire side by means of pack horses, mules and donkeys. No history of the traffic has been written and local historians make but the slightest reference to it, for instance, one historian states that in 1788 a procession of 70 pack horses started daily from an Inn in Dale Street for Manchester, but does not inform us of how many started for Preston and the North, Stockport and the South, etc. Dr. Aiken, who wrote in 1795 "A Description of the Country around Manchester," tells that from 1730 to 1770 pack horses were the chief means of communication between Manchester and Liverpool. Daniel Defoe gives some information about this slow and costly method of transport, and Ralph Thoresby, in his account of the History of Cloth Making, tells of how that Cloth Fairs were held in Leeds on a bridge over the Aire until 1684, and afterwards in Briggate until 1715, and of how the cloth was brought from the country around on the backs of horses. Manchester merchants and clothiers, as the weavers were called, used the pack horse, some as pedlars, trading from house to house, and others as wholesalers, dealing only with shopkeepers and at market places, similar to the old Richmond Cloth Market at Soho, Liverpool.

Among the Pennine Hills, which lie beyond Manchester, in the small towns and villages, weaving had been carried on from early in the 16th century; in the 18th century the majority of the houses contained one or more looms. The weavers often owned their own donkeys and would travel long distances to sell the cloth in the best market; the tracks to London and the South, Glasgow and the North, and throughout the Midlands and into Wales, were familiar with these shrewd traders. There is a large village among the hills called Farnley Tyas, it is known among the neghbouring towns as *finished* Farnley, the imputation being that it was built so perfectly, about 300 years ago, that there has been no need to try and improve it, and truly it is a quaint old-world spot as we see it to-day. Although this village is from fifty to sixty miles from Liverpool, one of its cloth weavers did business in the old seaport and exported his cloth from Liverpool to Ireland in the days of good Queen Bess, as the following extract from Gregson's " Fragments " (Liverpool records) shows:—

> 1574 To regester the losse of the small boat the Swanne of Liv'pole, Wynstanley's owners, Edmund Laurence of Liverpole Master under God. The good Marchaunt Mr. John Armetage of farnley tyes in the Countie of Yorke, alias clothier wth riche stocke pro Livpole to Knocfergus aft shipwrecke came to land & fell amongst the Rebell Kernes, and were there moost vilianouslie mrthered, slayne and cut in pecs as the vilest kynd of fleshe, contrie to the pleasure and will of God.

The Armitage family of Farnley Tyas have been a very numerous one, and, on the whole, enterprising, as we might expect from the ancestry. Among the most distinguished members of it to-day are the Venerable Archdeacon of Halifax, Nova Scotia, and Sir John Armitage (of Lancashire and Yorkshire Railway fame), of Kirklees Hall, Brighouse.

It is interesting to know, also, that the descendants of the Winstanleys, as Liverpool shipowners, are still with us.

It reads very strange in these days, it is like unto romance; it seems incredible that traffic should be carried on under the conditions of Tudor days—no roads from the town into the interior, and boats of puny size to carry goods for import and export.

On the Liverpool Burgess Roll of 1585 is a list of ship-masters (or captains, as we would call them), and the tonnage of their boats is always given; they averaged from 10 tons to 34 tons, the latter being the highest.

Amongst the records of the Town Council, " 1758, July 14th,—It is ordered that a horse-causeway be made from Doghouse Lane (then part of Richmond Row between Byrom and St. Anne Street) to the Township of Everton, near The Loggerheads, to meet the horse-causeway there."

The pack horse tracks of South-west Lancashire are now difficult to trace, the original 4ft. cobble tracks having been merged into roads suitable for waggons. The best known were those which ran between Liverpool and the centre of Lancashire, via Old Swan, between the ford at Hale and West Derby, via Wavertree, and between Ormskirk and Formby, via Altcar. No pack horse bridge, similar to those which can be seen in Cheshire and Derby-shire, is known to exist in S.W. Lancashire to-day. Rev. Wm. Warburton, late Vicar of Altcar, in an article entitled " Notes on Altcar Parish," says that a few years ago there was a pack horse bridge between Formby and Altcar, and

Childwall Almshouses and Columbarium. (Page 130.)

Childwall Hall. (Page 130.)

Childwall Church and Hearse House (Page 131.)

Leper's Squint, Childwall Church. (Page 131.)

Base of Cross, Childwall. (Page 133)

Scandinavian Font, Kirkby Church. (Page 144.)

Cross at Rainhill. (Page 147.)

that it had been pulled down. When Formby was a port, and a rival to Liverpool, its ships received packs of goods from East Lancashire for export; there was a regular charge of so much per pack, indicating that the bulk of their cargoes came in this way. As it is well known that S.W. Lancashire was settled with Scandinavian peoples, it is of interest to note that the word " pack " is derived from the Danish " pak," and the Icelandic " packi," meaning wrapped up bundles.

EARLY ROADS.

From the time when Liverpool was a large village near Prescot, a path must have existed between the Castle and ships of the port and the inland town, but seven miles away. Herdman states that in 1539 the path to Prescot was *via* Wavertree, Childwall, and Roby. An old pack-horse track is still to be seen here and there, narrow, and paved with small cobble-stones. It appeared to have led along Edge Lane, through Oak Vale Nursery and Broad Green. The first Act of Parliament dealing with the highway was that of George II., 1745. It showed that the road from Prescot to Old Swan was in bad repair in consequence of the heavy coal traffic from St. Helens to Liverpool. It mentions the existence of a road from Old Swan, over Broad Green, and through Roby town towards Prescot. Broad Green was then unenclosed moorland, and Roby a town devoted to sail-making, and having a market-place and green; a portion of the shaft of the old stone cross is still there. The last Act dealing with the road is dated 1831. The road was then an important highway; the Cattle Market at Stanley had been opened, and an immense volume of traffic passed along it to and from Lancashire, the Midlands, and even London. The coming of the railway, however, in 1832, made an immense difference to it, to be revived, however, in these days by cycles, motors, and tramcars.

PACK-HORSE TRACK.

A pack-horse track has been traced from Edge Hill Church, along Edge Lane, over Old Swan Hill, through the old Nursery, and across the fields towards Prescot. It lay two feet below the soil in the Nursery, and showed the small cobble-stones of which it was made much worn with the shoes of the horses. Evidently great traffic had passed over it. These tracks were narrow, and used for horse travellers only. In East Lancashire they were usually paved with small squares of millstone grit. Previous to the making of the turnpike road to Prescot, pack horses carried most of the merchandise between the seaport towns of Liverpool and Formby and the interior. The last proprietor of pack horses in South Lancashire lived at Old Swan, where he had his stables, in which one hundred horses were regularly kept. His name was Davies, and he was an ancestor of the writer. The Smithies at Blue Bell and Black Horse belong to descendants of Lawrence and Catherine Davies, his son and daughter-in-law, whose name-stone is still to be seen on a house in Prescot Road, with the initials and date as follows :—

D.

L   C

1803.

When Mr. Davies died, he left a fortune of £20,000, a very considerable sum of money in the 18th century. His son, Lawrence Davies, however, was a spendthrift, and made bad use of the money which had been left to him, leaving his home to spend his time drinking and gambling. On one occasion he sent a message from Lancaster Gaol to his wife, telling her that he was locked up for a gambling debt owing to a local lord, and in the diary which his wife kept it was recorded that she sold thirteen cows and a bull to raise the money to release her husband.

A LIVERPOOL TURNPIKE ROAD.
ORIGIN OF THE TURNPIKE SYSTEM.

The road out of Liverpool towards London became a turnpike in the reign of Geo. II, in 1745, when an Act was passed through Parliament for repairing and enlarging the road between Liverpool and Prescot, over the Broad Green and through Roby town. In the reign of Geo. III, in 1768, an Act was passed to widen and repair the turnpike causeway at Blacklow Brow eastward through Huyton to the sign of Blue Bell, to join the turnpike causeway in the road leading through Prescot to Liverpool. In the reign of Geo. IV, in 1821, another Act relating to the same road was passed, similarly worded to the previous Act, excepting that Old Swan is mentioned, and Petticoat Lane; the latter is now Broad Green Road.

The word turnpike originally indicated a frame consisting of two bars turning on a post, to hinder the passage of beasts ; it came to mean " any gate by which the way is obstructed in order to take toll." It is of interest to know how it came about that our roads became obstructed with gates and bars. As we know, the country remained for centuries almost without means for wheeled vehicles to travel from place to place, the reason being that the system of repair was based on parochial divisions, each parish lying nominally under the obligation of keeping in repair the highways within it. But country parishes did not see the force of maintaining roads which were simply links in the chain of communication between distant towns, with which they had no concern, and the result of adopting so small an unit of area as the parish was that roads were in complete disrepair, and so-called highways were mere tracks. We are all familiar with the tales of how even the King's coach would often stick fast in the mire, and of six horses being harnessed, not from ostentation, but from sheer necessity. This condition of things was general until the reign of Charles II, when, in 1663, an Act was passed for placing a portion of the Great North Road from London, extending as far north as Huntingdonshire, under toll to provide for its repair. This seems to have been the first attempt at remedy of any magnitude, though there were earlier toll-houses established for special purposes, e.g., the Highgate toll, supposed to have been collected from 1385 in consideration of the Bishop of London allowing the road over Highgate Hill to pass through his park, and not discontinued till 1769.

The adoption of the principle that the people who used the road, and no others, should pay for its repair, seemed fair enough, and an admirable solution of the difficulty ; but, as we shall see, it brought consequences in its train which more than counterbalanced the advantages gained. These, however, did not appear at first. A plan that provided roads at all, where none had been before, had much to commend it, and so quickly was adopted all over England that in less than 200 years there came into existence some 30,000 miles of turnpike roads. In 1802, Thomas Telford commenced a Government survey with a view of roads and bridges being constructed, and ultimately a complete system was built under his direction, composed of 920 miles of road and 1,200 bridges. This being an undertaking called for by the State, the necessary funds were partly furnished by the Government ; in part they were contributed by the large landowners. The work occupied nearly 20 years, and it then became clear that the Parliamentary allowance which was made, together with the county assessment, did not always furnish enough to maintain the roads, and arrangements were therefore made under Act of Parliament for levying tolls.

In this manner the turnpike system came to extend
over most of Great Britain, and under it a considerable
proportion of the now existing roads were either constructed,
or converted from mere tracks, into thoroughfares, along
which it was possible to travel without constantly sinking
into the muddy ground. It should be mentioned in passing,
that some vehicles were exempt from toll, *e.g.*, those
belonging to the Sovereign or the army. Nor was any toll
taken from clergymen, nor from voters, and in some other
cases.

As the system came more extensively into operation its
defects became emphasised. One of the chief objections was
the costliness of this means of providing funds to pay for
repairs. There was the expense of erecting and subsequently
maintaining the toll-houses, gates, and bars, to say nothing
of the wages of the small army of men and boys required
to collect the tolls. It was estimated that nearly half the
receipts went in meeting these charges, and in defraying the
cost of the legislation, under which the system was maintained. Further objections were the obstruction caused to
traffic, the annoyance to travellers, and the diversion of
traffic into wrong channels. A careful study of the adver-
tisements which appeared in a Liverpool paper in the last
quarter of 1843 indicate the number of toll bars. The first,
after leaving London Road, was in Fairfield, where Stanley
Station is now. The auction was held at the Court House
in Prescot.

TOLL GATE ADVERTISEMENT.

Tolls to be let.—Notice is hereby given that the tolls
arising at the several Toll Gates upon the sides of the Turn-
pike road from Liverpool to Prescot, Ashton and Warrington,
in the County of Lancaster, called or known by the several
names of the Yellow House, the Old Swan, the Huyton, the
Green Lane, the Derby Lane, the Edge Lane, the Black
Horse, the Knotty Ash, the Roby, the Twig Lane, the
Blacklow Brow, the Rocky Lane, the Nursery Lane, the
Eccleston, the Haydock, the Four-Lane-Ends, the Portico
Chapel, the Thatto Heath, the Rainhill, the Sankey, the
Rainhill Tavern, the Farnworth Lane Gates and Side Gates,
will be let by auction in one or more lot or lots to bidder
or bidders at a public meeting of the trustees of the said
roads to be holden in the New Court Room in Prescot
aforesaid on Tuesday, the 19th of September next, between
the hours of eleven o'clock in the forenoon and three o'clock

in the afternoon, in the manner directed by the Acts passed in the third and fourth years of the reign of his late Majesty King George the Fourth " For regulating Turnpike Roads," which Tolls produced last year the sum of £7,150 above the expenses of collecting the same. All persons desirous of taking all or any of the said Gates will be required immediately on making their first bidding to deposit £50 in the hand of the Clerk to the said Trustees as a guarantee, the same at the close of the bidding to be returned to all (except the highest bidder or bidders) under conditions then to be declared.

Whoever happens to be the best bidder or bidders must at the same time pay one month in advance (if required) of the rent at which such Tolls may be let, and give security with sufficient securities to the satisfaction of the Trustees of the said Turnpike Roads for payment of the rest of the money, monthly or otherwise, as may be then ordered. Dated this Fifteenth day of August, 1843.

W. Rowson.
Clerk to the Trustees of the said Turnpike Roads.

At the auction in 1842, a Syndicate of Old Swan inhabitants, Messrs. James Hoult, Moses Dickinson, Henry Yates and Thomas Leach, bid for the privilege of farming the tolls, and were the highest bidders. They took possession of the bars, but the speculation turned out a bad one, each partner losing £106 10s. after working at it all year. The turnover was large, as the following day's takings from the toll book indicate :—

Thursday, October 19th, 1843—Cash received :—

Yellow House £28 1s., Green Lane £2 10s. 11d., Old Swan £12 3s. 6d., Coaches £1 16s., Nursery Lane 5s. 4d., Broad Green 14s. 7d., Roby £5 2s., Twigg Lane 14s., Blacklow Brow £1 2s., Kendrick's Cross 14s. 4d., Rainhill £4 11s., Coaches £1 2s. 2d., Sankey £14 17s. 6d.—£73 14s. 4d.—(Signed) James Hoult.

Black Horse 8d., Knotty Ash £1 6s. 6d., Huyton £32 5s. 6d., Coaches £9 8s. 6d., Lane Ends £3 1s. 11d., Portico 14s. 7d., Eccleston £9 10s. 5d., Haydock £3 8s. 2d., J. Hoult's 'busses £2 9s.—£135 19s. 7d.

The pike-men, as the toll-bar keepers were called, lived a hard life ; the pay was poor, but the toll-house was rent free. The wages paid in 1842 were the highest (in one case only), 21s. per week, others 8s., 5s., and even 2s. a week.

The roads between Liverpool and Prescot were left in notoriously bad repair, and the pike-men often had to stand the abuse of the traveller. The Cattle Market at Stanley caused much traffic of sheep and cattle. The former paid 1½d. per score, and cattle and horses 1d. each. The Old Swan 'bus and the coaches paid a special rate, *i.e.*, the usual payment at one toll-bar franking the next, which would mean that having paid at Fairfield toll-bar, Old Swan toll-bar would be free, and so on.

James Hoult was the proprietor of 'buses which ran between " The Turk's Head Inn," Knotty Ash, and Liverpool. He derived some benefit from his interest in the toll-bars from the advantage which his 'buses had over an opponent's, the gate men opening quickly for his, while the opposition 'bus was delayed as much as possible.

When asked how it was that the farming of the toll-bars lost so much money, one of the partners replied that, " We had not the first handling of the money." This can be read in different ways, but it is significant to find that at the 1844 auction the successful bidder was a Mr. Greenwood, who bid £6,850 while the syndicate only bid £6,840. The first act of the new authority was to clear out most of the old toll-house keepers and put in fresh ones.

The present generation has never seen a pikeman. Such a one was a distinctive figure, and hardly to be mistaken for any other occupation. He wore a tall, black glazed hat, stockings and knee-breeches, and invariably a short apron with capacious pockets for coin and the giving of change. He generally wore a scowl on his face, and altogether was a pretty tough and ugly customer to deal with. Turnpike-keeping, on the authority of Mr. Weller, senior (who, it will be conceded, is a classic authority), was indeed a singular kind of life : " Werry queer life is a pike-keeper's," he informed Mr. Pickwick, " they're all on 'em men as has met with some disappointment in life, in consequence of vich they retires from the vorld and shuts themselves up in pikes, partly with a view of being solitary, and partly to revenge themselves on mankind by taking tolls. If they was gen'l'men you'd call 'em misanthropes, but as it is they only takes to pike-keeping."

Next in importance to the London Road was the Scotland Road ; the turnpike trust on it was from Liverpool to Preston, *via* Walton, Burscough, Maghull, etc. This trust was not dissolved until 1877. The James Hoult mentioned in this article was the grandfather of the writer.

III

LIVERPOOL, NEAR PRESCOT.

Early in the seventeenth century, letters to Liverpool were addressed to Liverpool, near Prescot, or Liverpool, near Ormskirk, both of which towns were much larger and more famous. In the first year of the century the Parish of Prescot contained 5,000 inhabitants, half of whom resided in the township, and it had a large free Grammar School; while the population of Liverpool was something under 1,900, and its church only a chapel of ease of the Parish Church of Walton. At the same time Ormskirk was an important market town, the Quarter Sessions of the district were held there, and many of the South Lancashire gentry had town houses in it. It was also the centre for heraldry, and when the Spanish Armada invasion was anticipated, it was at Ormskirk that powder and matches were procured for the 300 soldiers raised in the Hundred of West Derby. The little town of Liverpool, with its castle, its pool, its fleet of fishing boats, the yellow sands of its river front, and the background of heather-clad hills, with the beacon at Everton above all, would indeed be a lovely place, and, doubtless, the beauty spot of the district.

LIVERPOOL TO PRESCOT 100 YEARS AGO.

A hundred years ago the traveller leaving Liverpool by the turnpike road to travel to Prescot began to climb the hill in London Road, which became steeper and steeper until the tableland of what is now Kensington was reached. There the horses would require a rest; as they "winded," as the driver would call it, and the Coach and Horses Inn, at the corner of Low Hill, was the stopping place. Adjoining it, where St. Luke's Schools now stand, was the West Derby Workhouse, and a little below it was the Court House. A hamlet straggled at the rear, and a Baptist Chapel and burial ground lay in the hollow on the Everton side. Continuing the journey, the fields at Kensington soon gave way to trees and park-like grounds on nearing Fairfield, where Mr. Edward Falkner, J.P. and D.L. for Lancashire, had built a large house, which, from its appearance, was nicknamed Tea-caddy Hall; the grounds were very extensive, one of the lodges being where Jubilee Drive, Kensington, is now, and the other at the entrance to what is at present Laurel Road, Fairfield. On the opposite side of the road (where Elm Park is now) was a villa residence standing in extensive grounds; it belonged to a Quaker family. Lower down the hill, towards Stanley, was the yellow house. It was an H-shaped building of some antiquity, 1617 being upon a date stone; its name was derived from its being regularly coloured with yellow wash. The traveller would here meet his first toll-bar, and if he had horse or vehicle, a stop would have to be made while he paid toll and the gates were opened to allow passage for his steed or carriage. Continuing the journey, the road was shaded with large trees which grew at each side and whose branches arched overhead. On crossing over the stream called the Tuebrook, a truly rural Inn called the " Traveller's Rest " was approached : the quaint old building did not belie its name, for along its entire front was a seat for weary pedestrians. When sold about seventy years ago, it was found to have but a squatter's title. At some time in the distant past a man had built for himself a shanty on the roadside, on the border of a large estate belonging to a De Walton, or Molyneux. No notice had been taken of the poor fellow and bye-and-bye he added a pigstye or out-building to it and it became more of a proper homestead. In course of time the squatter died, his heir took possession and again enlarged the dwelling. The landowner, living at a distance, knew nothing about the place, and if he did happen to pass it, would suppose that the occupant was legally there and would not trouble about it. In this way the place came to be looked upon as the property of the innkeeper, for it had evolved into an Inn. Passing on, the traveller begins to climb Old Swan hill. At the top would be found a village picturesquely situated, and commanding extensive views over Liverpool, and to the east over West Derby ; the local industries were glass manufacture, an earthenware works, a ropery and a nursery. It had no church or chapel, but a charity school had been in existence for about sixteen years. There was a stone building called the bridewell, which had been built for highwaymen and sheep stealers ; evidently these two crimes were common at one time hereabouts. The Old Swan Inn was a stopping place for the coaches. It was kept by a Mr. Clithero, who had quite an extensive establishment. At Old Swan the road branched, one into Prescot Lane, a narrow, cobble-paved lane leading by a short cut to Prescot, and the other into the turnpike road, then called Petticoat Lane, leading to Prescot *via* Huyton. There were toll-bars on both roads and numerous inns, the nomenclature of which is of passing interest. Innkeepers for centuries have used the coat-of-arms of the great local families, as their trade signs show.

For example, " The Cross Foxes " has been adopted from the armorial bearings of Sir Watkin Williams Wynn, and is very common in North Wales.   In the name Old Swan, which was derived from the Inn, we have a reminder of a great local family, now extinct, but at one time owning all the land around the village, namely, the Waltons, of Walton, whose coat-of-arms had three white swans upon a blue shield.   The other inns upon the road to Prescot which can claim some antiquity are the " Eagle and Child " and the " Blue Bell " at Huyton, and the " Turk's Head " at Knotty Ash.   The present " Eagle and Child Inn " is a transfer, the original inn of that name was on the same high road, but nearer to Prescot; the present hostelry had been Huyton Toll-bar.   The sign of the " Eagle and Child " is very common in Lancashire, and is supposed to have originated in this manner : In the reign of Edward III., Sir Thomas Lathom, ancestor of the House of Stanley and Derby, had a legitimate daughter and an illegitimate son. This son he ordered to be laid at the foot of a tree on which an eagle had built its nest.   He led his wife past the tree, found the child, and persuaded her to adopt him. Sir Thomas then assumed for crest an eagle looking backwards. The boy was called Sir Oscatel Lathom, and considered heir to the estates.   For some reason the old nobleman disinherited the son, and left his property to the daughter. Out of ill-feeling towards the boy the crest was afterwards altered to an eagle preying on a child. The origin or significance of the signs " Blue Bell " and " Turk's Head " the writer is unable to explain.   Each are notable in minor matters, the former as having a very ancient bowling green, and the latter as having been the inn from which the first 'busses commenced to run into Liverpool from the outskirts.

CROXTETH AND SEFTON AND THE ROAD BETWEEN.

There is a romance and charm about an old road which the antiquary only can realise, for not only does he study names and dates, but in imagination he sees on it a panorama of travellers wonderful in variety, according to the time under contemplation : mail-clad warriors, pack-horse drivers, friars and ecclesiastics in gowns and various robes, minstrels, pedlars, and strangely-dressed ladies of high degree of more distant date, while soldiers, traders, hunts-men, and the clergy of more recent centuries make plenty of variety.   Near Liverpool, among the oldest roads is that

J

which runs between Sefton Village and the seat of Lord
Sefton at Croxteth. Starting from the front of the hall, and
following the road due north, the traveller will journey in
almost a straight line to Sefton; there is one turn only, and
that is at Netherton, a hamlet of Sefton. Farmhouses and
cottages all along the route look as if they belonged to a
past century, most of them being roofed with stone slabs,
and in some cases they appear to have been originally
straw-thatched.

The Molyneux family lived originally at Sefton, and a
very distinguished family it was. Perhaps the greatest was
Sir William Molyneux, who in the reign of Henry VIII. was
sent three times to fight the Scotch, and who at the Battle
of Flodden captured the banner of the Earl of Huntly. In
Sefton Church a brass can be seen showing him in his
armour and shirt of mail. The lands of Croxteth had been
acquired in the reign of Edward IV., and a house had been
erected there in the days of Queen Elizabeth, but the west
front of Croxteth Hall as we see it to-day was only completed in 1714. After the removal of the family and all their
belongings to Croxteth the hall at Sefton was destroyed.
Its site, however, near the fine old church, is still easily
to be distinguished, partly by the moat which surrounded it
and partly by the heaps of debris, covered now with grass.
When, in 1771, the King, wishing to honour the head of the
family of Molyneux, offered him an earldom, it was a
pleasant thought on his part to choose to be known by the
name of the village where his ancestors had lived for so
many generations. The present Lord Sefton lives at
Croxteth Hall.

DERBY AND MOLYNEUX.

Liverpool citizens have not yet settled the question of
how to pronounce the names of its two leading families.
Certainly the oldest and best known names in the city are
those of Derby and Molyneux. The West Derby township
and the title Lord Derby prove the close association of that
family with Liverpool. In West Derby itself the question
is often asked, do we pronounce it Darby or Derby? Some
favour Darby, from the idea that it is the old way; and
certainly some of the oldest maps and plans spell the word
Darby, but this is answered by the statement that " any
time beyond a hundred years ago " is out of count, as people
then had not learned spelling as it was taught to the parents
of the present generation. To-day most people pronounce

Derby as it is spelt, and this seems to be the sensible way. The name Molyneux also is pronounced in two ways. Some drop the " x," and others sound it. The late Lord Sefton, the head of the Molyneux family, was once asked the question, " How should the name be pronounced "? and his reply was, " Pronounce as it is spelt, sounding the ' x.' "

JOHN WESLEY AND PRESCOT.

Replying to " R.W.W.," who is inquisitive about the roads to Prescot and John Wesley's associations with that town. The direct road from Old Swan, through Knotty Ash, was in existence in Wesley's day, for a stage coach ran from Liverpool to Prescot in 1767, the fare being 1s. 6d. inside, and 6d. outside. He first saw Prescot in 1757, calling when on his way from Liverpool to Warrington. He would travel probably on horseback. As Roby was then a large village engaged in sailmaking, and Huyton almost a town, with its present Church, with stocks and village green, he may have travelled *via* those two villages. It is not known whether he preached at Prescot or its vicinity, but in 1775 a Mr. Job Preston, a watchmaker and farmer, of Rainhill, was made a local preacher. One of Mr. Job Preston's sons had exceptional ability as a preacher; but died suddenly after preaching at Prescot on April 22nd, 1798, aged 23 years. Methodists were persecuted in Prescot in those days, as elsewhere. As they preached in the open air, many came to hear, and sometimes a large crowd would gather in the Market-place and around the Fish Stones, on which the preachers stood. The enemy once turned out the fire engine and tried to pump the water over the preacher. However, friends captured it and turned the stream upon their assailants, greatly to their discomfiture. Lord Derby, the great magnate of Knowsley, was also against Methodism, and caused it to be published on the market day " that no innkeeper should entertain the Methodist preachers on any consideration." The earl did not have it all his own way, for the innkeepers said that as long as the Methodists paid money for lodging they should have it. He then forbade his servants to attend the services, and threatened with instant dismissal any who were found doing so. This ban caused him to lose the services of his head gardener, and Lady Derby lost her own maid, to whom she was much attached. Both were sorry to part with these, among the best of their servants; but, as her ladyship put it, it were best for them to go, for fear they should corrupt the whole household.

AMERICA AND SOUTH-WEST LANCASHIRE.

1650-1700.

That America owes much to Lancashire and that Lancashire is indebted to America is commonplace knowledge. To all students of early American history the place which South-west Lancashire occupies is conspicuous; its men were among the most active and useful pioneers, and did good spade work in the laying of the foundations of civil and religious freedom in the New World. In the Mayflower was Miles Standish, of Duxbury, near Wigan, who had been an officer in the army sent by Queen Elizabeth into Holland to fight against the Spaniards. Fighting men were needed in those days, and he was able to wage successful war against the Indians. The story of Miles Standish is beautifully told by Longfellow. Among the first to take an interest in American education was Richard Mather. He had been educated at Winwick Grammar School, and in 1611, at the age of fifteen, he had gone to Toxteth Park, near Liverpool, and started there a school. His school became famous, but through the preaching of a Mr. Harrison, of Huyton, he was converted. He went to Oxford, and after a term at Brasenose College he became a minister. The people of Toxteth Park having sent and asked him to return to them, not so much to instruct their children as themselves, he became teacher and preacher to the little congregation there. He was, however, a Puritan, and, after spending fifteen years of useful work, he was suspended as a Dissenter. He decided to go to America, and fourteen years after the Pilgrim Fathers had landed at Plymouth Rock Richard Mather came to take his place among the leaders of the colony. He founded a notable family. Of his sons the most famous was Dr. Increase Mather, president of Harvard College, and a faithful servant of his State in an important diplomatic mission to the old country. Three sons became ministers. One, Samuel, after graduating at Harvard, returned to South-west Lancashire and became minister of a little chapel at Burtonwood. Another, Nathaniel, went to minister to an English congregation at Rotterdam ; and the other remained in America, settling in the Connecticut valley. Dr. Cotton Mather was the grandson of Richard Mather. He was a most prolific author and the learned historian of the New England Churches.

Descendants of the family took a foremost place in the fight for independence.

Henry Ashurst, of Ashurst, a small hall between Southport and Wigan, was another friend to America in the early beginnings. He at the age of fifteen years was sent to London to make his fortune. He became a linen draper. When his father died he had a legacy of £500 and a small annuity chargeable on the estate, with which, and a loan of £500 from the Rev. Jas. Hyet, the Presbyterian rector of Croston, he started a business in London in partnership with a Mr. Rowe, a major in the Puritan army. Three years later he married Judith Heresby, with whom he got £1,000, and, leaving his partner, he started a business on his own account, which was extremely successful, and for thirty years of his business life he dedicated a tithe of his income to religious works.

His habit was to rise between four and five o'clock and spend two hours at his prayers before engaging in business; and for eighteen years he subscribed £100 per annum—no inconsiderable sum in those days—towards the support of Nathaniel Heywood, of Ormskirk, and other distressed Lancashire ministers, besides stocking their schools with Bibles and educational works. On December 14th, 1645, he was appointed one of the treasurers of the London Church Fund for the relief of the distress in Manchester after the siege, and on September 7th, 1648, treasurer of the London Church Fund for the relief of the maimed soldiers and the poor of Lancashire. He was for nineteen years treasurer of the Cromwellian Trust for the education of the poor children in the New England settlements of America, and after the restoration he successfully fought a legal battle in its defence. This trust was the foundation of the Society for the Propagation of the Gospel in Foreign Parts.

He declined to be sworn as a magistrate or alderman of London from conscientious objection to the oath and the execution of the cruel laws against Dissenters, but when master of the Merchant Taylors' Company he was a munificent donor to its charitable funds, and gave £300 towards the rebuilding of its hall. He had a country house at Henley, but his London house was burnt down in the great fire of 1666.

In March, 1672, he was consulted by the Presbyterian ministers of Lancashire and requested to ask permission of the bishops for them to hold services " in void chapels and churches where would give leave." This request was refused ;

but permission was granted to apply for a licence to preach in their own or any other house, and conduct religious services, and it was under this regulation that Chapel House, Ormskirk, was licensed for the ministrations of Nathaniel Heywood, the ejected vicar of Ormskirk.

In a transient gleam of recovery during his long illness, Mr. Henry Ashurst is reported to have said to his friend Nathaniel Hulton, of Hulton : " You and I will take care for Lancashire, that the Gospel may be more preached amongst them." He died in 1681, aged seventy, leaving by his will £50 to the New England Trust and £100 to the foundation fund of Harvard University, U.S.A. His funeral sermon was preached by his closest friend, the celebrated Richard Baxter, author of " The Saints' Everlasting Rest." He left four sons and two daughters. Men of the type of Standish and Mather have enriched America by their lives ; but the sympathy of an Ashurst has been but an example of that of numbers of South-west Lancashire worthies who have given generously to advance every cause which would in any way help their kin at the other side of the Atlantic.

Numerous articles might be written on the trade between Liverpool, the port for South-west Lancashire, and America, but it is worth remembering that as far back as 1697 the tide of emigration had commenced to flow, and that between 1697 and 1706 there left Liverpool for America no fewer than 1,456 persons. They were from all parts, like Thomas Bowling, of Euxton, who took out five emigrants, to two poor children of Aughton, named J. Woods and J. Taylor, orphans saved from the workhouse and given a chance to lead useful lives in a new country.

America then wanted people, and South-west Lancashire did its best in supplying its needs. The good seed sown by our Lancashire forefathers soon bore good fruit, and Harvard College, which had been helped with men and money, returned to our shore its special and peculiar Puritan culture. Peter Ambrose, of Ormskirk and Toxteth, sent his two sons to be educated at the New England College—Joshua in July, 1650, and Nehemiah in November of the same year. They took a three years' course and returned home in 1655. These two students eventually became ministers. Joshua was curate at West Derby in 1662 and vicar of Childwall in 1664. He died and was buried at Childwall in March, 1710. Nehemiah became minister at Kirkby, and because of his Nonconformity was ejected in 1662. He died in 1668 and was also buried at Childwall.

FAMOUS LOCAL WELLS.

Some years ago the writer was at Sefton, and he saw gathered together around the old well of St. Helen a number of girls; they were in their summer frocks, were laughing and evidently enjoying a holiday in this rural spot. He stopped to see what caused the fun and found that each girl was provided with a pin and was dropping it vertically into the water; there was a great eagerness to see how the pin descended and settled at the bottom of the well; if it lay at the bottom with the point towards the church, it was supposed that the owner of the pin would be married within the next year; the whole picture was pretty and the innocent merriment of the girls was pleasant to see and hear.

At Wavertree there is a well of great antiquity, and within the lives of people still living it was the place to which the villagers of Wavertree went for their water; it was never known to run dry, and in hot, dry summers people sold the water from it in Old Swan and neighbourhood of Wavertree at the rate of a halfpenny per Hessian can. It is known as Monks Well, and has the following Latin inscription above it :

" Qui non dat, quod habet daemon,
    Infra ridet, anno, 1414."

Translated very literally it runs :
    " He who hath and wont bestow,
    The demons will reckon with him below."

The moral of the warning seems to be that just as Nature has given the most precious gift of water so generously, so Man in his turn ought to give generously of his abilities and goods to his less fortunate brothers.

Within the Hundred of West Derby in mediæval days there were a number of holy wells rivalling the famous one of Holywell, in Flintshire. There was the Well of St. Thomas, near Windleshaw Chantry; it is to be seen to-day in an enclosed field, and only with difficulty; the writer, wishing to photograph it, had to climb over a very high wall and trespass. Its sides are of stone with recesses and shelves, upon which healed people placed their crutches and splints; at the head it bears this inscription : St. Thomas Well, W.E., 1798." These initials represent the names of William and Elizabeth Hill, owners of the adjacent land, but the well is much more ancient than the inscription suggests. There are two or three legends about the well, the most popular being that a saint of the old faith was being pursued for his religion, was overtaken where the well is now, was struck down, and his head cut off, and that the water burst forth where the head fell. There are two or three stunted trees leaning over the turbid water of the well; the place is desolate to a degree, and an appropriate motto for the times would be : "Ichabod"—"Thy glory has departed."

At one time, there was a famous well adjoining Lathom Park, dedicated to Saint Mary Magdalene. It was deemed a Holy Well, having unusual medicinal and healing qualities; it was converted into a fashionable spa-well during the Cromwellian period, by a son of the seventh Earl of Derby, who hoped thereby to bring riches to the family in his generation or the next. However, when coal mines were sunk at Skelmersdale, the spring dried up.

An old and historic well also is situated in Aughton, known as Cromwell's Well. This well, which is in the centre of agricultural land off Swanpool Lane and Moss Delph Lane, is supposed to have been used by Cromwell's soldiers during his campaign in Lancashire, for the purpose of watering the army horses. There is still a footpath to the well.

Before the Liverpool Corporation brought water from Rivington, the supply was obtained from wells only, and they were very numerous. At Old Swan, Knotty Ash, and Thingwall, they were very deep ones; at the latter place, when one well ran dry, the drains were turned into it.

All around, and even in Liverpool, there have been famous wells, most of them famous for the goodness and purity of the water, like the one which Sir John Moore tells of in his rentals. He tells of sinking a well in Moore Street, at a cost of £6. He goes on to state that : He found water at a depth of 14 yards, and that two or three of his tenants said that the water from this well, with four measures of malt, will make stronger and better ale than most of the town wells with five measures, whereas there are several scores of wells about the town, yet none were known to stand soap so to wash with, but the whole populace sends to a place called the Fall Wall Well, a quarter of a mile from the town. This well was situated at the edge of the heath, by where Lime Street is now; it was crowned by a dome supported by arches; it was removed about 1790. Other well-known wells were Dyehouse Well, one at Stanhope Street, where a brewery now stands, and Gregson's Well by the Necropolis, at the corner of Everton

Edge Lane Hall, demolished 1913. (Page 93.)

Prescot Market Place in 1750. (Page 111.)

Ancient Knowsley. (Page 114.)

Monk's Well, Wavertree. (Page 119.)

Speke Hall. (Page 121.)

St. Anne's Church, Stanley, now demolished. (Page 127.)

A Childwall Tithe Barn.   (Page 129.)

Childwall Abbey Inn.   (Page 129.)

Road. In St. James' Cemetery there is a stream of water which 50 or 60 years ago had a reputation for curing sore and weak eyes, and crowds of people were at times seen bathing their eyes, others filling bottles and taking it away. When the churchyard of St. Peter's was encroached upon on the widening of Church Street, a few of the bodies had to be removed, and it was found that some of them were as hard as stone, and it was thought that the mineral spring from St. James' Cemetery had run in that direction and had caused petrification of the bodies.

SOUTH-WEST LANCASHIRE AND THE WARS WITH SCOTLAND.

Liverpool and district, in these days, produce men to be captains of commerce. There have been times when from the same localities men came who were equally famous as military leaders, viz., of the families of Molyneux, Moore, Stanley, and Norreys. There is an incident of Henry VIII.'s time which is worth remembering, when local leaders and their men of West Derby distinguished themselves. England had been invaded by the Scotch, led by their King, James IV., who took the border fortresses of Wark, Etal, and Ford, at the latter of which he found the beautiful Lady Heron, whose attractions kept him waiting upon her until the English had time to muster forces to oppose his army. Ultimately the two armies met at Flodden Field, and the Scottish army was disastrously defeated, losing the king, twelve Scottish earls, thirteen lords, fifty chiefs, knights, and men of birth, and ten thousand soldiers. The Lancashire and Cheshire men, led by Sir Edward Stanley, especially distinguished themselves. There are several old poems referring to the Lancashire men and the field of Flodden. One of these is well over 350 years old. It has been printed by the Chetham Society (Vol. 39) and consists of about 700 lines. The following is a sample :

```
Lancashire, like lyons,
layden them about!
All had been lost by our Lorde !
had not these leddes (lads) bene.
For the care of the Scottes
increased full sore,
For their King was downe knocked
and killed in their sight,
Under the anner of a bishop
that was the bold Standley !
Then they fetilde them to fly
as fast as they might.
```

In 1544 Sir William Norris, of Speke, took part in the famous Lancashire raid into Scotland led by Lord Hertford, when many waggon loads of trophies were captured and brought to England. Sir William, who seems to have been a scholar as well as a raider, left behind him a note attesting that, " Md yt Edyn Boro Wasse Wone ye viii daye o Maye Anno xxxvjo H viii et Anno Dmi moccccco xliiiio and yt yis boke called Bartolus sup prim Degesti Veteris was gotty and brought awaye by me Wm. Norres of ye Speke K(nt) ys xi daye of Maye foursaide and now ye boke o me ye foursaide Sir William gene, and by me left to remayne at Speike for an ay loome. In witnesse whe'of (I have) wryty vis wt my none hand and subscribed my name. Me Will'm Norres night."

Sir William's share included fourteen volumes taken from the plunder of Holyrood, and a great deal of the wainscotting of that famous palace. He commandeered horses and waggons from Edinburgh and brought down to his house at Speke much treasure. In Speke Hall to-day we can see some of the beautifully-carved wainscot and panels and grotesque heads. One row of panels contains the following inscription : " Slepe not :till :ye :hath :considered : how : thou : hast : spent : ye : day : past : : if : thou : have : well : don : thank : God : if : other : ways : repent : ye." Other plunder from Holyrood is now in the Athenæum, Liverpool—a number of very large books, almost a cartload in themselves. They were worth bringing. Each volume represented the labour of years ; the writing is nearly as uniform as printed matter, and a great deal more attractive, the capitals being in many cases coloured. The paper, ink, and leather bindings are marvellous in excellence, considering the date. Other plunder which Sir William Norris brought home were four volumes, including a Bible from the Augustinian Monastery of Cambuskenneth.

At the Battle of Musselburgh Sir William lost his son, when resisting a desperate charge by the highlanders ; he had the consolation of knowing, however, that victory had again been on the side of the English ; also that he was able to bring home to Speke the Jennon or gwyddon of the noble Scotch family of the Boswells.

Among the trophies which Sir William Molyneux won were some banners of Scottish nobles. The poles upon which these banners hung, were until recently in Sefton Church. A brass in the chancel of the church, which commemorates Sir William, has upon it a representation of the

" pennon " of the Earl of Huntly, which had been taken
at the Battle of Flodden by Sir William Molyneux.

MISCELLANEOUS.

From " HARROGATE HERALD," *December* 11th, 1912.

AT A PACK HORSE BRIDGE.

Every object of interest in or about Harrogate ought
to be made the most of. Visitors usually have a good deal
of time on their hands, and they like to be able to go and
see things. One characteristic of them is that for the time
being they are all antiquaries. There is, about a mile out
of the town, a genuine pack-horse arched bridge, just the
kind of object to go and see in an afternoon's walk. The
same kind of a bridge in a Derbyshire resort is called a
Roman bridge, and every visitor to the town goes to see it.
The Harrogate pack bridge is part of a very historic track.
It is said that King Charles I. passed along it when a
prisoner in charge of Parliamentarian soldiers in 1646, when
travelling from Newcastle to Holmeby House, in Northamp-
tonshire, from " Leeds, Dewsbury, Almondbury, and
Farnley Tyas," as a centre. Pack horses and pack donkeys
travelled in the seventeenth century, and well into the
eighteenth century, east, west, north, and south. The
Yorkshire clothiers, as they were called, were familiar
travellers, even to Scotland and Ireland. At Farnley Tyas
the weavers had a special large breed of donkeys ; they were
kept as being more suitable for the carriage of cloth. It
was usual to wind the cloth round the body of the donkey
and fasten it with straps. Generally the cloth went to cloth
markets in the towns, but in some cases the owner went
with his donkey and cloth and traded for other goods in
return for the cloth, receiving general stores, such as sugar,
salt, ironmongery, etc., which he would take home. The
Harrogate pack bridge, at the present time, is in a field
protected with locked gates and high barbed wire fences.
It is for those in authority to have it made accessible.

ALDERMAN SNAPE'S STAFF.

Numbered amongst the treasures of the late County
Alderman Snape was a special constable's staff which he
inherited from his father, who in William the Fourth's
reign apparently acted in that capacity in Salford, of which

borough the late alderman's own brother was mayor in the
year 1910. For a token of such a nature the staff is
remarkably handsome, it being made of polished baywood
and ornamented with blue decorations, while the King's
monogram appears in gilt letters in company with a figure
of the crown. Alderman Snape took this interesting heir-
loom to the Liverpool Town Hall, and it was admired by
Lord Derby, as well as by his predecessor in the chief
magistracy, Mr. S. Mason Hutchinson. A point which is
not clear is the occasion which led to the enrolment of special
constables in Salford. King William's reign was a short
one, extending only from 1830 to 1837, but it is at least
probable that the ' civilian police '' were enrolled in connection with the fierce national agitation which followed the
rejection of the Reform Bill by the Peers in 1831, and
preceded their acceptance of that far-reaching measure in
1832.

A 1778 BALLAD, TOPICAL IN 1913.

The enclosed ballad, dated 1778, and printed at
Lancaster, is interesting to-day, showing as it does that the
evils which the Rev. Walter Cresswell, of Harthill, Cheshire,
is seeking to cure, were as rampant 134 years ago.

Mr. Cresswell states in a letter to the Press last week
that there are 1,491 clergymen who only receive £67 a
year, and he asks that people should think of the life of
genteel poverty which these men and their unfortunate wives
are compelled to live.

Tho' "Rectors'" livings do exceed,
And they have more than they do need;
They'll neither lose tyth, goose, nor pig,
Which makes 'em strut both fat and big.
They will not favour rich nor poor,
Tho' they have plenty in great store;
To love abenefit, they'll not yield,
Neither in Church nor in the field.
Old Ellis's (?) sons we find of old,
With th' people's offerings make too bold;
By taking what they lik'd the best.
For sacrifice they left the rest.
It's much the same in these our days,
He seems to imitate their ways:
Lets nothing pass him, great or small,
But strove at sharing part of all.
Such things as these came not to pass,
When Jesus rid upon an ass;
Nor did it ever yet appear;
Th' Apostles rid in coach or chair.
But, now, we see the clergy ride
In showy grandeur, pomp, and pride;

Which is not comely for to see,
In patterns of humility.
But (as we find most things are brittle)
Rectors have too much, curates too little;
Might justice rule, I must confess.
Curates should have more and rectors less.
Curates do most of all the duty
(If well performed, religion's beauty);
To pay them well they should engage,
Who do most work should have most wage.
To go no further, make a stand,
And speak no more of this in hand;
Composing rhyme to th' brain's a toil,
So here I'll stop and rest a while.

The unequal division of wealth and privilege is a problem to all thinkers, and appears to come within the scope of the proverb which tells us that, "The poor will be always with us." But if there is any profession or organisation which ought to aim for *greater justice and equity* between man and man, and practice these virtues within its *own walls,* surely it is the *Christian Church.*

A comparison between the salaries of bishops and rectors, and of the curates is very instructive.

BYROM HALL'S HISTORICAL POSITION.

Byrom Hall, one of the historic chapels of the Baptist denomination, was built in 1789 for the Rev. Samuel Medley and his congregation, who had removed from a smaller building, but which building, with additions, afterwards became St. Stephen's Church, in Byrom Street. Byrom Hall is notable as being the chapel from which the Rev. Mr. Birrell (father of the Right Hon. Augustine Birrell) seceded. He, with the majority of the congregation, left it and built Pembroke Chapel, where they established the principle for which they seceded —that of open communion. Mr. Samuel Medley himself was a character well adapted to his time and to this city, in which he was very popular. He had been a sailor in the Royal Navy. and had seen something of war. He was in 1755 a midshipman on the "Intrepid," and sailed under Admiral Boscawen. After being in several small engagements against the French, he, with his ship, was in the terrible conflict off Cape Lagos on August 18th, 1789. Many of the soldiers and sailors were killed, and among the wounded was Samuel Medley, who was crippled by an injury to one of his legs. On the return of the fleet he decided to settle down and live a quieter life ashore, and, as he had received a good education, opened a school. He was successful, but, happening to hear a sermon preached by Dr. Watts, he became converted, and soon commenced to preach. He received a call from the Baptist congregation in Liverpool, and his maritime expressions and open, hearty ways endeared him to the people of the seaport. Mr. Medley was a poet, and wrote several hymns, the best known being, "Mortals awake with angels join," which is still to be found in the Wesleyan, Congregational, and Baptist hymn-books. Many anecdotes are told of Mr. Medley. The following is characteristic :—Preaching in a chapel where the singing was anything but artistic, Mr. Medley looked over the pulpit to the leader and choir below and asked, "What tune do you call that, Mr. Leader?" "'Glory,' Mr. Medley," was the reply. "Then call it 'Ichabod'; the glory has departed," came the retort from above. A portrait of Mr. Medley is to be seen in the vestry of Pembroke Chapel.

MAGHULL CHURCH AND ITS FONT.

Sir,—In a recent issue of your paper you allude to an article on Maghull Church and its font, which appeared also in "Home Words," a magazine which has been localised by many churches, and appears as the "Parish Magazine." The article on "Font Hunting" was written by Mr. H. Jenner Fust, jun. As an antiquary he evidently enjoyed the sport, and had examined and photographed a large number, finding his finest specimens in the South of England. In search of fresh fields he visited S.W. Lancashire, had quite an adventure, and find (?) at Maghull. He thus describes his discovery of the old Unsworth Chapel, "but dedicated to St. Andrew."

"He noticed at a little distance the remains of what must have been either a small chapel or a bit of the original church. He investigated, only to meet with a firmly-barred door. But a peep through a window revealed a small object in a corner which must surely, he thought, be a font, and an old one.

"Ten minutes sufficed to find the grim custodian, talk him out of a 'don't-care-about-anything' frame of mind into a condition of sweet reasonableness, and got the door unfastened. Ten minutes more proved sufficient by the exercise of much ingenuity in camera-stand making, and the pressing of coat, waistcoat, cap, shoes, and (whisper it) stockings into the service to photograph the most deliciously simple (?) Saxon font that ever man set eyes on. The result well repaid a several miles' bicycle ride, over the bumpy setts of those northern roads, and five minutes without shoes or stockings in that charnel house of a chapel with a temperature uncommonly near the freezing point."

Mr. Jenner Fust, jun., was in too great a hurry when in Maghull, so was not able to learn what local antiquarians could teach him about Maghull fonts. In Mr. Wm. E. Gregson's notes on the old chapel, as they appeared in the "Lancashire and Cheshire Historic Society's Transactions," vol. 11, page 253, we have this reference to the fonts : "There is a Georgian baptismal font built in the wall over the modern door of the Chancel, and a prism-shaped holy water receptacle close to the same door, set on a fragment of a circular pillow." From the illustration in "Home Words," the latter is what Mr. Jenner Fust, jun., has discovered as a "Saxon's font."

It looks as if a pre-reformation holy water stoup had been mistaken for a baptismal font.—Yours truly,

Old Swan, Liverpool.   JAMES HOULT.

ST. ANNE'S CHURCH.

Mr. R. D. Radcliffe, M.A., F.S.A., my friend and helper, wrote the following account of the Church :—

Where St. Anne's Church now stands there was formerly an iron-foundry, standing back some distance from the high road, abutting on which were the necessary offices, and somewhat to the rear and side of them was a row of cottages with gardens for the workpeople. Tue Brook, then an open stream of clear water, flowing past the works, furnished the necessary water supply for the foundry.

About the year 1830 this property was bought by Thomas Gardner, who had a son of the same name in Holy Orders, married to the daughter of a retired Jamaica planter, Samuel Hilton, then living in Anfield. These gentlemen, assisted by a grant from a Church Building Society, put up the first church at Stanley, the site of which, and of the churchyard, were conveyed to William Barton, the younger, of Elm House, West Derby (at the top of Edge Lane), ironmaster, and Peter White, of Liverpool, master mariner, as trustees. The church was not endowed, but the pew rents were estimated as likely to provide the minister with an income of £150 a year. Mr. Gardner, senior, built and furnished a house for his son at the east end of what had been the foundry offices, and the remainder of his purchase was laid out as a garden to the parsonage.

The Church (or, as it is called in the deeds "chapel"), which was consecrated 13th October, 1831, was a plain building of red sandstone, with a low-pitched roof and squat tower, consisting of a nave, south transept (added later) and shallow chancel with round headed windows. Internally the flat ceiling was supported by iron columns, and there was a west gallery. The pulpit, reading desk and clerk's place were of the old "three decker" style—afterwards altered—the pews were high, and all the fittings were of the plainest description.

There seems to be no record of the Rev. Thomas Gardner's institution. He resigned the cure 25th March, 1880, and nominated his son, the Rev. Hilton Gardner, as his successor, it being provided that for a period of fifty years from the consecration of the church the right of presentation should remain with the founder's family. The Rev. Hilton Gardner was instituted 1st August, 1880, and died 16th February, 1886. His successor, the Rev. Walter J. Scarlin, was instituted 11th May, 1886, and died 18th October, 1907, when he was succeeded by the present Vicar, the Rev. W. J. Elsley, instituted 21st March, 1908, on the nomination of the Rector of West Derby, who is now *ex-officio* the patron of the living.

In 1845 the schools in Derby Lane were built, in the erection of which Mr. Gardner was largely assisted by old Anfield friends, Mr. Cliff, of Belmont Road, Mr. William Preston, of Rock House, and by others. In the big schoolroom there still remain plaster busts of Mr. Gardner and Mr. Preston, wonderfully like them, as the writer of this notice can testify.

For over fifty years St. Anne's was without a legal district, but on 16th August, 1886, one was assigned to it by an Order of the Privy Council.

On 22nd July, 1891, No. 8, Derwent Square, was acquired by the Ecclesiastical Commissioners as a vicarage for St. Anne's, Stanley.

On Saturday, 27th September, 1890, the new church of St. Anne, built by Mr. Thomas Fenwick Harrison in memory of his most worthy father, who formerly lived at Brook House in Green Lane, and who lies buried in our churchyard, was consecrated by Bishop Ryle. The church, which seats 700 people, is Early English in character, of the style prevalent in this country between the years 1200 and 1250, and of excellent proportions and admirable design. The architects were Messrs. Aldridge and Deacon; the builders Messrs. Jones and Sons, of Pleasant Street, Liverpool. Externally the most striking features are the massive tower, the south porch and the west window of five lancets. The exterior is of Woolton, the interior of Runcorn, stone, chosen with great discrimination. The stone pulpit was the gift of one of Mr. Harrison's daughters, the east window in the Lady Chapel of another, the east window of his son, both designed by Walter Lonsdale and executed by Messrs. Heaton, Butler and Bayne; the font of his grandchildren. These, with reredos, choir stalls, altar rails and sacrarium pavement and all internal fittings, are of the handsomest and most appropriate description. Indeed, the munificent donor, architects, builders, vicar and congregation are to be congratulated on the erection of so beautiful a church in a little over a twelvemonth, the foundation stone of which was laid in June, 1889, by the young son of the donor, now a Lieutenant in His Majesty's Royal Horse Guards.

Since the completion of the church, Mr. Fenwick Harrison has greatly increased our indebtedness to him by purchasing from the Gardner family land formerly the garden of the old parsonage to the east of the churchyard, to which, with a handsome lodge built at his expense, it makes a most valuable addition, and preserves the amenities of the church in perpetuity.

At Easter, 1909, the Lady Chapel was fitted up as a Memorial for his Parents, by the writer of these notes, in the ecclesiastical style prevalent in England in the year 1400. The Altar is a copy of the lower portion of Gower the poet's monument in Southwark Cathedral, the Reredos of the screen to William of Wykeham's tomb, in Winchester Cathedral. Both are of brown oak from St. Thomas's Church, Liverpool, built in 1750 and recently taken down. Other oak used, as hard and close in grain as marble, is from Boulton's Hall, Finch Lane, West Derby, built about 1400, and pulled down in 1907. The canopy from the dining hall in this building was set up in Liverpool Museum by the writer a few years since, when he built the Lych Gate at Knotty Ash Church out of oak from the same building. The wrought iron gates of the chapel are of exquisite design, copied from ironwork on a door in Durham Cathedral, believed by experts to be French and of the year 1135, and quite unlike anything else of its kind in England.

KIRKBY AND ST. CHAD.

St. Chad's Day is on March 2nd. St. Chad was a British hermit monk who lived at Lichfield, of which diocese he became Bishop in 669. At Kirkby, about eight miles from the city, between West Derby and Ormskirk, are the remains of an old Church, which was built and dedicated to St. Chad about the year 870, in the days of King Alfred. Dug out of the soil, and now covered with grass, is to be seen the ground plan of the original, tiny kirk, which was for so many centuries the spiritual home of the farmers and villagers of the moss-land of Kirkby and Simonswood. A stone cross (modern) indicates the position of the altar, and on it are engraved these words, " Here for a thousand years stood a table of the Lord." As is well known to antiquaries, the Danes conquered the people on both sides of the Mersey; they formed settlements, and became permanent dwellers in the land. It is pleasant to think, however, that in those early days Christianity was well organised, and that Lancashire, which remained in the diocese of Lichfield until 1542, had its religious needs supplied.

The 200 years which passed between the time when Bishop Chad became St. Chad were sufficient, in days when the people were only partially educated, to weave around the story of his life much that was legendary and of the miraculous. It was related of him that, being disturbed by the nightingales while at his devotions, he prayed that they should cease their evening song—the prayer was answered, and the sweet songsters of Stowe Wood were henceforward silent; that a snow-white doe came daily from a distant forest to supply him with milk; and that when the holy man was dying, a cloud of angels descended from the heavens and sang hymns over his cell.

FRIAR'S CROFT.

Friar's Croft sounds like the fancy name given by an ardent antiquarian to his garden. It is, however, the name of a field on the Old Swan side of West Derby, and it has borne that name for centuries. It lies at the rear of an old house, now falling into ruin, lately occupied by a Mr. Jeff Roberts, nurseryman, and adjoining a road afterwards closed and appropriated by a local landowner which ran between Old Swan and the Old Mill at Mill Bank. The house one hundred years ago was the parsonage of the old West Derby Chapel.

CHILDWALL PARISH.

Busy, populous, and rich Lancashire had not always this happy character. Time was when the population was so small and the people so poor that it took from 15,000 to 30,000 acres to keep a population equal to supporting a church. Its parishes were the largest in the kingdom. Manchester was perhaps the largest with 35,000 acres, but local ones were very similar. Childwall parish embraced ten townships, and covered 16,043 acres of land and 4,500 acres of foreshore. Walton had 29,615 acres, and formerly included Formby, Bootle, West Derby, and Liverpool. Winwick covered an area of 26,502 acres, and became the richest parish in England, owing to the great development of coal mining at Haydock and Newton. It was originally a vicarage attached to the abbey of Nostell. In 1291 its annual income was £26 a year. In 1835 it was worth £7,000 a year. Through the generosity of one of its rectors in 1841, an Act of Parliament was passed which divided some portion of its great income with the new parishes which had been formed out of the old one, leaving, however, £1,600 a year for the parent church. The chances of an ordinary clergyman succeeding to this fat living are very slight. The patrons are the Earls of Derby; the lucky vicar is always a relation of the earl. Since 1740 there has not been a single break in the succession of sons and cousins of the house of Stanley. Childwall in its most prosperous days was never so wealthy, although it had a fair estate of land. There was a time, however, when its vicars did tolerably well out of the tithes. The parish had three tithebarns, one at Lea, one at Woolton, and one at Garston, and among the products which paid this impost were hemp, flax, pigs, geese, corn, lambs, cows, calves, and wool.

Childwall the picturesque is also Childwall the historical, and is the Mecca to which artist and antiquary journey to pay their homage. For many years past no autumn exhibition of pictures in Liverpool has been held without sketches of the Hall, the Church, the Inn, or the Lake being exhibited. To the student of the past it teems with interest. There is the story of the Manor of Childwall dating back to Saxon

K

days, of its township with its Court Leet, and of its Hall with its notable owners; but the characteristic of the whole hamlet is its savor of an ecclesiastical past; at one time there were no fewer than three stone crosses within a stone's throw of the church, the base of one (of a large Market Cross) is still to be seen behind a hedge of the road to Woolton; a pond in a field (one side still lined with stone) is called the Monk's Bath, and the legend is still believed that the man who first ploughed up to it was seized with illness and died within a short time after.

"CHILDWALL ABBEY."

A farm house near by is called the Priory, and the Inn is called Childwall Abbey. It is a pity to have to say it, but there is no evidence to prove that either Priory or Abbey ever existed at Childwall. It is on record in Domesday Book that there was one priest at Childwall, and he is put down as holding half a caracate of land (about 30 acres), not for his use, however, but for the poor of the parish which was then a very large one, extending to the Mersey, and taking in the foreshore from Garston to beyond Hale, embracing 10 townships, and covering 20,500 acres of land. The name "Abbey" probably came to the Inn from the fact that when Bamber Gascoyne built the Hall in 1780, from its resemblance to a Monastic religious house it was nicknamed "The Abbey"; the Inn, the Hearse House, and the Church Porch, were castellated to match the Hall, and the Inn, having a number of "a kind of" Gothic shaped windows of a kind favoured by a local builder, we can easily understand would get the nickname of the "Hall," especially as that building became more known by its name of Childwall Hall. The door, dated 1608, shown to visitors, came from an old farm house at Allerton, when it was demolished.

THE HALL.

Childwall Hall stands on the site of a previous building. It is now a beautiful place, embowered among venerable trees, and having all its original appearance of modernity toned down by the sunshine, storm and frost of a century and a quarter it has received that finishing touch which only Nature and age can give. The Hall itself was built from the plans of John Nash, the most celebrated architect of his day, the man who planned Regent Street and Regent's Park, London, and drew the plans for Brighton Pavilion. Bamber Gascoyne, the owner and builder of the Hall, has left his mark upon it; on the metal spouts, etc. we can see to-day his initials, "B.G." There is one tower standing apart from the hall itself, and close to the cottages, which was built to be a pigeon-house. There was a time when all large houses had their columbarium: the birds were not only a pleasure, to have them about when alive, but in winter they furnished a welcome change in the food of the inhabitants of the hall, in days when there was little variety of fresh meat. Standing on the slope of a low hill, the highest point of which is only 223 feet high it yet commands an extensive view over the Childwall Valley. Its prospect embraces the Aughton hills, near Ormskirk, Prescot Hill, Rainhill, a distant view of Halton Castle, and a range of hills beyond; while villages with their church spires or towers are numerous in the middle distance. The most notable family to live at the hall has been the Gascoynes. The present Lord Salisbury is descended from this family. The name Gascoyne used to be pronounced Gaskin.

THE CHURCH.

Childwall Church is a veritable Campo Santo for that part of South Lancashire, of which it is the centre; in it have been placed the bones of the illustrious dead, and on its walls are the memorial tablets, crests, and armorial panels of the departed representatives of the local families. Before the renovation of the church in 1851, the floor was of earth, and children kicking into it, with their heels, would sometimes dislodge a human bone. There was a time when all were anxious to be buried within the precincts of the sacred building. Perhaps the most distinguished family in the past worshippers in the church to be remembered to us is that of the Norres or Norrey's family of Speke; as far back as 1487 a Thomas Norrey of Speke founded a Chantry here. It was dedicated to St. Thomas á Becket, and a Chantry Priest was attached to it. The part of the church occupied with the Norrey's Chapel is known and can be pointed out by the caretaker of the church. There is in the South wall a brass representing Henry Norrey and his wife, with date 1524, he as a warrior in plated armour and his lady in the costume of Henry VIII's days. The Norreys were a typical Lancashire family, and an account of them would be a delightful story. One Edward Norrey built Speke Hall, the most picturesque black and white half-timbered house in South Lancashire; it is embellished and partly furnished with spoil from Holyrood Palace. The family were always honoured in the Church register of births, marriages, and deaths by better writing and a fuller description of the events recorded. They, on the whole, remained of the "old faith," and suffered severely for their recusancy. One of them was fined £1,000 for knocking down an informer who came to ask if he regularly attended the service at the church (the fine was afterwards reduced). The Norreys family remained at Speke Hall until the male line became extinct, about the year 1736. Another brass in the old church is of Richard Percival, who died in 1701, aged 84. He was a Puritan, and must have been a fine character. On the brass it states : " He passed so inoffensively through the world as scarce to have an enemy, and died in great peace and serenity "; but his life's record is of more value in reckoning up his worth than the flattering words of a memorial tablet. We find that he had been the Bailiff and Mayor of Liverpool, and was an Alderman in 1662, and that he refused to take the oath or to sign the declaration required by the Test Act of 13th of Charles II., and was accordingly dismissed from his office. He was a man of principle, and was willing to suffer for his opinion, if need be. He lived at Hart Hill, Allerton. His eldest son John was one of the original founders and a trustee of the ancient Nonconformist Chapel at Gateacre. Among the armorial panels by the clerestory windows of the church is one of Nicholas Ashton, of Woolton Hall, in his day a county magistrate. He bought the Hall from Viscount Molyneux, largely improved the house, and adorned it with lead statues. There is another of the Onslow family of the time of Henry VIII.; the name is not a local one, and nothing seems to be known of them. There is another, belonging to Joseph Reed Walker, dated 1828. He was a noted lead merchant of the firm of Walker, Parker and Co., did a large business in Liverpool, and erected a shot tower at Chester; he built Calderstones, now the property of the Corporation. Like the bootmaker, who said there was nothing like leather, he believed in lead, and it was used very freely in his building; the passages were floored with it, and it is remembered that it made a very silent floor to walk upon.

There are two memorials of the Hardman family, one dated 1755 This family is famous for its litigation. There have been law cases regarding their Manor of Allerton, extending through 150 years. It was a local saying that it would be easier to get out of hell than for a Hardman to recover the estates; one claimant to the estates was recently an employee at Lime Street Station, Liverpool.

Of course, the Gascoyne family has its tablets, as they had the squire's pew; this pew, by the way, is claimed as private property by Lord Salisbury. Bamber, who was the founder of the family, lived at Childwall Hall, and was M.P. for Liverpool. He is remembered as a good specimen of the gentleman of the old school, and very superior to the county squires of his day; he was well educated, and his tastes were refined and literary. Rather proud and aristocratic in his bearing, he did not get on well with the Liverpool merchants, and was deprived of his seat by them, but it was given to his brother, General Isaac Gascoyne. The change was not a good one, for the General had no ability and was known by friend and foe as "cunning Isaac." The coat of arms of Charles II, dated 1664, the year of the passing of the Act of Uniformity, is also to be seen here. It was usual at the time to place it in churches, as a token of loyalty.

RELICS OF THE PAST.

The crest of the Lord of Knowsley, the Eagle and Child, is to be seen here, beautifully carved out of wood. But there is much also of interesting matter of the museum order—an old church becomes a repository of relics of the past. There is the ancient piscina, into which the ablutions of the sacramental vessels were poured, in pre-reformation days. There are the collecting boxes, one pair dated 1703, and another of copper, like warming pans, with wardens' names on and dated 1779. The old font, which was once put outside and used as a flower pot. A candelabra (brass), dated 1737, ornamented with the Fleur de Lys. An oak chest, with three locks and three keys, each set different, two belonging to the wardens of the church, the other to the Vicar, so that it cannot be opened without all three being present. There used to be a three-decker pulpit, which was sold to a Liverpool gentleman and sent to Abergele; and we must not forget the parish hearse. This hearse was for the use of the parishioners, and it was usual for them to provide the gears and make a payment of 2/6 each time that the hearse was required.

As an educational agent, an old church, if studied properly, cannot be surpassed, as Ruskin has shown us. Entering Childwall Church by the south porch, which, by the bye, was built about the 15th century, out of material of a former one, the visitor notices, above his head, four stone heads, one in each corner, and the emblems beneath each of an axe, a cup, a human head, and a bull's head, teaching by symbol that the heads represent the four evangelists. In the wall are to be seen carved stones of very early date, probably Scandinavian. On the building are some mason's marks; these are the marks of the Guilds of Church builders of the middle ages, and we can recognise to-day by these marks something of their work. There are two mason's marks here, the same as are to be seen on Lichfield Cathedral, and we are reminded that for centuries Childwall was in the diocese of Lichfield. There is another mason's mark, identical with one on the tower of Halsall Church, indicating that the same workman had been engaged on the two churches. The door into the church proper is a study of simple strength. It will be about 500 years old, it has never felt the plane, and is as originally adzed out. Its outside is decorated with iron studs, and the latch, handles and hinges are fine specimens of local blacksmith's work. Instead of iron nails oak pegs have been used. Chiselled out of the masonry at each side of the door are holes which indicate that the door was wont to be fastened from the inside by means of a beam of wood being across. A noticeable feature of the church is that of the west end, it is much below the level of the churchyard. The reason for this is that when the present spire-surmounted tower was built, the debris from the old tower was allowed to remain, it being simply smoothed over. The tower, which is at the west end of the building, was built by the Old Swan firm of J. and P. Barker, and stones of the original tower were used in the construction of the interior of it. The reason why the old tower was demolished was that on the Sunday morning of February 11th, 1810, the spire of St. Nicholas' Church, Liverpool, fell, killing 22 persons, one or more of whom were buried at Childwall. Attention was called to the condition of other towers, and on an examination of the one at Childwall it was deemed unsafe, and accordingly was taken down and the present one erected. Another result of the accumulation of debris at this end of the church is to be seen in the position of the leper's window. Originally it was about three feet above the ground, so that people in pre-reformation days could see the altar at the end of the church while standing outside the building. The window is now almost hidden, being below the level of the soil. It is sad to think of a time in this Lancashire of ours when there were lepers. The foul disease of leprosy disappeared in Tudor days, and its departure coincided with the general improvement of the condition of the people, cleaner linen and better food no doubt were the curative agents. Not only was the window used as a leper's squint, but only through it could excommunicated persons see into the church. At different times the Bishops of Chester have used the powerful weapon of the church very freely at Childwall. For instance, in 1592, during his visitation, the Bishop excommunicated "the Church-wardens for allowing the church to be in bad repair"; also Henry Hale and Ralf Whitfield, for piping on the Sabbath day in the churchyard; some for talking and standing about in the churchyard during sermon time; others for being in the ale-house during time of service; one man for not making his wife go to church; and another because " His children came not to be catechised." In the 1635 visitation a Thomas Huche, of the Broad Green, was " presented for sleeping in our Church of Childwall at time of Divine Service." In the beautiful God's acre at Childwall are the graves of many Liverpool notabilities of the past, perhaps the most famous being that of Bishop Ryle.

FONTS IN NONCONFORMIST CHAPELS.

In Nonconformist chapels one usually looks in vain for a baptismal or christening font, while in the Anglican Church it is placed in a conspicuous place at the entrance, teaching, in this way, its own lesson on the matter of baptisms. The Nonconformist, when infants are to be sprinkled and named, is in the habit of requisitioning a vessel from the chapel-keeper, and usually it is the slop basin of the Sunday best tea set. Without thinking at all over the matter, the Nonconforming Methodists (Wesleyans excepted), Presbyterians, Congregationalists, &c., are following in the footsteps of the earliest Dissenters. They, in their day, had a strange objection to the ancient fonts of the parish churches, and during the time when the Puritans were in power they were dispensed with. In the accounts of the parochial chapel at Didsbury, under date 1645, is the following item :—" Paid for one Pewter Basson to Baptise Children in, £0 3s. 5d." After the Restoration many of the fonts were replaced, but not all, especially in the Liverpool district. For instance, the ancient font at Walton was for many years used as a mounting-stone and a seat in front of the public-house adjoining the church. It is a specimen of early Norman workmanship, and its carvings are worth seeing. It is now in the church. The font at Kirkby was placed as a receptacle to hold the water discharged from a spout of the old schoolhouse, and it was used by the children to sharpen their pencils and knives upon. It also has interesting carvings, and is generally considered to be the work of Saxon masons. At Huyton and Childwall the old fonts had been degraded into flower-pots.

EARLY NONCONFORMITY.

The Liverpool Liturgy of 1763 was the outcome of Nonconformists' darkest hour in S.W. Lancashire. A century had passed since the great event of the year 1662, when so many Ministers of the Established Church had given up their livings and become Nonconformists. The heroism of this act, combined with the saintly character of many of these Ministers, had a great effect upon their congregations. A great impulse was given to the Puritan Movement ; Meeting Houses, some of them large and well furnished, were built, and crowds gathered to follow the ministrations of their ejected pastors. Within the century following, however, a change came over the religious sentiments of preachers and people. Calvinism, Arminianism, Arianism, and Sabellianism were preached and wrangled over, while the Evangelical spirit of Christianity with its message for erring mankind was apparently forgotten. The Meeting Houses became neglected, and religious life sank low. It was at this time the idea of a Nonconformist Liturgy took shape. It was thought that a form of service consisting of Praise and Prayer could be compiled which would be an improvement on that of the Established Church. It was even suggested that the Bishops might copy it. The Ministers chiefly concerned in the matter were Mr. Goodwin, of Gateacre, Mr. Seddon, of Warrington ; Mr. Holland, of Bolton ; while the secretarial work was undertaken by Mr. Thomas Bentley, a layman of Liverpool. He was a porcelain manufacturer, and late in life joined partnership with Josiah Wedgwood. The result of their labours can be seen to-day ; copies of the Service are still extant, but for the ordinary reader there is no need to re-publish it. It is sufficient to say that the service book was a failure. It was beautifully worded, and contained the most pious of sentiments, but for all that it was condemned as being vague, indefinite, and unsatisfying. Everywhere where introduced it caused dissension, the Puritan element of the congregations would not have it at any price.

A few Meeting Houses tried the Liturgy, but all gave it up in short time. In Liverpool, however, some wealthy Dissenters, either ashamed of the simplicity of their fathers' worship, or expecting to attract some members of the Established Church, erected a Meeting House at which the Liturgical Service was to be the chief feature. It was called the Octagon Chapel. This building was the first dissenting place of worship to assume the name of Chapel, and it derived the name Octagon from its shape. It was situated in Temple Court.

Mr., afterwards Dr., Clayton became Minister. He was a popular preacher, and had scholarly attainments, yet the enterprise was a failure. Few Church people came, and those who did found fault, while the Presbyterians preferred the old associations of Benn's Garden Meeting House, and the Puritan simplicity of its services. Eventually the Octagon Chapel was sold to a clergyman, who had it licensed for "the genuine worship of the Church of England."

From the date of the closing of the Octagon Chapel, Nonconformity in Liverpool and S.W. Lancashire took a new lease of life, and it came from the very opposite source to that of read prayers from a formal Liturgy. Methodism had come with its revival enthusiasm. A Meeting House had been erected in Liverpool in 1764; it was, however, in 1763 that the first Methodist Prayer meetings were held (during the previous 20 years of the evangelical labours of the Wesleys they had not been known). John Wesley himself mentions the Prayer Meetings starting at Dukinfield, Ashton, Davy Hulme, and Stockport. The effects, he says, were surprising, large numbers being added to the Society as a result of these Meetings for extempore prayer; but another great development also resulted, lay exhorters and preachers were trained in them, and these men went out and spread Methodism in all directions. The other Nonconformist sects were influenced; they caught something of the religious zeal, and again began to flourish. The Baptists of Liverpool had a small Meeting House in 1772 in Byrom Street, when the Rev. Samuel Medley became its Minister; but it was soon found too small to hold the large congregations who thronged to hear his earnest and eloquent sermons, and in 1789 a new chapel was built, now known as Byrom Hall. (See section "Byrom Hall's Historical Position.")

The Nonconformists of Liverpool in 1912 do not as a rule use a Liturgical Service. The Wesleyans at two or three Churches use the Prayer Book of the Established Church. The Unitarians have a Service book, but the others are content with a more or less plain order of service. The Wesleyan position is quite logical, for, as followers of John Wesley, they do not rank as Dissenters, they are Nonconformists only. John Wesley, as is well known, loved the Prayer Book. In a letter to a Miss Bishop, one of his most esteemed correspondents, he writes, " I find more life in the Church Prayers than in the extemporary prayers of the Dissenters; nay, I find more profit in sermons on good tempers or good works than in what are called Gospel Sermons." In contrast to this, the great Apostle of Dissent, the late C. H. Spurgeon, says in his "Lectures to my Students," p. 55, " It would be difficult to discover when and where Liturgies began; their introduction was gradual, and, as we believe, co-extensive with the decline of purity in the Church."

1662 IN S.W. LANCASHIRE.

We hear a good deal about the Act of Uniformity and the great ejectment of Bartholomew's Day, 1662. The Act required that any Parson, Vicar, or Minister should freely and publickly declare his unfeigned assent to all and everything contained in the book entitled the Book of Common Prayer. The result was that 2,000 ministers gave up their living rather than conform to the Act, and about 100 of them were of Lancashire. It is worth while in these days of tolerance to look back and see how our local ministers acted at this time of stress. It was a serious matter; it had to do with conscience and also with board and lodging. Of whatever shade of creed we belong to, it is gratifying to find that the majority were willing to suffer deprivation for what they considered the right.

John Fogg, the minister of St. Nicholas' Chapel, Liverpool, was a Lancashire man, but had been educated at Oxford. He was described as a man of fine abilities, good learning, a serious Christian, and useful preacher. He chose, on the passing of the Act of Uniformity, to give up all; he retired to Budworth, in Cheshire.

Henry Finch, vicar of Walton, had laboured there with great success from the year 1656. He was anxious to remain with his congregation (with whom he was on the best of terms), and as he had a growing family dependent upon him was loth to give up his living. Conscience won, however, and he removed to Manchester, which town, strange to say, was not then a Corporation. Liverpool, in the days of Charles II., returned a member to Parliament, but Manchester did not.

The ministers of Toxteth Park Chapel were Nonconformists, but were fortunate in being able to keep their chapel. It appears that it had never been consecrated, although it had been considered a chapel of the Parish of Walton. No doubt but that the great local landowner, a Catholic, one of the Molyneux family, assisted them to retain their building as a Nonconformist place of worship.

The curate of West Derby, Joshua Ambrose, M.A., conformed, and was advanced to the position of vicar of Childwall, where he lived until his death, in 1710. His brother Nehemiah, minister at Kirkby, had conscientious scruples respecting the teaching of the Prayer Book. He paid the price—was ejected in 1662, and four years later died, and was buried at Childwall. It is worthy of note that William Roscoe, the historian, and author of the "Life of Lorenzo de Medici," one of Liverpool's noblest sons, married the great-grand-daughter of Joshua Ambrose, the Conformist, just mentioned. Joshua and Nehemiah were the sons of Peter Ambrose, of Toxteth Park, who must have been well-to-do, and also a man of good character. In his will he directed that various payments should be made from his estate for the benefit of the poor, and it is interesting to notice how he divided it: to the poor of Wavertree 5s., of Toxteth 40s., of Orrell 10s., of Much Crosby 10s., and of Ormskirk 10s. He stipulated that preference should be given to them of the Household of Faith.

The vicar of Huyton, William Bell, M.A., was famous as a scholar and as a preacher. He had been one of the King's preachers. He had been ordained, and was willing to accept episcopal government, but could not assent to the teaching of the Prayer Book. He therefore became a Nonconformist and had to retire. He went to what he called the " godly " town of Manchester.

At Prescot, the vicar, John Withers, conformed, and from the warden's account we gather that the surplice was again introduced, and a " faire linen clothe " once more placed upon the Communion table, and handsome silver was procured for the service. The Communion table was moved back to the east end of the church, and railings set around it.

Joseph Thompson, of Sefton, refused to conform, and was ejected from his pleasant parsonage. He was a Lancashire man, and educated at Oxford. He was very rich, and generously helped his less fortunate brethren of the ministry in their need. He retired to Ormskirk.

The vicar of Melling, John Mallinson, refused to conform, as did also a more famous preacher, Nathaniel Heywood, vicar of Ormskirk, a Lancashire man, educated at Cambridge. Heywood continued to reside in the neighbourhood, and went about visiting the sick and preaching at lonely homesteads in the remote parts of the parish. He was under the protection of Lady Stanley, and when soldiers came to arrest him when preaching she stood upon the pulpit steps and forbade them to touch him.

At St. Helens, the minister, Thomas Gregg, was a Nonconformist, but he continued to preach in the chapel as if there had been no Act. The building remained in the hands of the Dissenters until 1710, when is was surrendered to the Bishop of Chester.

The Act of Uniformity found a good scholar, Samuel Mather, minister of a wooden chapel at Burton Wood, a hamlet between St. Helens and Warrington. In this humble sanctuary was a man acting as minister who was a graduate of four Universities, had been a Fellow of two Colleges, and a chaplain to the Lord Protector's son. It was a poor place, the income being £32 5s. a year, besides the few pounds which his poor parishioners gave him; yet he was expelled from this quiet spot, and had to find refuge elsewhere. He went to Ireland.

There were others notable in other parts of Lancashire who took part in the great drama, but they were of lesser interest to us of West Derby Hundred.

In most places the people were glad to get back to a more ornate church service. They had not really liked the plain order of worship which had been imposed on them, nor the regulations of the Presbytery, by whom the congregation were authoritatively commanded to " abstain from all private whisperings, conferences, salutations, or doing reverence to any persons present or coming in; as also from all gazing, sleeping, and other indecent behaviour in church. The prayers offered up by the minister were to be 'conceived' or extemporary, and so directed as to get his hearers' hearts rightly affected with their sins, that they might mourn thereof with shame and holy confusion of face." The Nonconformists of to-day, heirs of the past, do well to remind each other of the heroes of 1662, and of the principle for which they passively resisted—i.e., that each individual should be free to worship according to the dictates of his or her conscience.

1662 AND THE CHURCH.

We are indebted to Canon Grensted for the following interesting information :—

In your issues of Tuesday Mr. James Hoult has given us some details as to the Act of Uniformity and the great ejectment of Bartholomew's Day. He gives local instances of ministers who, all honour to them, obeyed the call of conscience and resigned rather than conform. Will you allow me a little space to point out that some honour is also due to those Church of England clergy who, about the year 1645, when their archbishop was beheaded and their Prayer Book was forbidden under penalties, had been ejected? Mr. Hoult mentions Joseph Thompson, of Sefton. Now, what are the facts of the case? On the north wall of the chancel of Sefton Church is the monument of Edward Morton; he became rector in 1639, he was ejected in 1643. The Parliamentary survey of the Rectory of Sephton, 1649—1658, has come down to us. It says : " . . . the present incumbent being Mr. Joseph Thompson an able and godly Minister painfull in his cure : and dilligent in observing such dayes as have been sett a part by the Parliament either for ffasts or days of thanksgiving . . ." It also states that he had to pay to " Mrs. Morton, wiffe of Doctor Morton, a Delinquent late Rector of Sephton, a ffift

part of the said pffits according to an order from the Comittie."
Walker, however, in his "Sufferings of the Clergy," London, 1714,
says Mrs. Morton got nothing. In 1662, Joseph Thompson was ejected
and Edward Morton reinstated. He died 1674, and his tombstone
speaks of him as one who had lived as a banished man—"Bonis
Omnibus Spoliatus." Stripped of all his goods.

Let us also honour, if we will, Henry Finch, who, as vicar of Walton,
bowed to conscience in 1662 and retired to Manchester; but let us
no less honour Andrew Clare, who was ejected in 1643, when the tithes
were sequestrated by Parliament and William Ward was intruded
into his place. We may not forget that the years preceding 1662
had been years of suffering for the Church of England. We remember
that Dr. Jeremy Taylor, the noblest preacher of his day, was
imprisoned under Cromwell's edict of 1655 because he had preached
to a small congregation which had met for secret worship in London.
We remember the entry in Evelyn's Diary against December 25, 1655 :
"There was no more notice taken of Christmas Day in churches.
I went to London when Dr. Wild preached the funeral sermon of
preaching, this being the last day, after which Cromwell's proclama-
tion was to take place that none of the Church of England should dare
either to preach or administer Sacraments, teach schools, &c., on paine
of imprisonment or exile." But we also remember, and we will ask
Nonconformists to remember, that it was in 1660 that Henry More,
the Cambridge Platonist, wrote in his "Mystery of Godliness" :—
"A mutual agreement of bearing with one another's dissents in the
non-fundamentals of religion is really a greater ornament of
Christianity (that is, of the whole Church of Christ) than the most
exact Uniformity imaginable, it being an eminent act or exercise of
charity, the flower of all Christian Graces. And it is the best way,
I think, in the long run, to make the Churches uniform as can justly
be desired." And we will ask the Nonconformist of to-day to consider
whether in 1662 all the heroism had been on one side and the lack
of charity on the other.

EARLY DISSENT IN S.W. LANCASHIRE.

Here in West Derby Hundred the religious controversy was waged
quite as zealously, but not as acrimoniously, as in the neighbouring
hundreds of Leyland and Salford. Without further dealing with the
local situation, I wish to point out the different attitudes of two
classes of the literature of recent years, the novelist and the historian,
in their treatment of Dissent and Dissenters. In most fiction the
attitude is of contempt, and the dislike is very marked ; the contempt
may be good-natured, but it is there. The most is made of the curious
names of some of their leaders, their stern faces, the strict Sabbath,
and their hatred of what to them was idolatry have been used to the
utmost to influence thought against the ordinary, peaceful, chapel-
loving Dissenter. They have been charged with being opposed to
art, and music, and poetry, but the fact is that their unlovely and
plain form of service in the churches was the outcome of an opposite
form of service, one in which music and art became a substitute for
true religious life.

The charge of desecrating the churches had some truth behind it.
But again, the other Cromwell, he of Henry VIII.'s reign, and his
minions, did not scruple to plunder Westminster Abbey, to rob even
the shrine of Edward the Confessor of its golden ornaments, and melt
them down to enrich the treasury of the "Defender of the Faith";

but the idea that Puritanism was antagonistic to art was preposterous. What about John Milton, one of the noblest English poets, and his "Paradise Lost"; John Bunyan, and his dramatic idyll, "The Pilgrim's Progress"? The first English opera was performed under the Commonwealth, and it is to Cromwell himself that the country owes the preservation of the Raphael cartoons. But sober historians, men of thought, those who have sought for the moral foundations of the State, give us their summing-up of what Dissent has done for the country. Lecky says : "It is difficult indeed to overrate the debt of gratitude that England owes to her non-episcopal churches that they 'only' clung fearlessly to the banner of her freedom." Macaulay says : "The Church of England continued for more than 150 years the servile handmaid of the Monarchy and the steady enemy of public liberty." Such testimonies might be multiplied, but writers who have studied the times of early Dissent and Nonconformity do great service in giving to the world their findings.

EARLY NONCONFORMIST MEETING HOUSES.

Few of the original buildings of the old Nonconformist meeting-houses now exist. In some cases a chapel (more or less modern) has taken the place of the original building. In 1715, only twenty-seven years after the passing of the Act of Toleration, a Dr. John Evans compiled a list of Nonconformist congregations, and gave the name of each minister. There were in Lancashire forty-three congregations. Each town and large village had its meeting-house. In Liverpool there was one in Castle Hey, now Harrington Street, built about 1688, minister the Rev. Christopher Richardson, the ejected minister of Kirkheaton, in Yorkshire. In 1707 a meeting-house was erected in Kaye Street, minister the Rev. Christopher Basnett, who is mentioned as preserving the good old Puritan habit of preaching extemporaneously. In 1700 the house of Dr. Daniel Fabius was licensed as a meeting-place of the Baptists; it was near the present Fabius Chapel in Everton Road. Previous to that date Baptists from Liverpool travelled for Sunday worship to Hill Cliff Chapel, near Warrington, a place hallowed with its historical associations, and admired for its position, being beautiful for situation. In 1714 a church had been formed and a minister appointed, the Rev. Peter Devonport. His successor, the Rev. John Sedgfield, left to become minister of the famous Tottlebank Chapel, the oldest Nonconformist chapel in Lancashire. At the present time services are held in chapels, on the sites of original meeting-houses, at the following places in Lancashire :—Cloughfold, dated 1675 ; Bacup (Ebenezer), dated 1710 ; Sunny Bank, dated 1678 ; Goodshaw, dated 1756 ; Accrington (Cannon Street), dated 1760 ; and at St. Helens, the old meeting-house called Mary in Ellens, dated 1710 (in which the last Nonconformist sermon was preached by Matthew Henry).

HILL CLIFF CHAPEL.

Hill Cliff Chapel was a thriving church in Cromwell's day, for he went to a service there and heard one of his troopers preach. The "original" of the Ancient chapel of Toxteth also is older, dating from 1618 ; but the chapel then, and until the Restoration, strange to say, belonged to the Establishment, and was of the parish of Walton. Gateacre Chapel is of fair age, having been built in 1700. It was built, according to its trust deed, to be used by a congregation of

Protestants "dissenting from the Church of England," and was licensed under the Toleration Act. At the present time the chapels of Toxteth and Gateacre belong to the Unitarians, while those at Hill Cliff and Tottlebank belong to the Baptist denomination.

MOST ANCIENT CHAPEL IN LANCASHIRE.

Tottlebank Chapel, the most ancient Dissenting chapel in Lancashire, was built to accommodate a congregation of the Church of Christ, now Baptist, which had been formed from the people of Broughton Fells, and dates from August 18th, 1669. It was the parent church of Sunny Bank, Hawkeshead, Ulverston, Coniston, Barrow, &c. The history of these Nonconformist chapels takes us back to the days of the penal code. The last man to perish at the stake for his religious belief in England was a Baptist named Edward Wightman, who was burned at Lichfield on April 11th, 1612; but for years after this suffering, fines, imprisonment, and banishment were the lot of those who refused to conform to the religion of the State Church. Dissenting congregations met by stealth in fear and secrecy, with one of their number keeping watch, that they might be warned of the approach of danger. During the Commonwealth toleration was granted to Dissenters, and they were able to meet openly and in security; but no sooner was the Restoration an accomplished fact than hostilities commenced again. By the Act of Uniformity, which came into force on St. Bartholomew's Day, 1662, upwards of two thousand clergymen of the Established Church were ejected from their livings for refusing their adherence to the Thirty-nine Articles and the Liturgy of the Church of England. Many of these clergymen, with their adherents, formed congregations of their own, and others joined existing Dissenting bodies.

One of these ministers, a Gabriel Camelford, had been curate of Staveley Chapel, and the newly-formed church at Tottlebank called him to be its first minister. The writer has seen the original book of the church, and it commences : "This book is for the use of the Church of Christ in Broughton, whereof Mr. Gabriel Camelford is teaching elder." It appears as if the congregation wished to drop the name of curate or minister and use a more Scriptural one. They, like the Quakers of their day, were anxious to get back to primitive ideals, and were afraid that minister would evolve eventually into priest. The Quakers, fearing that the Lord's Supper would evolve into the Mass, dispensed entirely with that ordinance. Camelford was described as "a godly and painful man in his calling." A "leading spirit" in the formation of the church was a Colonel Roger Sawrey. He had been an officer in Cromwell's Ironsides, and had received the nickname of "Praying Sawrey." He owned, and lived in, Broughton Towers. There were a number of well-to-do families among these Dissenters. One of them, who had his house licensed for religious Dissenting services, was a Myles Sandys, an ancestor of Colonel Myles Sandys, late M.P. for Bootle. At a later date the church was so well-to-do that it lent money freely to members of the congregation. On July 18th this year the Baptist Association of Lancashire and Cheshire organised a pilgrimage to the old chapel, and about sixty ladies and gentlemen travelled to it. The minister, the Rev. W. Osborne, gave an account of the most noted events in its history, and they sang together a hymn which had been written by a former minister.

141

ORIGIN OF COMMUNION RAILS.

The custodians of some of our historic churches frequently try and prevent visitors from entering within the communion rails, it being assumed that there is something peculiarly sacred about that part of the building. It may not be generally known that the original introduction of the altar or Communion rails was partly due to the presence of dogs in church. They were first ordered by Archbishop Laud, with the stipulation that the rails should be close enough to exclude the body of a dog. In 1636 Bishop Wren, of Norwich, issuing orders for the performance of divine worship, directed "that the rayle be made before it reaching crosse from the north wall to the south wall neere one yard in height so thick with pillars that dogs may not get in." In the Aughton parish books, under the heading of churchwardens' accounts, there are several entries with references to moneys paid to the dog whipper. This person appears to be an important official in the parish, who drew a yearly salary of 10s. An entry to this effect is recorded in the accounts as follows:—
1758. "Pd the Dog Whipper 10s." Fortunately, we are not exposed to such distractions now, and the ancient office of dog whipper is now extinct.

DR. ADAM CLARKE AND MILLBROOK.

Dr. Adam Clarke's connection with Liverpool was associated with two interesting epochs of his remarkable career. The first was that in our neighbourhood he wrote his famous "Biblical Commentary," and the second that he interested himself in Brunswick Chapel, Moss Street, where he baptised two ex-Buddhist priests whom he had educated in Christianity and the sciences of Europe. He also threw himself into the local organ controversy, and from one of his letters addressed to his friend Daniel Isaac, and dated 1828, it would appear as if the first organ erected in a Methodist chapel was set up at Brunswick Chapel, Liverpool. The extract reads : "You have a blessed work, and shall doubtful disputations and ungodly music be permitted to destroy all this? You and I had the honour of being numbered with the seventy-five preachers who wrote and signed our protest against the first organ, which the eloquence of Dr. Bunting set up at Brunswick Chapel, Liverpool, and which to my own knowledge has been an unmixed curse to that chapel and, I doubt, to the society in general.—Yours affectionately, A. CLARKE."
Dr. A. Clarke was President of the Conference three times—namely, in 1806, 1814, and 1822, and was esteemed as one of the greatest men of the Connexion. Of his literary work, the Commentary was the chief, 8 vols., 4to., a learned work, for its time extraordinarily so. A "Biographical Dictionary," 8 vols., 12mo., a "Clavis Biblica," &c., were minor efforts. Clarke's early education was given to him by his father, an Englishman. He was born in Ireland, and became a linen draper's assistant in Coleraine, but in 1778 he met John Wesley, who took him in hand and sent him to Kingswood School. He did not remain there long, but became an itinerant preacher in 1780, being ordained in Bristol. His early attitude towards the Church of England was that of John Wesley, of not desiring separation from her, and it is noticeable that he was confirmed by Lewis Bagot, Bishop of Norwich, after his ordination. He encouraged his followers to apply to the bishops for confirmation, and he loved to communicate at the altars of the Mother Church.

When, however, he became president of the Irish Conference, he had come to see that Methodism was destined to become a separate Church, and he advocated the holding of Methodist preaching services in church hours, and the receiving of the Sacraments from the hands of Methodist preachers. He said that where it had been done in England it had been marked by the most distinguished approbation of the Almighty. In Dr. A. Clarke's life, written by his son, it is recorded that at one time his health suffered, and he wrote, " I must hide my head in the country, or it will shortly be hidden in the grave," and that in 1815 he purchased a country residence near Liverpool. The house was Millbrook, and he lived in it for eight years, and in it he wrote the " Commentary of the Bible " and the " Memoirs of the Wesley Family," and it was here that he entertained, at the instigation of Sir Alexander Johnstone, the two Buddhist priests. He publicly baptised them, amid a scene of great emotionalism (both priests weeping copiously), on March 12th, 1820, at Brunswick Chapel, Moss Street, to the Christian faith. It was a great trouble to the worthy doctor to hear in after years that, on their return to Ceylon, they threw off Christianity, and reverted to their original faith. Millbrook is at Eccleston, about two miles from Prescot. The brook which gave the name to the house is still there, but of the mill only the foundations remain. When he came there, on September 20th, 1815, he was fifty-six years of age.

Being concerned about the spiritual welfare of his neighbours, he built a chapel and started a Sunday school. The congregation of the chapel was small, and consisted of the village smith, the schoolmistress, and shoemaker, and a few colliers. The school, however, which was staffed with members of Dr. Clarke's family, did better, and had at one time as many as seventy scholars. The chapel schoolhouse was afterwards made into two cottages, and it can be seen to-day.

The houses are called Chapel Cottages, and are at the corner of Chapel Lane and Gracious Street. Millbrook had a considerable amount of land attached to it, and the doctor farmed it himself, taking great interest in the operations of nature as seen in garden and field. He also went in for stock raising. It is remembered of him that he would not eat flesh or fowl which had been reared on his farm

In 1816 there was much distress among sailors, shipping going through a time of crisis in Liverpool. Dr. Clarke brought a number of the most poverty-stricken out to some cottages which he had built ; he provided them with bedding, &c., food, and grog. He, however, objected to tobacco. He had many arguments with them about it, but at last gave way on being told what a solace tobacco had often been when exposed to hunger, cold, fatigue, and the hardships of a sailor's life. He employed them in fine weather to make a road to his house. Dr. Clarke was visited by many distinguished people, among them being the Earl and Countess of Derby, Lord Dartmouth, Lady Essex, &c. Lady Derby, who had been a notable actress—Miss Eliza Farren —was a frequent visitor to Millbrook.

The study in which Dr. Clarke worked is still kept almost as he left it. He was a great worker, rising at five o'clock each morning. He had no time for idlers, and once wrote on the window-pane of the study, a Latin verse, which, translated, ran :—

" Good friend, whosoever thou art,
That comest my study to see,

Be short, and be quick to depart
Or work in the vineyard with me."

Millbrook House is remarkable as having been at different times
the home of families whose names are familiar to Liverpool and
Prescot people. After Dr. Clarke there have been the following
occupants of this house :—In 1824 a Mr. Hadfield, a cotton spinner,
who tried to establish that industry at Eccleston, but who had to
remove to Warrington; in 1850, William Pilkington, founder of the
great glass business, and father of William Pilkington, J.P. and D.L.,
of Roby Hall; in 1860, William Whitley, brother to Edward Whitley,
M.P. for a Liverpool Division, lived there; in 1884, Thomas Swift,
barrister, of Liverpool and St. Helens, lived there. He was the father
of Rigby Swift, K.C., M.P. for St. Helens; Dr. S. W. Swift,
of Huyton; E. E. Swift, registrar of the County Courts of St. Helens
and Widnes, and other sons all in the profession of law. Other
tenants have been Mr. J. H. Leather, a chemical manufacturer;
David Gamble, son of Colonel Gamble, C.B.; and the present tenant
is Mr. John Hamill, a gentleman well known in St. Helens, and
who keeps the house and grounds in excellent condition.

LIME STREET CHAPEL.

In October, 1803, a new Chapel was erected at the corner of Elliot
Street, but in Lime Street; its Minister was the Rev. James Lister,
an alumnus of Glasgow University, the denomination was Baptist,
and the membership numbered 45. The cost of the Chapel was about
£1,900. Mr. Lister was an eloquent preacher and an active organiser,
and the cause grew under his ministry. In 1809 the Church had
grown to 90 members, and by 1818 to 159 members. In 1841 the
Corporation of Liverpool purchased the Chapel in Lime Street, the
site being wanted for a town improvement. Minister and congregation
thereupon removed to Myrtle Street and built the now famous Baptist
Chapel, it was opened in 1842. Mr. Lister, however, began to fail
in health and felt called upon to resign, which he did in 1847. He
was succeeded by the Rev. Hugh Stowell Brown. Mr. Lister was
esteemed as a leading Nonconformist Minister in his day, not only
in Liverpool, but in England and in Scotland, where his preaching
attracted large crowds. On one occasion he visited Leicester and
preached for the great Robert Hall. Mr. Lister was a man of very
regular habits, always retiring to rest at ten o'clock, and rising at
five. Mr. Hall asked him about these matters, questioning him very
closely, and in his own characteristic style, about getting up at
five a.m., a point on which Mr. Hall seemed rather incredulous.
Mr. Lister's lodgings were near Mr. Hall's residence. The morning
after the aforesaid conversation, at a few minutes before five o'clock,
there came a vigorous rapping at the door of the house where
Mr. Lister was staying, which, after some delay, was responded to by
the servant. On opening the door, she found Mr. Hall outside, very
imperfectly arrayed in dressing gown and slippers, and insisting on
being shown immediately to Mr. Lister's bedroom. The servant
hesitated, said Mr. Lister was not up, and so forth, but Mr. Hall
would have his way. Meanwhile the clock on the staircase struck
five. Mr. Hall was shown Mr. Lister's bedroom, and in he walked
without knocking. Mr. Lister was at the washstand, performing
his morning ablutions. Surprised at such an intrusion, and fearing
some misfortune had happened, Mr. Lister exclaimed, " Why, what is

the matter, Mr. Hall?" "Matter, matter, why nothing is the matter. I simply came to see for myself that you are a man of your word, and I find you are, sir. Good morning, sir!" and, turning about, he returned to his own house and bed. He never doubted Mr. Lister's word after that. The name of this Glasgow minister is remembered in Liverpool to-day, and will be for generations to come in Lister Drive, Lister Drive Baths, and Lister Drive Reading Room and Library. Lister Drive was so named to honour a descendant of Rev. James Lister, who became a leading citizen, and who is still with us—Alderman James Lister, of Basil Grange, Sandfield Park.

MEDIÆVAL FONTS OF S.W. LANCASHIRE.

Older than the churches to which they belong are the christening or baptismal fonts of most of our local churches; some are Norman or pre-Norman, but the majority of them date from Mediæval times.

Perhaps the most ancient is that of Kirkby. Kirkby Church, dedicated to the British saint Chad, had been erected by Saxon or more probably Scandinavian settlers after their conversion to Christianity. It was originally of wood and very small, as the ground plan as seen to-day, marked out in the churchyard, indicates. The font now stands on a circular plinth at the west end of the nave of the beautiful modern Church. It was, however, at one time thrown out of an older church as useless, and, according to an article in the "Gentleman's Magazine" of 1845, it was found by a Mr. W. J. Roberts [Mr. Roberts resided at Aughton], neglected in the churchyard, under the spout, by the door of the old schoolroom, and was used by the school children to sharpen their knives and pencils upon. The font is of Scandinavian or Saxon origin. The bowl is massive and circular, with a series of ten arcades, formed by semi-circular arches, which are irregular in width and height, and pillars with well marked capitals and bases. The spandrills of the arches are occupied by ornaments of a floral character, which spring from the centre of the capitals. The bowl rests on a support formed of a coil of serpents, the heads of three of which project above the coil. The compartments of the arcade contain rude sculptures. Compartment 1, facing east in the present position of the font, represents the temptation of Adam, wherein Eve hands with her left hand the forbidden fruit to her spouse, who is receiving it with his right; between the two figures is the tree of life, round which winds a serpent with a wolf-like face directed towards the legendary mother of the human race. One may notice Eve's remarkable coiffure, for her hair hangs nearly to her feet in a huge coil or plait.

In Huyton Church is a large circular font; it was examined by Mr. H. Ecroyd Smith, who wrote an article on it which appeared in the Historic Society's Transactions for 1873. He thinks that this font dates from the 8th or 9th century, and that it owes its Roman character (the arcading and the six petalled flowers) to the influence of the presence of Roman altars and other carved work upon the Saxon sculptors of that time; it is well known that these sculptors copied Roman work when possible. A font found at Grappenhall, about 20 miles from Huyton, is very similar in design, and both fonts might justly be described as of "debased Roman style." The Huyton font has sculptured around it a series of eleven compartments, and each compartment contains a head, presumably of an apostle or a saint; there are no symbols, however, to enable one to learn who they are intended to represent. The font has traces of the staples by means of which a cover has been attached to it (in 1236 Edmund, Archbishop of Canterbury, ordered that all fonts should be provided with a cover in order to preserve the water which it contained from witchcraft). These early covers in the South of England developed into the magnificent spires of tabernacle work which are still to be seen suspended over the font here in Lancashire; however, the covers were always flat, where tabernacle work is seen it is modern. There are two more fonts at Huyton, one a massive plain one of millstone grit, which can be seen in the churchyard, and dates probably from the 13th or 14th century and the other the one now in use, of local sandstone, is in excellent preservation. The height is 31 inches, the diameter of the bowl inside 21 inches, and depth inside 9½ inches; it is a comparatively modern copy of a 15th century font.

At Aughton the mediæval font is still in use, and stands beneath the tower, which in this Church occupies an unusual position on the north side of the nave. It has at some time been subjected to rough usage; it is of finely-grained, light-coloured sandstone, and stands upon four semi-detached columns; it is of 14th or 15th century workmanship.

At Walton-on-the-Hill is an ancient font, which has passed through many vicissitudes. Turned out of the Church in 1754, it was for many years used as a mounting stone and seat at the door of the adjacent public-house. Matthew Gregson saw it, called public attention to it, and in 1817 the font was removed into the churchyard. Now, however, it is again in its rightful place, i.e., in the Church. The font consists of a massive circular bowl of sandstone, having around it an ornamentation of six panels with rough carvings, now much obliterated with the destructive agencies of the weather and human hands and feet. The only portions of the sculpture to be recognised now are (1) a serpent coiled round the tree of life, with Adam and Eve on either side; (2) a figure with a nimbus around the head, seated on an ass, and preceded with another on foot carrying a child; the first apearing to represent the temptation, and the second the flight into Egypt. The font is an excellent example of early Norman workmanship, and probably dates from the time of Edward the Confessor. Just as we regard the flint-scratched bones of Paleolithic cave men and recognise them as the beginning of pictorial and decorative art, so we may see in the rude and quaint sculpture on our oldest fonts a development in ecclesiastical art, for they were intended to convey to the unlettered peasant some scriptural story or moral lesson.

At Formby and at Altcar the ancient fonts had been turned out and left in their respective churchyards to the tender mercies of children, gardeners, and the weather. At Burscough the sacrilege (if so it could be called) went even further, for in the yard of an adjoining farm (Worthington's) at one time could be seen the font from the ancient Priory being used as a mixing trough for mixing pig's food. I am glad to say, however, that thanks to the Misses Wilbraham, it was rescued, and it now occupies a position of honour in Lathom Chapel, in Lathom Park.

It is passing strange that, considering the importance of Baptism according to the creed and liturgy of the Church, so little reverence has been attached to the font. If Baptism is a sacrament, then the font should be treated as a sacramental vessel.

At Sefton is a handsome font in excellent preservation. It is, of

L

course, sandstone, and each face of the octagonal bowl is occupied by a deeply-cut panel, with a six-leaved ornament in high relief. It has a heavy pyramidal oak cover, which bears on its rim: RR : HM : CW, with the date 1688. The initials are those of the churchwardens who provided the cover. The font at one time had been covered with plaster, this, no doubt, accounting for its superior state of preservation. The font is of unusual pattern, and is thought to be 15th or 16th century work.

At Halsall the ancient font was probably a handsome structure, if one may judge from the remnants of it. Part of the base of the bowl and the supporting pillar have been incorporated in the present modern font and stand, an admirable arrangement whereby the venerable vessel has been preserved. It would appear to date from about 1300 A.D.

At Maghull is a portion of an old chapel (it was there in 1100) called the Unsworth Chapel. The chancel arch is destroyed and now blocked up; the nave was pulled down about 1800, when the new church of St. Andrew was built. There is a Georgian font built into the wall over the modern west door of the chancel, and a prism-shaped holy water stoup set on the fragment of a circular pillar, near to the same door. This latter is sometimes mistaken for a Baptismal font. The font from the original chapel I cannot trace.

At Melling the font, from its size and general character, is probably pre-reformation. It stands in the S.W. corner of the nave; it is of sandstone, but has been covered with a thin coat of paint. The height of the bowl outside is 30 inches, inside 21 inches, and in depth 10 inches.

At Ormskirk the Norman font has disappeared, and the one now in use bears the date 1661. There seems good reason for believing that the font was originally given by some one of the Stanley Family. It was first used on January 2nd of that year by the Rev. Nathaniel Heywood, the vicar, who was ejected in 1662, and who may have had something to do with the obtaining of the font. From some extraordinary and unintelligible cause the font was removed about the year 1773, and at one period was placed under a spout to receive the downfall, and at another time it was the companion of rubbish. In 1862, at the expense of a parishioner, it was renovated and replaced. The following subjects are sculptured on the six panels which surround the bowl :—1st, date, 1661 ; 2nd, the Royal Crown, surmounted by a Lion, and the initials " C.R." ; 3rd, the Eagle and Child, the crest of the Stanleys ; 4th, a Latin Cross ; 5th, a St. Andrew's Cross ; 6th, an hour-glass.

At Childwall and Roby fonts have been converted into flower pots ; at the former place at one time in the garden of the Abbey Hotel, the one at the latter had come from Prescot. At Prescot the font now used is a handsome Italian one of peculiar design, and around it is carved the following, " The gift of Daniel Willis of Halsnead Hall, Esqre, 1755."

In Liverpool there are no fonts so far as I can trace older than the 17th century.

Many of our readers are ecclesiologists, some, perhaps, without being conscious of it. They love to examine an old church, and try to understand what they see. The font, if properly placed, is by the entrance door, at the west end of the Church, thus indicating that Baptism is the first stage or at the beginning of the Christian life.

Broadly speaking, fonts follow in their design the architectural period to which they belong. Saxon fonts are, as a rule, rude and plain, but towards the end of that period, when it begins to emerge into the Norman, you may occasionally find a specimen which is astonishing in its wildly intricate ornateness.

Norman fonts, while often fanciful and grotesque, retain the general grand massiveness of their period. Those of Early English date are lighter, more scientifically economical of material, and exhibit scarcely anything of the Norman grotesqueness. In the decorated period, instead of following the usual rule of progress, the font shows signs of decline. And this is the more curious since that period in general church architecture is admittedly the most beautiful of all.

In the succeeding or Perpendicular period the font, according to the best opinions, so far from continuing to decline, recovered and reached in design, ornamentation and general beauty its zenith. And this again is curious. For if there be many who admire the Perpendicular in general church architecture, many more cordially detest it, and all are agreed that in its later stages it cannot challenge comparison with the Decorated Style.

Earlier than the earliest font or Baptistry was the river, and it is worthy of note that on the conversion of Northumbria (of which Lancashire formed a part), King Edwin and his niece, the Lady Hilda, were baptized by immersion, and according to Camden, multitudes at once desired to follow the royal example. He says, "that Paulinius, after he had consecrated the River Swale, commanded, by the crier and principal men, that they should by faith go in, two by two, and in the name of the Holy Trinity baptize each other." Bede also relates that Paulinius spent 33 days from morning to evening baptizing the crowds.

STONE CROSSES.

In several of the villages near Liverpool these interesting relics of the past have been preserved, as at Garston, Roby, Rainhill, Cronton, Crosby, Formby, Lydiate, &c. At Childwall, however, there is a large base which, with little expenditure, could be restored to somewhat of its original condition as a complete wayside cross. At present it lies in a field belonging to Lord Salisbury, and in the tenancy of Mr. Hale, and it is hidden by a hedge. At some time between a hundred and a hundred and fifty years ago the local landowner brought the hedge to the centre of the broad road, and enclosed along with a strip of land the old cross. The shaft and cross piece have gone, but local Catholics knew of the whereabouts of the "Weeping Cross," as it was called, and the procession of mourners has often stopped and rested the coffin beside it in the now narrow thoroughfare.

The Lancashire and Cheshire Historic Society are now considering ways and means for restoring to the community this bit of antiquity. The two ways suggested are :—(1) To remove it to the churchyard; (2) to remove the fence which hides it, allow it to remain in its present position, and in some way to restore it to somewhat of its original appearance, and to be within view of passers-by.

As memorials of the past, stone crosses are especially worth preserving. They are of various kinds—market, wayside, and memorial. The most noted of these latter were erected by Edward I. in affectionate remembrance of Queen Eleanor. She died at Harby, in Nottinghamshire, in the house of Robert de Weston, in 1291, and crosses were erected in her memory in every town and village where the body rested on its way from Hardby to Westminster. These

L2

crosses were beautiful examples of mediæval sculpture. Of the fifteen crosses said to have been erected, only three now remain, namely, at Northampton, Geddington, and Waltham.

The crosses of Liverpool and district were market and wayside, and were at one time very numerous. In a map prepared by Mr. Henry Taylor and shown to the Lancashire and Cheshire Antiquarian Society at Chetham College, Manchester, the sites and remains of no fewer than one hundred ancient crosses were marked, all within the hundred of West Derby. Many of these crosses were put up in the 13th century or earlier. Near Ormskirk there was a remarkable group of crosses within a circle four miles in diameter. There used to be no fewer than eighteen crosses. Several of these were in existence at the time of the first ordnance survey. The group of crosses appeared to lead in three lines from Scarisbrick Priory to the churches at Halsall, Ormskirk, and Burscough Priory, and until quite recently they were used by Roman Catholic funeral processions for devotional purposes, the mourners stopping at the site of every cross to offer prayers for the dead. Another noticeable group of crosses was found in the neighbourhood of Ince Blundell, Little Crosby, and Sefton. The one at Little Crosby is said to have been removed there from the village green at Great Crosby, and at its foot the custom of proclaiming the decision of the mayoral court was kept up.

In the twelve miles of country between Liverpool and Warrington the remains of sites of upwards of twenty of these ancient crosses were recorded on the early ordnance maps. Few of these remain, but some have been restored or rebuilt. The best examples are those at Rainhill and Cronton. At Roby there is a portion of a shaft to be seen at the roadside. It is on the brow of the hill and on the road going down to the village. At Garston the square base and shaft of a cross stood at the head of the mill dam. It is shown by Troughton as having two steps, and probably marked a well. It was buried when St. Mary's Road was made. It was found again when making a drain, and was kept for many years by Mr. Owen, stonemason, and was finally re-erected on a new site by a local Roman Catholic priest, Father Smith. At Farnworth there is a fine cross about nine feet high. It stands at the south side of the Church by the Cuerdley Chapel. It stands on three steps, the upper one forming the base—a massive square stone. The shaft is square, but the writer thinks that a crosspiece originally stood above the present cap and gablets. At Childwall there were originally three crosses, but none are now to be seen. The base of one of them has been previously alluded to in this article.

In the central parts of South-West Lancashire, owing to the number of landowners who adhered to the ancient faith, crosses are perhaps more abundant than elsewhere. At Lydiate—a manor which, from the time of William Gernet (to whom it was given by Paganus de Vilars soon after the Conquest, and who was the progenitor of the De Lydiates), has never passed out of Catholic hands—no fewer than six crosses may be traced within a mile of the hall. Of these the remains of three are still visible, one of which was found in the year 1870 buried in a cop on the road to Downholland. This cross has been restored, and is now the cemetery cross at the Roman Catholic church, not far from which it was discovered. Mr. Blundell, the diarist, mentions the setting up again of the village cross at Little Crosby in his own time In several passages, a few of which are here given, he speaks of the above ceremony :—

1707, June 24th. I went to Ince with the intention to go to the flowering of Ince Cross with Mr. Blundell if he went, but he not being at home I came back. Some of the servants went.

1708, June 23rd. I gathered some flowers for flowering Great Crosby Cross to-morrow.

June 24th. My wife and I were at the flowering of Great Crosby Cross.

1715, June 24th. My children went to the flowering of Ince Cross.

The uniform day for these celebrations was the 24th June, being the Feast of Nativity of St. John the Baptist, a very appropriate time, seeing that it is midsummer when flowers are most abundant. Moreover, it was a term day in ancient grants, and much land was held under the fee of a red rose at the Feast of the Nativity of St. John the Baptist. The festival was a very popular one, both with the adults and the children, and in pre-Reformation days would take the place of the flower services as held at many places of worship to-day. The parish priest and clergy joined with the young people in gathering flowers, making them into garlands and decorating the crosses. Part of the festival consisted of a procession between the church and the various crosses, and the singing or chanting of hymns.

In " Brook's Liverpool," in 1775 to 1800, we have the following item relating to Liverpool crosses :—" We can scarcely doubt that Liverpool had a market from about the time of its becoming a borough, but it is not known where the market was held until after the middle of the sixteenth century, when it was established at the High Cross for butcher's meat, fish, and vegetables." This cross was at the junction of the four main streets of the town, and was removed in 1673 on the occasion of the preparations for the building of the then Exchange or Town Hall. The general market was held for a considerable time in the vicinity of High Street and of the Exchange, and another was established at the White Cross, little more than about 100 yards distant, at the upper part of Chapel Street, near the place where the north entrance of the Exchange Buildings now is. The place for holding the White Cross market was changed to St. John's Market in 1822.

Another market, which afterwards became the principal one for the sale of provisions, vegetables, butter, and other articles usually sold in a market, was established early in the last century in Derby Square, and on the south side of St. George's Church, where Alderman Tarleton afterwards erected an obelisk of red stone, which was called the Red Cross or Tarleton's Obelisk, and after its establishment the most ancient market, in the vicinity of High Street and the Exchange, became disused. except as to the butchers' shambles which remained there many years after 1775. At the spot where the north entrance of the Exchange Buildings now is, and near the third pillar on the right of the centre iron gate entering from Chapel Street, was a portion of the ancient cross called the White Cross, and close to it the White Cross Market used to be held.

The lower end of Tithebarn Street, between Hatton Garden and Cheapside (formerly called Dig Lane), was then called Patrick's Hill, at the foot of which, and at the end of Pinfold Lane (now Vauxhall Road), stood a portion of St. Patrick's Cross. The remains of it were there three or four years after 1775. The Town End Cross was near where St. Stephen's Church, in Byrom Street, now stands. St. Patrick's Cross, and the Pinfold near it, are both laid down in Mr. Perry's Map of Liverpool of 1769. The Market Cross originally stood in the Market Place, and the country people, as they brought their butter, eggs, poultry, &c., for sale, gathered round it; the pedlars also, with their cloth and cotton goods, their cutlery from Sheffield, and hardware from the Midlands. All had in view the Cross, that symbol of the Church, with its message of self-denial. Probably the buyers and sellers of bygone days would be as keen to make bargains as the same classes are to-day, and the emblem would be forgotten. In the base of some of the crosses are found basin-shaped hollows, in which vinegar was placed in time of plague. It was usual for money to be dipped in this old-time antiseptic before changing hands.

Everton Church was a round pillar, standing about four feet from the top of the three square stone steps, and stood in the centre of the village, about one hundred yards eastwards of the once-famous Prince Rupert's cottage. It was the last monument of antiquity that Everton possessed. About one hundred years before its surreptitious removal it appears to have been fitted with a sundial on the upper surface of the shaft, and the following charges for its repair are taken from the accounts of the township :—

1736—The cock of the dial repaired..
1774—One shilling was paid to a mayson for squaring the dial.
1785—The cross repaired, and 1s. paid for same.
1787—Fifty-five shillings and fivepence paid for repairing the cross.

In the year 1820 it disappeared in a most extraordinary way.

APPENDIX.

THE ANCIENT CHAPEL OF WEST DERBY.

In the centre of West Derby, in front of the Parish Church, flanked by the Old Manor Court House, and near the pound and stocks is a pillar, locally called Heyworth's Monument. It was erected by Mrs. J. P. Heywood, of Norris Green, upon the site of the altar of the ancient Chapel of West Derby.

The first mention that we have of the Chapel is in a law case. A certain John del Brakes struck and wounded Richard le Jay in the Chapel of West Derby, on Sunday, after Ascension Day; this was in 1360. In 1494 it was reported as being in bad repair, and King Henry VII. allowed 5 marks out of his Manor of West Derby towards making it suitable for divine worship. In 1552 it was recorded that the ancient chapel had only two little bells; it is also mentioned as poor.

At the time of the Commonwealth, a godly minister, a Mr. Norcott, was placed there, and it was recommended that another Chapel should be built to the south, somewhat in the direction of what is now Knotty Ash.

After the restoration, Bishop Gastell found, on his visitation in Lancashire, a curate there, with a stipend of £43 2s. 8d. There had been many alterations of the building, and it was mentioned that sacrament day was observed five times a year. The steeple had been rebuilt in 1745, and the Chapel itself in 1786. The Parsonage was built in 1793.

The Chapelry consisted of four quarters, each represented by a warden; from the minute book the writer was interested to find that an ancestor of his, Lawrence Davies, farmer and blacksmith, was chapel warden for a quarter called Accersend quarter, in 1793-4. Lawrence Davies' smithy and dwelling house are still to be seen in Prescot Road, almost facing Black Horse Lane; his farm was called Accers-end farm, and consisted of about twenty-three acres. It is now part of the Highfield Estate.

When the old Chapel was demolished about 1853, among the debris were found stones which had been shaped in such a way as to indicate that they had been part of a straw thatched roof. It is quite probable that the first Chapel, which would be contemporary with the Castle, would be a wooden building, thatched with straw

There is a legend in West Derby to the effect that when in Reformation times the Commissioners came to the Chapel, the Priest who had retained possession hid the sacrament vessels and the plate beneath the pulpit, and that they had never been recovered.

The altar and rails, the former being beautifully carved with leaves and fruit, are now adorning a staircase in the house of Dr. P. Judson, at Heatherby, the Bourne, Farnham, Surrey.   Dr. Judson took them with him on removing from Mill Lane, West Derby, in July, 1910.   The two little bells before mentioned had given place to one larger bell, and it was taken to the Church Schools.   From calling the parishioners to worship, it has still the useful function of calling the children to learn their lessons.   The font was rescued by Rector Percy Stewart, M.A., and is now used for its original purpose in the Church of the Good Shepherd, in Carr Lane.

The Sun-dial which was on the wall, on the south side of the old Chapel, on the flat with a finger indicator, went to Moss House, but has been restored to ornament the Church.   It is now on the wall of West Derby Parish Church.   The two old doors, strong, and ornamented with iron studs, are, one in the vestry of the new Church, and the other securing an outbuilding of Ivy Cottage, in Almonds Green.

Inside the Chapel was quaint.   It had high pews, so high that children could not see the minister, excepting when standing, and it had a three-decker pulpit.   The clerk, Thomas Lawton, a blacksmith, of Leyfield Road, occupied the clerk's pulpit.   It was usual at West Derby for the minister to retire to the vestry before the sermon, and to exchange the white surplice for a black gown; in those days it would have been considered as unorthodox to preach in any different colour than black.

MILLER'S HOUSE, WEST DERBY.

Boltons, as it was locally called, was the Miller's House, belonging to a West Derby Mill.   The house was Tudor in design.   It was of two storeys, the upper one having a clay floor.   It was considered, until demolished about 10 years ago, as the oldest house in West Derby Township.   The Mill belonging to John del Accers in 1342, it and the Miller's house were in Finch Lane, near to the famous yew-tree, and almost adjoining the Farm (Rainfords), beneath which coal has recently been found. It was called Accers' Mill for centuries.

Finch Lane was formerly called Mockbeggar Lane. It would be interesting to know the origin of this curious name.

FAIRFIELD HALL.

From the supposed similarity to the Caddy of our Grandmothers, it has been nick-named " Tea Caddy Hall." It is now (in 1913) in process of demolition. It was built by Edward Falkner, a Liverpool Merchant, who removed here from Old Hall Street, when that, " at one time" fashionable thoroughfare, changed its character. He was a man of influence in the good old town and even further afield, and became High Sheriff of Lancashire in 1788. He also raised a troop of Volunteer Cavalry, which he commanded himself. The family name will be perpetuated in Falkner Street and Falkner Square.

The most notable family after the Falkners, father and son, to reside at Fairfield Hall, was that of Mr. Charles Shand, who had lived at a large house in Rupert Lane, Everton, and who came to live at Fairfield when the property was sold to the Government, and converted into Cavalry Barracks. Judge Shand, the noted County Court Judge, belonged to this family.

KING'S MILL, WAVERTREE.

Wavertree Windmill is a standing monument to the progress of milling and to the spirit of freedom in the English people, the advance being enormous in each case, from the slow grinding of the corn by the wind, to the high pressure pulverising by the roller mill of 1913, and from the tyranny of the soke system, to the absolute freedom of the people to grind their corn where they liked. From 1475 to 1629 the Mill was the property of the reigning King or Queen, and all tenants of the Manor of Wavertree were compelled to bring their corn to it to be ground; the Royal right of soke, as Queen Mary once observed, was " for the maintenance of our mills and our inheritance." King Charles I. sold his rights in the Mill, along with the Manor, to James, Lord Strange, son of the Earl of Derby. In 1675, William, Earl of Derby, owned the Mill, and enforced the soke of the Mill upon his tenants. The unfortunate tenant who took his corn to be ground at another Mill was liable to have his flour, waggon, and horses confiscated.

In 1768, Bamber Gascoyne, M.P., held the Mill as Lord of the Manor, and in that year the Act for enclosing the Wavertree Commons was passed through Parliament. To protect his Mill, Gascoyne had inserted in the Bill a clause prohibiting the erection of any house or building, or the planting of any trees, or the growth of any existing trees within 200 yards of the Mill to such a height as to prevent the going of the said Windmill. Presumably this was to guarantee that the wind should not be impeded in turning the sails. Early in the 19th century the Mill was in the possession of the Bourne Family. At a later date, when belonging to Sir James Bourne, a son of his coachman was killed, the lad playing beneath the sails while they were revolving and striking him on the head. The last miller to grind corn was Mr. Charles Taylor, who became tenant in 1857, and worked the Mill for 16 years. His eldest daughter was unfortunate in being caught by the hair by the revolving sail. She was scalped and was rendered insensible for 12 hours, but happily she recovered.

C. Tinling & Co., Ltd., Printers, 53, Victoria Street, Liverpool.

Cronton Cross. (Page 147.)

Cronton Stocks. (Page 147.)

Old West Derby Chapel, now demolished. (Page 151.)

King's Mill, Wavertree. (Page 153.)

Boltons, West Derby. (Page 152.)

Fairfield Hall, demolished 1913. (Page 153.)

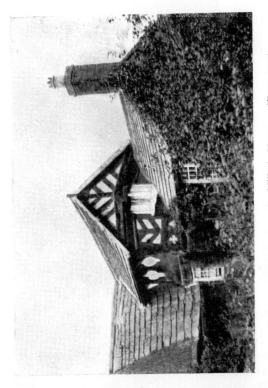

Boltons, West Derby, the Miller's House. (Page 153.)

INDEX

Accers	92
Accers, John del	152
Accers End Farm	151
Accers Mill	153
Adam, William Son of	21 – 23
Aiken, Dr.	103
Aldridge & Deacon, Messrs	128
Allerton	130
Allerton, Manor Of	132
Almonds Green	15, 71, 152
Altcar Font	145
Ambrose, Joshua	118, 136
Ambrose, Nehemiah	118, 136
Ambrose, Peter	118, 136
America – Associations with South West Lancashire	116 – 118
Ancient British Burial Ground	66
Ancient Chapel of Toxteth Park	15, 136, 139 – 140
Andrews, Constable Wm	66
Armitage, John	104
Armitage Family	104
Ash House	74 – 75
Ash House Meeting House	74
Ashfield	92 – 93
Ashton, John	62
Ashton, Nicholas	62, 131
Ashurst, Henry	117 – 118
Assembly Room, Old Swan	45
Ather, William	52
Atherton, William	8
Atholl, Charlotte Dowager Duchess of	30
Atholl, John, Duke of	30
Aughton	72, 120
Aughton Font	145
Aughton, Manor of	78

Aughton Well	120
Austin, Mr	35, 39
Aymount, Annie	15
Aymounts (Almonds) Green	15
Babthorpe, Father Albert	97
Badnall, Rev William	57, 66, 68
Baptist Chapel, Everton	111
Baptist Chapel, St. Oswald Street	45
Baptists, Old Swan	44 – 46
Barker, J & P	133
Barker, Paul	28 – 29, 49
Barker, Richard	28, 49
Barker's Row	29
Bartley, T B	69
Barton, William	127
Basnett, Rev. Christopher	139
Bates, Sir Edward	13 – 14
Bates, Percy	13
Bell, William	136
Bellefield, West Derby	13 – 14
Benn's Garden Meeting House	135
Bentley, Thomas	134
Bibby, John	68
Bibby Street	102
Billinge, Father Richard	97
Birch, Sir Joseph	61 – 62
Birrell, Right Hon. Augustine	40, 69 – 70, 125
Birrell, Charles M	70, 125
Bishop Eton Church, Woolton Road	53
Black Horse Lane	102, 151
Black Horse Smithy, Old Swan	106
Blackburne, John	53
Blackburne House	53
Black Moor	102
Blackmoor Moss	102
Bland, John	54

Blind, School for the	93
Blue Bell Smithy	106
Bluecoat School	5 – 6, 70 – 71
Blundell, Lt. Col.	17
Blundell, Mr	19
Blundell, Bryan	5 – 6
Blundell, Henry	17
Blundell, Jonathon	6
Blundell, William	5
Blundell Family	5 - 6
Blundell Hollinshead Family	16 – 17
Bolton's Hall, Millers House, Finch Lane	128, 152 – 153
Boulton's Hall **see** Bolton's Hall	
Bourne, James	69, 154
Bourne Family	154
Bowling, Thomas of Euxton	118
Brammall, Mr	90
Brandreth, Dr. Joseph, Snr.	85
Brandreth, Joseph Pilkington, MD	84 - 85
Breres Family	26
Bridewell, Old Swan	46 – 47, 112
Bright, Allan H	92
Bright, Henry	92
Broadgreen	71, 72 – 85
Broadgreen Hall	83 – 85
Broadgreen Railway Station	80 – 81
Brookland Road	102
"Brothers of Charity"	76
Brown, George	70 – 71
Brown, Rev. Hugh Stowell	74, 143
Brunswick Chapel, Moss Street	141 – 142
Bull baiting	19
Bullen, Mr	48
Bunting, Dr.	141
Burscough Font	145
Byrom Hall Chapel	125 – 126, 135

Calderstones	51, 131
Camelford, Gabriel	140
Carr, William	62
Castle, West Derby	9 – 10, 99, 151
Castle Field	9 – 10, 19
Castle Hey	139
Catholic Reformatory for Girls	39
Cattle Market, Stanley	44, 81, 105, 110
Cavalry Barracks	153
Chaloner, Edward	29 – 30, 50
Chaloner Schools	29
Chapel Cottages	142
Chapel House, Ormskirk	118
Charity School, Old Swan	40 – 43, 57, 84, 112
Chester, Bishop of	42, 52, 133
Childwall	129 – 134
Childwall Abbey Inn	129 – 130
Childwall Church	28, 55 – 56, 61, 129–134
Childwall Court Leet	130
Childwall Cross	147 – 148
Childwall Font	134, 146
Childwall Hall	3, 94, 129 –130, 132
Childwall Manor	1 – 2, 60, 129
Childwall Market Cross	130
Childwall Monks Bath	130
Childwall Parish	51, 129
Childwall Priory	130
Childwall Valley	130
Christy, Dr. T W	74 – 75
Claighton, James	52
Clare, Andrew	138

Clark, Rev. W L Hutching	56
Clarke, Dr. Adam	141 – 143
Clarke, James	61
Clarke, John	84, 93
Claughton, William	67
Clayton, Dr.	135
Clemens, James	92 – 93
Clemens, Thomas Crowden	93
Cliff, Mr	127
Clithero, Mr	112
Coach and Horses Inn	111
Cock Pits	46
Congregational Church, Wavertree	52
Conley, Betty	58 – 59
Constable, Old Swan	47
Constable, Wavertree	54 – 55, 58 – 59, 63 – 65
Constable, West Derby Parish	6 – 7, 63
Copyhold Court of West Derby	63
Country Lanes	7 - 8
Coupe, Father	97
Court House, West Derby	1 – 3, 8, 111, 151
Cresswell, Rev. Walter	124
Cricket Ground, Knotty Ash	76
Cromwell's Well, Aughton	120
Cronton Cross	147 – 148, 150
Cronton Stocks	150
Crosby, Great, Cross	147 – 148, 150
Crosby Hall	5
Crosby, Little, Cross	148
Crosse, Humphrey	23
Crosse, Rector John	22 – 23
Crosse, Richard	23

Crosses	130, 147 – 150
Crowther, Thomas	76
Croxteth	113 – 114
Croxteth Hall	96 – 98, 114
Cuerdley Chapel, Farnworth	148
Cunard Offices, Rumford Street	6
Cunningham, George	44 – 45, 81 – 83
Cunningham's Nursery	81 – 83
Curnock, Rev. George	39
Dallinger, Rev W H	37
Dannes, Rev Thomas	63
Davies, Mr	47, 90, 106
Davies, Catherine	106
Davies, Lawrence	106, 151
Dawson, Dr.	11
Deaf and Dumb, School for the	93
Defoe, Daniel	103
Dell, Mr	48
De Nash, John	95
Derby, Earls of	39, 52, 69, 88, 90, 99, 114 – 115, 124, 129, 142, 153
Derby, James, 7th Earl of	2, 30, 120
Derby, William, 9th Earl of	2
Derby, 12th Earl of	46
Derby Lane	102
Derby Lane School	127
Derby Square	149
Derwent Square	127
Deys Family	17
Deysbrook	16 – 17
Deysbrook Hall	16 – 17
Dickinson, Moses	109

Dig Lane	149
Ditchfield, E	65
Doghouse Lane	104
Dove, C E	37
Dovecot	85 – 89
Dovecot House	85 – 89
Dugdale, Adam	86 – 89
Dunbabin, John	62 – 63
Dutton, Sam	63
Dwerryhouse Green	71 – 72
Dyehouse Well	120
Eagle and Child Inn	113
Earle, Thomas	61
Edge Hill Station	81
Edge Lane	94 – 96
Edge Lane Hall	93 – 96
Elsley, Rev W J	127
Eltonhead, Thomas de	20
Emmott, Rev Father	97
Enclosure Act, Wavertree	58, 71
Etches, John Clifford	44
Evans, Dr. John	139
Everton Church	150
Everton Cross	150
Exchange Buildings	149
Eyes, Charles	57, 62
Eyes, John	68, 72
Fabius, Dr. Daniel	139
Fabius Chapel	139
Fairfield Hall	61, 94, 153
Falkner, Edward	60 – 61, 64, 111, 153
Falkner Square	153
Falkner Street	153
Fall Wall Well	120
Farnworth Cross	148
Ferrers, William	99

Finch, Henry	136, 138
Finch House	87 – 88, 90
Finch Lane, West Derby	152 – 153
Firgrove House	10 – 12
Fleetwood, Caryl	72
Fogg, John	136
Fonts	126, 133 –134, 144 - 147
Footpaths	16
Formby Cross	147
Formby Font	145
Fraser, Mr	35
Fraser, Sam	36
Free Library, Museum and Art Gallery	69
Friar's Croft	129
Gamble, Colonel C B	143
Gamble, David	143
Gardner, Rev. Hilton	127
Gardner, Thomas	127
Gardner Family	128
Garston Cross	147 – 148
Gascoyne, Bamber, MP	2, 55, 59 – 60, 63, 71 – 72, 102, 130, 132, 154
Gascoyne, Frances Mary	3
Gascoyne, General Isaac	3, 132
Gascoyne, Mary	2
Gascoyne Family	132
Gascoyne Street	102
Gastrell, Bishop Francis	87, 151
Gateacre Nonconformist Chapel	131, 139 – 140
George's Dock	102
Gibson, Michael	50

Gildart, Mr	88
Gildart, Francis	90
Gildart, Rev. James	88, 90
Gildart, Richard	90
Gill Moss	96 – 98
Gladstone, T S	69
Glassworks, Old Swan	43 – 44
Good Shepherd, Church of the, Carr Lane	152
Greaves, Thomas	52
Green, Isaac	2, 52, 60
Green, Mary	60
Green Lane Well	49
Greenfield Road	37, 39
Greenwood, Mr	110
Gregg, Thomas	137
Gregson, Matthew	28, 62, 86 – 88, 145
"Gregson" Ship	84
Gregson's Well	120
Gylee, Thomas	56
Hadfield, Mr	143
Halsall Font	146
Hamill, John	143
Hardman Family	132
Harkirk, Sefton	78
Harrington Street	139
Harrison, Mr, Huyton	116
Harrison, Thomas Fenwick	127 – 128
Harrogate Pack Horse Bridge	123
Hart Hill, Allerton	131
Harvey, Mr	53
Heap, R R	102
Heaton, Butler & Bayne, Messrs	128
Herculaneum Pottery	28
Herdman, William Gawin	11
Heywood, Francis	94
Heywood, Mrs J P	151

Heywood, Nathaniel	117 – 118, 136 – 137
Heywood's Bank	76
Heyworth, Lawrence	7, 90
Heyworth's Monument	151
High Cross, Liverpool	149
High Street, Liverpool	149
Highfield House	30 – 34
Hignett, Samuel C	85
Hill Cliff Chapel near Warrington	139 – 140
Hilton, Samuel	127
Hind, Mr	64
Holt, John	27 – 28
Holy Trinity Church, Wavertree	52, 56–57, 68
Honeys Green	71
Hornabrook, John	37
Hornby, Hugh	52, 68
Hornby, Thomas Dyson	68
Hornby Dock	68
Hornby Library	68
Hoult, James	48, 65, 86 – 89, 94 – 95, 101, 109 – 110, 126, 137
Hoult, Joseph	48
Howard, Hon. Charles Wentworth George	31
Hulton, Nathaniel	118
Hume, Canon	73
Hurst, Mr	35
Hurst Street	102
Hutchinson, S M	39, 50, 124
Huyton Church	87, 144
Huyton Font	134, 144 – 145
Huyton Grammar School	87

Hyet, Rev. Jason   117

Ince Family   6
Ince Blundell Cross   148 – 149
Isaac, Daniel   141
Ivey, Professor John   39, 50
Ivy Cottage   152

Jackson, Joseph   10, 40, 72, 84
John, King   3, 10, 20, 26,
                                    79, 98 – 101
Jones, Rev. Daniel   45
Jones & Sons, Messrs.   128
Judson, Dr. P   152

Kaye Street Chapel   139
King John   3, 10, 20, 26,
                                    78, 98 - 101
King's Mill   92, 102
King's Mill, Wavertree   153 – 154
Kirkby   128
Kirkby Church   144
Kirkby Font   134, 144
Kirkham, Kitty   60
Knight, Sir John Tobin   29
Knotty Ash   85 – 93
Knotty Ash Church   28, 75,
                                    86 - 87,
                                    91 – 92, 151
Knotty Ash Church, Lych Gate   92, 128
Knotty Ash Church School   41
Knotty Ash Cricket Ground   76
Knotty Ash Well   120

Lancaster, Henry, Earl of   51
Lance, Mr   62
Lance Lane   62
Lathom, Sir Oscatel   113
Lathom, Sir Thomas   113

Lathom Chapel	145
Lathom Park	120
Lawton, Thomas	152
Leach, John	64
Leach, Thomas	109
Leather, J H	143
Lee, James	73
Leech, John	65
Leech, Thomas	64, 109
Leigh, John	94
Leigh, John Shaw	68, 93 – 94
Leigh Street	68 – 69, 94
Leyland, Thomas	26 – 27
Leyland & Bullen's Bank	26
Lime Street Baptist Chapel	143
Lister, Alderman James	144
Lister, Rev James	45, 143–144
Lister Drive	144
Lister Drive Baths	144
Lister Drive Library and Reading Room	144
Littledale, Alfred	31
Littledale, Bolton	75
Littledale, H	31
Littledale, St. George	31 – 33
Littledale, Thomas	31
Liverpool, Adam de	21 – 23
Liverpool, William de	21 – 23
Liverpool Abattoir	44
Liverpool & Manchester Railway	54, 82
Liverpool Dispensary	85
Liverpool Mercury	34, 91
Local Board, Wavertree	52
Lock Up, Wavertree	64 - 65
Londini, Dr.	12
London & North Western Railway	79
Lonsdale, Walter	128
Lowther, Hon. William	31
Lunatic Asylum & Hospital	93
Lydiate Cross	147 – 148

Lyon, Ellen	11
Lyon, Matthew	11
Lyon & Parr's Bank	11
McCullagh H H	37
McIver, Charles	86
Maddocks, Canon	102 – 103
Maddocks Street	102
Maghull Church Font	126, 146
Maghull, Unsworth Chapel	126, 146
Maher, Mrs	16
Maher's Cottages	16
Mallinson, John	136
Manchester to Liverpool Railway	75, 79
Markets	149
Marsden, Thomas	27
Mary Magdalene Well, Lathom Park	120
Mather, Dr. Cotton	116
Mather, Dr. Increase	116
Mather, Ellis	15, 90
Mather, Nathaniel	116
Mather, Richard	15 – 16, 116
Mather, Samuel	116, 137
Mather Family	88
May Place	35, 39 – 40, 70
Medley, Rev. Samuel	125 – 126, 135
Melling Font	146
Methodism, Old Swan	35 - 39
Mildway, Walter	23
Mill Lane	102
Millbrook House	141 – 143
Miller's House, West Derby see Boltons	
Mitchell, Rev J L	57
Mockbeggar Lane	153
Molyneux, Viscount	97, 131
Molyneux, Charles William	97
Molyneux, Edward	75

Molyneux, Ellen 75
Molyneux, Horatio Nelson Crichlow 75
Molyneux, Margaret 86, 88 – 89
Molyneux, Hon, Thomas 97
Molyneux, Rev. William 97
Molyneux, Sir William 114,
122 – 123
Molyneux, William 20 – 21
Molyneux Family 75, 96 – 97,
112,
114 - 115,
121, 136

Monk's Bath, Childwall 130
Monkswell, Wavertree 66 - 67,
119 – 120
Monuments 91, 149,
151
Moore Family 121
More, William de la 20
More Street Well 120
Morton, Mrs 137 – 138
Morton, Edward 137 – 138
Morton, James 98
Moss House 17, 102
Mount Vernon Green 72
Murray, Lord Henry 30
Myers, John 64
Myrtle Street Baptist Chapel 143

Nash, John 95, 130
Nelson Monument, Springfield 91
Newsham House 94
Newton, Rev. R 36
Norcott, Mr 151
Norrey, Edward 131
Norrey, Henry 131
Norrey, Thomas 131
Norrey's Chapel, Childwall Church 131
Norris, Sir William 122

Norris Family, Speke	121, 131
Norris Green	71
Nursery Lane	102
Oak Hill House	29 – 30
Oak Hill Park	28 – 29
Oak Vale Nursery	81 – 83
O'Connell, Daniel	50
Octagon Chapel	134 – 135
Old Hall, The	14 – 15
Old Swan	28 – 50
Old Swan Assembly Room	45
Old Swan Baptists	44 – 46
Old Swan Bridewell	46 – 47, 112
Old Swan Charity School	40 – 43, 57, 84, 112
Old Swan Constable	47
Old Swan Glassworks	43 – 44
Old Swan Inn	34, 112
Old Swan Methodism	35 - 39
Old Swan Methodist Chapel	35
Old Swan Police Station	28
Old Swan Postal Arrangements	34
Old Swan Rock House	48, 102
Old Swan Sunday School	37 – 39, 49 – 50
Old Swan Water Tower	49
Old Swan Well	120
Olive Mount	80
Olive Mount Cemetery	51
Omnibus, First	48 – 49
Omnibus Service	53 – 54, 80
Onslow Family	131
O'Reilly, M	95
Ormskirk	111
Ormskirk Church	63
Ormskirk Cross	148
Ormskirk Font	146
Owen, Geronwy	24

Osborne, Rev W   140

Pack Horse Bridge, Harrogate   123
Pack Horse Tracks   104 – 106
Pack Horses   103, 106
Page Moss   96
Palmer, John   28
Papayanni, Mr   39
Parke, Mr   30
Parke, Celia Anne   31
Parke, Charlotte Alice   31
Parke, James   30 – 31
Parke, Mary   31
Parke, Robert   65
Parke, Thomas   40, 84
Parr, John   11
Parr, Joseph   10 – 11
Parr, Roger   10
Parr, Thomas   11
Parr Street   11
Parr's Bank   11
Parsonage, West Derby   8, 151
Pase – Egging   4 – 5
Patrick's Hill   149
Pembroke Chapel   125 – 126
Percival, John   131
Percival, Richard   53, 131
Percival Family   53
Perry, George   72
Perry's Plan   17, 93, 150
Picton, Sir James A   65, 69, 101
Pilkington, William   143
Plimsoll, S   14
Plumbe, Thomas   62
Police Station, Old Swan   28
Poor Relief, Wavertree   59 – 60
Postal Arrangements, Old Swan   34
Potter, William   38 – 39, 50
Pound, Wavertree   66

Pound, West Derby	8 – 9, 66
Prescot	111 – 113
Prescot Font	146
Prescot Grammar School	111
Preston, Elizabeth	11
Preston, Jane	11
Preston, Job	115
Preston, Judith	11
Preston, Margaret	11
Preston, Robert	11
Preston, William	11, 127
Pugin, Welby	30, 53
Quarries	28, 65 – 66, 102
Radcliffe, Sir David	76
Radcliffe, R	28, 92
Railways	54, 75, 79 – 81
Rainhill Cross	147 – 148
Rainhill Hall	102
Rathbone, William	69
Redish, James	54
Reynolds, J	12, 16
Richardson, Rev. Christopher	139
Richmond Cloth Market	103
Ridley, Sir Matthew White	31
Rigby, Peter	17
Rigg, John	65
Rigg, William	65
Roads, Early	105
Roads, Turnpike	106 - 110
Roads, Wavertree	67 – 68
Robin, Edward	84
Robinson, Sir George	87
Roby Cross	147 – 148
Roby Font	146

Rock House, Old Swan   48, 102
Rocket Hotel   80
Roddick, George   44
Rooklands   70
Rope Making   102
Roscoe, William   136
Round House   14
Rowe, Mr   117
Rowson, W   109
Royal Institution   11
Royal Insurance Buildings   43
Ryle, Bishop   127, 133

Saint Andrew's Church, Maghull   146
Saint Anne's Church, Stanley   126 – 128
Saint Chad's Church, Kirkby   128 – 129
Saint George's Church   149
Saint James' Cemetery   121
Saint John's Church   17
Saint John's Market   149
Saint Katherine's Chapel   23
Saint Margaret's Church, Anfield   11
Saint Nicholas' Church   21 – 22, 25,
                                                       55, 90.
                                                       92 – 93,
                                                       133, 136
Saint Oswald's Church   44, 50, 103
Saint Patrick's Cross   149 – 150
Saint Paul's Methodist Church, Old Swan   37
Saint Peter's Church, Church Street   91, 121
Saint Stephen's Church, Byrom Street   125,
                                                       149 – 150
Saint Swithin, Roman Catholic Chapel of   96
Saint Thomas' Church   128
Saint Thomas, Well of   119
Salisbury, Lord   2 – 3, 102,
                                                       130
Salisbury Street   102
Sandfield   14 – 15

Sandford, F W	33 – 34
Sandstone Road	28
Sandys, Colonel Myles	140
Sawrey, Roger	140
Scarlin, Rev. Walter J	127
School for the Blind	93
School for the Deaf and Dumb	93
Score Lane	72 – 73
Sefton	113 – 114
Sefton, Charles, William, 1st Earl	97
Sefton Church	114, 122, 137
Sefton Cross	148
Sefton Font	145 – 146
Sefton Hall	114
Sefton, Harkirk	78
Sefton Park, Palm House	76
Select Vestry of Wavertree	52, 65 - 66, 68 – 69
Shand, Judge	153
Shand, Charles	153
Shaw, Corporal John	90 – 91
Shaw, John	90
Smithdown, Manor of	98 – 99
Smith, Egerton	34
Smith, John	53
Snape, Alderman	123 – 124
Speke Hall	122, 131
Spekelands	61
Spence, Mr	35
Spooner, Archdeacon	25
Springfield Monument	91
Springfield Park, Knotty Ash	91
Stamp, Rev. William Wood	35
Standard, T	35, 38 – 39
Standish, George	15
Standish, Miles	15, 116
Standish, Ralph	15
Standish, William	15
Standish Family	15

Staniforth, Samuel	84
Staniforth, Thomas	40, 84
Staniforth, Rev. Thomas	84
Staniforth Family	84
Stanley, Lady	137
Stanley, Sir Edward	121
Stanley Family	113, 121, 129, 146
Stanley Cattle Market	44, 81, 105, 110
Stanley Park Palm House	76
Stanhope Street Well	120
Staplands	75
Stephenson, George	81
Stewart, Mr	37
Stewart, Rector Percy	152
Stocks, Cronton	150
Stocks, West Derby	1, 8 – 9, 46, 66
Strange, James, Lord	52, 153
Stubbs, Bishop	53, 57
Summerhill	76
Sunday School, Old Swan	37 – 39, 49 - 50
Swan, James	57, 62, 65
Swan Hill Farm	44
Swift, E E	143
Swift, Dr. S W	143
Swift, Rigby	143
Swift, Thomas	143
Tarleton, Alderman	149
Tarleton Family	61
Tarleton's Obelisk	149
Taylor, Charles	154
Tea Caddy Hall	111, 153
Telford, Thomas	107
Temple Court	134
Thingwall	77 – 79

Thingwall, Hugh de	79
Thingwall, Margery de	79
Thingwall, Richard de	79
Thingwall, Robert	79
Thingwall, Roger	79
Thingwall, William de	79
Thingwall Family	79
Thingwall Hall	75 – 76
Thingwall Well	120
Thompson, Anna Marie	76
Thompson, Edward P	76
Thompson, Henry Yates	76
Thompson, Joseph	136 – 138
Thompson, Samuel Ashton	76
Three Swans Inn	45 – 46
Thurston, Richard Son of	79, 98
Thwaites, Jeff	12
Tipton, Mr	44
Tithebarn Street	149
Tobin, Sir John	29
Toll Gates	108 – 110
Toll Houses	108 – 109
Torbock, John	86 – 89
Torbock, Sir William	88
Torbock, William	86 – 88
Torbock Family	86 – 87
Torbock Chapel	86
Torbock Green	86 – 87
Torr, John	31
Tottlebank Chapel	139 – 140
Town End Cross	149
Town Hall, Liverpool	93, 149
Town's Well, Wavertree	66 – 67
Toxteth Park, Ancient Chapel of	15, 136, 139 - 140
Toxteth Park Chapel	136
Toxteth, Royal Park of	98 – 101
Transport	103 - 114
Transport At Wavertree	53 – 54

Traveller's Rest	112
Travers, Henry	9
Tunnel Hotel	80
Tunnel Road	80
Turnpike Roads	106 – 110
Unsworth Chapel, Maghull	126, 146
Urban District Council, Wavertree	52
Village Greens	71 – 72
Wainwright, John	63
Wakefield, Sir Charles C	39, 50
Walker, Mr	40
Walker, Joseph Reed	131
Walker, Parker & Co.	131
Walton	20 – 28
Walton, Henry de	3, 9, 26, 51, 99
Walton, James de	26
Walton, John de	26
Walton, Nicholas de	26
Walton, Thomas de	26
Walton Family	45, 112–113
Walton Church	22 – 23, 25, 27, 94, 111
Walton Church, Old	24, - 26
Walton Churchyard	27 - 28
Walton Font	134, 145
Walton Grammar School	17, 23 – 24
Walton Hall	26 – 27
Walton Parish	129, 139
Wapentake Court	3 – 4, 99
Warburton, Rev. William	104
Ward, William	138
Waterhouse, Rev. L	37
Water Tower, Old Swan	49
Watt, Richard	29, 40, 84
Wavertree	51 – 72,119

Wavertree Academy	57
Wavertree Chapel	56 – 58
Wavertree Common	52, 58, 154
Wavertree Common School	57
Wavertree Constable	54 – 55, 58 – 59, 63 – 65
Wavertree Enclosure Act	58, 71
Wavertree Green	52, 71
Wavertree Hall	53
Wavertree Holy Trinity Church	52, 56 – 57, 68
Wavertree Lane	54, 80
Wavertree Local Board	52
Wavertree Lock-Up	64 – 65
Wavertree Lodge	69
Wavertree Mill	153 – 154
Wavertree Monks Well	66 – 67, 119 – 120
Wavertree Park	96
Wavertree Poor Relief	59 – 60
Wavertree Pound	66
Wavertree Quarry	65 – 66
Wavertree Roads	67 – 68
Wavertree Select Vestry	52, 65 – 66, 68 – 69
Wavertree Towns Well	66 – 67, 119
Wavertree Transport	53 – 54
Wavertree Urban District Council	52
Wavertree Wakes	64
Wavertree Windmill	69, 153 – 154
Wedgwood, Josiah	134
Wells	49, 66 – 67, 119 – 121
Wensleydale, Lord	30 – 31
Wesley, John	74, 115, 135, 141
Wesley Chapel, Old Swan	35 – 37
Wesleyan Methodists	35 – 39

West Derby Castle	9 – 10, 99, 151
West Derby Chapel, Old	129, 151 - 152
West Derby Chapel, Sun Dial	152
West Derby Church	28, 136, 152
West Derby Church Schools	152
West Derby Court House	1 – 3, 8
West Derby Hundred	3 – 4, 26, 78, 98–99, 111, 119, 137 – 138
West Derby Manor	1– 3, 51 – 52, 151
West Derby Mill	152
West Derby Parish Constable	6 – 7, 63
West Derby Parsonage	8, 151
West Derby Pound	8 – 9, 66
West Derby Stocks	1, 8 – 9, 46, 66
West Derby Village	8, 46
West Derby Wakes	18 – 19
West Derby Workhouse	111
White, Peter	127
White Cross Market	149
Whitley, Edward	143
Whitley, William	143
Whitstone, Ann	60
Wilson, Rev. T	39 – 40, 70
Winwick, John de	20
Winwick, Richard de	20 – 22
Winwick Parish	129
Withers, John	136
Woolton Hall	62, 131
Workhouse, West Derby	111
Worthington, William	8

Yates, Henry   109
Yates, Samuel Ashton Thompson   76
Yates, William   72
Yates & Perry's Plan   72
Yellow House   112
Yewtree Field   18
Yewtree House   18

LIST OF SUBSCRIBERS TO THE
2005 EDITION

Ablewhite,   Miss Rita
Adams,   Geoffrey
Alcock,   John
Alecock,   Cynthia & Ethel
Ancient Chapel of Toxteth
Anderson,   David
Anderton,   Eric
Andrews,   Morton
Ardrey,   Jean
Armitage,   John
Atherton,   Mike & Sue
Atherton,   Roger
Ayre,   Joan
Bailey,   Mrs F G
Baldwin,   Christine
Balshaw,   Lisa, Mark & Zoë
Bancroft,   George
Barklem,   George
Barlow,   Lyn
Barnes,   Mrs B
Barrett,   Niamh Marian
Barrett,   Philip Gordon
Barrett,   Sian Elizabeth
Basnett,   Sylvia
Beaumont,   Tim
Beesley,   Audrey J
Benham,   Margaret
Berry,   S
Berthelsen,   Bertel

Bisson,	John & Elaine
Blackwell,	Ruth
Blanchard,	Edward
Blease,	A J & R J
Boardman,	Dr Frank
Boardman,	Mark & Joyce
Boardman,	Dr Terry & Margaret
Bonney,	Mr James
Bowen,	Marjorie
Bradley,	Emma & Ling, Kevin
Bradshaw,	Eric
Brennen,	M M
Brett,	Margaret & Bernard
Brian,	Michael E
Brinkman,	M
Broadbent,	Adam & Sara
Brocken,	Christine
Brooks,	Walter
Brooks-O'Sullivan,	Sean Paul
Brown,	Anita
Brown,	Ron
Browning,	Barbara M
Brunskill,	Mr Harry
Bullock,	Evelyn V
Burden,	Mrs B
Burgess,	Norman
Burnip,	Jan
Burnip,	Tony
Burquest,	Tony
Burton,	John William
Burton,	Kenneth V
Butler,	Gordon J
Butler,	Paul E

Butler,	Peter A
Buxton,	Alfie
Byrne,	Denis V
Byrne,	Mr Peter
Bythell,	Sarah
Cahill,	Peter
Callan,	Jackie & Michelle
Callender,	Mr B R
Campbell	Ian J F
Campbell,	Margaret & Bill
Campbell,	Ronald Terence
Carder,	Mr & Mrs
Carrick,	Susan
Cato,	Joyce
Chesters	Lhind & Dorothy
Chidda,	Sandra
Chin,	Patricia
Christie,	Stuart
Claeys,	T
Clark,	Elaine
Clark,	Margaret
Clarke,	Margi
Cliff,	Vivienne
Cliffe,	Patrick & Alison
Cliffe,	Richard & Tek Lee
Clitherow,	Vanessa
Clougher,	Muriel
Clubmoor Youth Centre	
Coleman,	Amy
Colley,	Mr M
Collins,	Ron
Collins,	Stan
Cook,	Karen Severud

Cooke,	Anne
Cooper,	Ena
Corbett,	Peter
Corkish,	John A
Corlett,	William Roy
Cossons,	Lady Veronica
Costello,	Thomas
Cotter,	Frank
Cotton,	Prof Brian
Couche,	Mary
Cox,	Les & Dianne
Cragg,	M J
Crawford,	Marie & Ray
Cregeen,	Mr W A
Crimes,	Ralph
Crompton,	Arthur Gordon Ellis
Crosby,	Terry
Cross,	Lady
Crossey,	Paul
Culling,	H & J
Cunningham,	Roger & Doreen
Custance,	Joan
Dale,	John & Anne
Darley,	Margaret
Darley,	Tina
Davies,	Ms Edith
Davies,	Geoffrey
Davies,	Professor J K
Davies,	Malcolm
Davies,	Sylvia
Davis,	John B
Day,	A F
Dix,	Margaret

Dodd,	Betty
Dolman,	Frank and Margaret
	(Fairfield)
Doughty,	M
Douglas,	Corrina & Balmer, Ray
Dovedale Junior School	
Drakefield,	Sandra
Dunn,	Alexandra Pauline
Dunn,	Mrs E A
Durkin,	Len
Dutton,	D J
Eastwood,	Tanya J
Edwards,	John
Edwards,	Ruth & Tommy
Ellis,	Bill
Ellwood,	John
Elston,	Noreen
Evans,	Winifred
Everett,	Mrs Cherie E, MBE
Everett,	Christine
Evetts,	Naomi
Fairbrother,	V E
Fairfax,	Margaret
Faragher,	R G & B A
Farrington,	Pauline M
Farthing,	Mr & Mrs
Fawcett,	Diane
Fawcett-Smith,	Richard
Fellows,	D W
Fellows,	Sheila
Fennah,	Robert Mark
Ferns,	Arthur Dominic
Fitzgerald,	Mrs J

Flack,	J A
Fleming,	M
Fletcher,	Duncan
Flood,	Mr Dennis
Floyd,	Mr S
Fogarty,	Audrey
Ford,	Mrs J
Forster-Dean,	Peter
Foster,	J
Foulkes,	Mrs D
Fowler,	Myra & Ray (Skelmersdale)
Fraser,	Marjorie W
Fredson,	Frederick George (Australia)
Freeth,	Christine
Gallimore,	Peter & Ann
Galloway,	Angel Rose
Gamble,	Frank
Gambles,	David
Gane,	K
Gardner,	Joseph
Garrity,	Michael
Gee,	David
George,	William
Georgeson,	Mrs W D
Gersten,	Florence E
Gibb,	Barbara
Gilbody,	D
Gilmore,	John
Gleave,	Katherine & Matthew
Goodwin,	Peter
Gooseman,	Marj & Bill
Gornall,	Mrs R

Gradden,	Mrs J L
Graham,	H C
Graham,	Janet
Gray,	Florence
Greene,	Doris & Richard
Greenland,	Alfred
Greenwood,	Veronica E M (nee Dillon)
Grey,	Doreen E
Griffiths,	Dominic
Griffiths,	Joe
Griffiths,	Joyce A
Guinan,	Lorna
Gustafson,	Helen Louise
Guy,	Stan
Guy,	Stephen
Hall,	Peter A
Hankin,	Cath
Hardy,	John W
Hargreaves,	Mr & Mrs A
Harkins,	Mary
Harpur,	Kathleen
Harrison,	G J C
Haskell,	David T
Hawthorn,	C W
Haydon,	Norman
Haymes,	Donald
Heaton,	James Mulgrave
Hedley,	Doreen & Bill
Heery,	Margaret
Hemmings,	Mrs D
Henderson,	Bernard
Henley-Smith,	Pam
Hennessy,	Gillian

Hibbert,	Jim & David
Higham,	E
Hinds,	Martin
Hird,	Alison
Hodges,	Frank & Dorothy
Hodgetts,	Lilian
Holland,	Frank
Holmes,	Leonard Thomas
Holmes,	Teresa
Holt,	Jennifer S
Hosker,	Donald
Hoult,	Ken
Housbey,	John & Valerie
Howard,	Rosemary
Howson,	Peter & Marina
Hughes,	Emrys
Hughes,	Ken
Hughes,	Michael James
Hulse,	Enid
Hunt,	Robert
Hunt,	Mr & Mrs F C
Hunton,	Mrs Maureen
Hurrell,	Carol
Hurst,	Mrs Pauline J
Hussey,	Anthony
Hussey,	John
Irving,	Cllr D
Isherwood,	K H C
James,	E B & S
James,	P M
Jamieson,	Marjorie & Robert
Jenkins,	Barbara
Jennion,	Arthur

Jerabek,	Jean
Johns,	Hannah
Johnston,	Allan, Barbara & Jody
Jones,	David H
Jones,	Gary Philip (In memory of)
Jones,	Geoffrey
Jones,	Joan T
Jones,	June
Jones,	Keith
Jones,	Malcolm R H
Jones,	Pam & Peter
Jones,	Peter G
Jones,	R G
Jones,	Stephen
Jones,	Trevor
Kay,	Margaret
Kearns,	Joan
Kearns,	John & Molly
Keig,	Betty
Kelly,	Avril
Kelly,	D L
Kelly,	Frank
Kelly,	Ivy
Kenneally,	Kevin Patrick
Kennedy,	Ron
King,	Neville
King,	Ms Sara Elizabeth
Kirwan,	Elaine & Barry
Knowsley Historical Society	
Lamb,	Charles J
Lancaster,	Bob
Lane,	Diana M

Latimer,	Val
Lawrence,	Vera
Lea,	Norman William
Leather,	Brenda
Lee,	Deborah
Lee,	Maureen
Lee,	Olivia
Leech,	Harry
Lempereur,	Mrs Elda
Lennon,	Michael
Lewis,	Susan E
Lindsay,	Bet & Sid
Livingston,	Ray
Lloyd,	Heather M
Logan,	Mrs N
Longworth,	Frank
Loughran,	Sue
Lowe,	John MA
Lowe,	Tom
Lowthian,	Mrs J L
Loynes,	Mrs B J
Lucy,	E G
Lunt,	Peter John
Lutas,	Mrs J
Lyons,	Patricia-Maria
Lyons,	Vincent
Maddocks,	John
Maginn,	Poppy Deane
Manion,	Howard P
Martin,	Ron
Martindale,	George Holme
Matthews,	Hilda
Matthews,	Roy

Mayer,	Philip S
McCarthy,	Jean
McCarthy,	Prof K
McConville,	Simon James
McCormack,	Breffni
McCrea	A J
McDonald Family	
McDonald,	Philip
McDonough,	Brian
McFarlane/Hesketh,	Margaret
McGhee,	R
McGill,	Bill
McGill,	L
McGovern,	Peter
McGuinness,	Kevin
McIntyre,	Mrs N
McKenzie,	Mrs I S
McKenzie,	Ian
McKeown,	John
McLoughlin,	Joseph
McQuaid,	Anne
McShane,	Mrs Pat
Meeson,	Mrs Jean
Melluish,	Hazel
Molyneux-Berry,	D B
Monaghan,	Julie
Moody,	Mrs V
Mooney,	Len
Moorhead,	Claire Natasha
Morris,	Pauline Ann
Morton,	Michael
Mothershaw,	Diana
Moulsdale,	N F

Moyneux-Johnson,	Russell
Mudd,	Philip K
Muraski,	Patricia
Murphy,	John J
Museum of Liverpool Life	
Naylor,	D
Netherway,	Robert & Hilary
Newcombe,	Brian
Newett,	Julie
Northway School, Wavertree	
Nowell,	Diane
Nugent,	W T
Nuttall,	John
O'Brien,	Avril
O'Brien,	Melanië
O'Brien,	Peter A
O'Brien,	Peter N
O'Connell,	Leslie
O'Reilly,	F
Organ,	E E
Owen,	J D
Owens,	G
Park,	George
Park,	James
Park,	Robert
Parkins,	Elsie
Parr,	Karen
Parr,	Pauline
Parrott,	Kay & Tim
Parry,	Mr & Mrs G
Parsons,	Philip James
Pat,	Bill
Patterson,	S W & N

Pearce,	Andrew
Peers,	W L
Pennell,	Mr & Mrs A V
Perry,	Kate
Pierpoint,	Brian
Pilkington,	Tina
Platt,	Peter
Poole,	Norman
Pooley,	R J & N E
Porter,	Sarah
Powell,	Neville
Preston,	Eric J
Price,	Dr Geoffrey L
Price,	Jim
Price,	Marie & Bob
Price,	Mike
Pritchard,	Steve
Pritchard,	Walter
Purcell,	Margaret
Pye,	Colin
Quade,	Anne
Quilliam,	Cerena
Quinn,	Michael
Quinn,	Mr Richard
Quirk,	Mr G
Radley,	Gordon
Rannard,	G E
Rattray,	Pamela
Rawes,	Jean
Reader,	Simon
Redpath,	Fiona M H
Reeves,	John
Reppion,	Phyllis

Richardson,	Andrew
Rimmer,	Henry
Roach,	Anthony
Roberts,	Margaret (Campbell)
Robertson,	Alec
Robertson,	John
Roche,	Joseph A
Rockliff,	Lilian Agnes, nee Macmillan
Rose,	Samuel
Rossiter,	William James
Rowan,	Thomas
Ryder-Jones,	Peter & Angela
Sanders,	Edward
Sarrar,	Russell
Schofield,	David
Seabrooke,	Herbert
Sedgwick,	Shirley
Segrave,	Nina
Sewell,	Peter
Shapton,	Margaret
Shipsides,	Mr & Mrs R
Shuttleworth,	Milly
Shuttleworth,	Thos H
Simpkin,	Mr George
Simpson,	Edward
Simpson,	Rod
Sinclair,	Roy
Sixsmith,	Kathleen Sandra
Skillend,	W E
Skillicorn,	J R
Slack,	Veronica E
Smart,	Mr James A

Smethurst,	John B, MA
Smith,	Alex & Rita
Smith,	Muriel & Jim
Smith,	Robert J
Smith,	Vivienne A
Smith,	Wendy
Smith,	Charles H
Smith,	Joan Geddes
Smith,	Les
Sorenson,	Mrs Rhoda
Spencer,	Colin
Spencer,	Elizabeth
Spencer,	Richard & Sandra
St Francis Xavier's College	
St Mary's Cof E School	
Stafford	Robert Edward
Stanley,	Maureen
Still,	Christine (nee Crummey)
Stock,	Doreen
Stoker Family	
Stoker,	Pat & Terry
Stott,	Susan
Stubbs,	John & Pat
Sunners,	Derek C
Sunners,	Sheila
Taylor,	John
Taylor,	Kenneth G
Taylor,	Ms M Iris
Taylor,	Margaret
Teese,	Mr & Mrs R W
Thompson,	Gerard
Thompson,	Mr J
Thompson,	Madeline

Thompson,	Margaret
Thompson,	S N
Threadgold,	P M
Threlfall,	Alan
Thwaite,	Roy
Tiernan,	John & Diane
Tinkler,	Ken
Todd,	Mrs L
Toman,	Cornelius
Tonkin,	Marguerite T
Townley,	A W
Tufnell,	Gordon F
Twells,	Alex
Tyrer,	David
Urquhart,	Peter
Vaughan,	J E
Walker,	Michael
Walmsley,	Thea Alice Emily
Walsh,	Michael Anthony
Walsh,	Peter & Sue (Jersey)
Walsh,	Roger & Dot
Walton,	Maureen
Watson,	Mrs Ivy
Webb,	Neville & Eileen
Whelehan,	Katherine Mary
White,	Mr Alan E
White,	Mrs June M
White,	Sheila M
Whitlow,	Charles R (Senior)
Whittaker,	Frank & Helen
Wilcott,	Thomas
Wilkinson,	Pat
Willdridge,	John

Williams,	Allan
Williams,	Beryl
Williams,	Colin
Williams,	George
Williams,	J D, MRSC
Williams,	Mr Michael
Williams,	Pam & Bob
Williamson,	Eileen
Willridge,	John
Wilson,	David & Joy
Wilson,	Leslie
Wilson,	Paul
Winterburn,	Ruth
Wisdom,	Jackie
Wolfenden,	John L
Wood,	Dave
Woodcock,	Mrs Nora
Woosey,	Elizabeth
Worthington,	Alan Francis
Wright,	Elizabeth
Wylie,	Angela
Young,	Walter